Transforming Children's Spaces

How can young children play an active role in developing the design of learning environments?

What methods can be used to bring together children's and practitioners' views about their environment?

What insights can young children offer into good designs for these children's spaces?

With the expansion of early childhood education and the move to 'extended schools', more young children will spend more time than ever before in institutions. Based on two actual building projects, this book is the first of its kind to demonstrate the possibilities of including young children's perspectives in the design and review of children's spaces.

Situated at the heart of the debate about the relationship between the built environment and its impact on children's learning and well-being, *Transforming Children's Spaces*:

- provides insights into how young children see their environment;
- discusses children's aspirations for future spaces;
- develops the Mosaic approach, pioneered by the author, as a method for listening to young children and adults.

Emphasising the importance of visual and verbal methods of communication, this fascinating book demonstrates how practitioners and young children can articulate their perspectives, and shows how participatory methods can support new relationships between children, practitioners and architects.

This book is essential reading for those who work in children's spaces and for those who design them, as well as being of general interest to those studying education and childhood studies.

Alison Clark is Senior Lecturer at the Centre for Childhood, Development and Learning at The Open University, UK.

Transforming Children's Spaces

Children's and adults' participation
in designing learning environments

Alison Clark

Routledge
Taylor & Francis Group

LONDON AND NEW YORK

First published 2010
by Routledge
2 Park Square, Milton Park, Abingdon, Oxon, OX14 4RN

Simultaneously published in the USA and Canada
by Routledge
270 Madison Avenue, New York, NY 10016

Routledge is an imprint of the Taylor & Francis Group, an informa business

© 2010 Alison Clark

Typeset in Garamond
by Keystroke, Tettenhall, Wolverhampton
Printed and bound in Great Britain
by TJ International Ltd, Padstow, Cornwall

British Library Cataloguing in Publication Data
A catalogue record for this book is available from the British Library

Library of Congress Cataloging-in-Publication Data
Clark, Alison.
Transforming children's spaces : children's and adults' participation
in designing learning environments / Alison Clark.
        p. cm.
    Includes bibliographical references and index.
  1. Early childhood education. 2. Classroom environment.
  3. Children and adults. I. Title.
  LB1139.23.C53 2010
  372.21—dc22   2009034068

ISBN10: 0–415–45859–5 (hbk)
ISBN10: 0–415–45860–9 (pbk)
ISBN10: 0–203–85758–5 (ebk)

ISBN13: 978–0–415–45859–7 (hbk)
ISBN13: 978–0–415–45860–3 (pbk)
ISBN13: 978–0–203–85758–8 (ebk)

Contents

Figures

Tables

Foreword

Peter Moss

This book is the culmination of ten years of work by the author, Alison Clark. She explores the concept and practice of listening to young children. During that period I have had the privilege and pleasure to work alongside Alison, providing such support as I could and watching the evolution of this work with admiration and fascination. I am delighted to write a few words of introduction for the book and to commend it and the experience it relates as a major contribution to the field of early childhood studies, whilst also being highly relevant to the fields of education and architecture. With its rich mix of theory and practice and its extensive use of photographs and fieldnotes, the book offers a vivid account of a unique project, accessible alike to researchers and educators, parents and policy-makers, architects and designers.

At the heart of Alison's work over the last decade has been her development and application of the Mosaic approach, the key elements of which Alison has described as: multi-method, participatory, reflexive, adaptable, focused on children's lived experiences and embedded into practice. This book provides many examples of the Mosaic approach in practice. In brief, it uses a variety of methods – including observation, child interviewing, photography (by children themselves), tours and map making – to generate documentation with children. The documentation so generated is then subject to review, reflection, discussion and interpretation by children and adults in a process of participant meaning making.

The Mosaic approach shows the effects on Alison's work of several influences. First, has been the view of the child promoted through the sociology of/for childhood as an active subject, someone worth listening to, not least as an expert in her or his own life. Second, has been the field of international development, in particular the Participatory Appraisal techniques devised to give voice to the least powerful voices in communities. Third, has been the theories and practices of the municipal schools in the Italian city of Reggio Emilia, an example of a sustained local project in early childhood education, which has achieved worldwide attention and acclaim. Thus the multi-method approach recognises what Reggio has termed the 'hundred languages of children', the many different ways in which children represent, communicate and express their thinking. Alison, for example, makes much use of visual languages. The Mosaic approach shares much in common with the Reggio's practice of pedagogical documentation, which involves making practice and learning processes visible and thus subject to dialogue, reflection and inter-pretation. Alison, too, has benefitted from and been active among the growing international community of researchers and educators who have wanted to extend listening to the youngest children.

The Mosaic approach is multi-purpose, as well as multi-method. Its first use, and a recurring theme, has been to better understand the perspectives of young children about the early childhood services they find themselves attending. 'What does it mean to be in this place?' has been a consistently important question for Alison, and one that the adult world should pay more attention to as it extends early childhood services to more and younger children. While being a long-term advocate of such services, I also try and remember Foucault's words of caution: 'everything is dangerous'. Greater institutionalisation of childhood should bring with it a responsibility for considering its potential dangers, as well as its many possibilities; this calls for better understanding of what matters to young children and what meanings they attach to their nurseries or schools, as well as what they like and dislike about them.

Over time, Alison has increasingly come to use the Mosaic approach to enable the participation by young children in the design of outdoor spaces and now, in this book, buildings. She has shown that children and professionals (architects, in this case) can have a fruitful relationship that can contribute to the design process by helping architects to understand the environment from the perspective of the child – what it means, what is important and likes and dislikes. Children, of course, cannot determine the final design any more than any other interested group can, but they can help to shape it; this book shows that there is no excuse for omitting their participation in the design process.

The Mosaic approach has therefore come to be a means of supporting the rights of children, in particular Article 12 of the UN Convention on the Rights of the Child, which refers to the right of the child to express his or her own views in all matters affecting him or her, with these views being given due weight. Viewed from a slightly different perspective, the Mosaic approach also provides one means of bringing democratic practice into the nursery and school since it enables children to offer their point of view and for other participants to listen. Indeed the democratic potential of the Mosaic approach need not be limited to children. In this book, Alison discusses how its use might enable practitioners and parents to participate more fully in the design process. She convincingly demonstrates how the Mosaic approach is able to facilitate, in her words, 'an intergenerational approach to involving "end users" of different ages in the design process from design brief to post-occupancy reviews'. This broader perspective, so well illustrated in the book, raises a big and generic question: How might we make nurseries and schools more democratic for children and adults alike?

Alison has written about the Mosaic approach as 'embedded into practice'. It is not for use just by visiting researchers, but it has the potential, which

Alison would like to see widely realised, to be used by practitioners to embed listening into their everyday work. It is appropriate, therefore, that she closes the book by considering the implications of her work not only for architects, designers and researchers, but also more generally for learning communities. She asks: 'Can schools and early childhood institutions become "living spaces" for children and adults, more attuned to each person's capabilities and needs?' The book is, as its title says, about *Transforming Children's Spaces*, but not just in terms of children and adults' participation in designing environments, but in terms of the possibility of creating within these environments more democratic communities.

Peter Moss
Professor of Early Childhood Provision
Thomas Coram Research Unit
Institute of Education
University of London

Acknowledgements

This book is testament to the many conversations that have taken place with young children, practitioners, architects, early childhood studies students and colleagues across national boundaries and institutions. I am very grateful to all those who gave their time to be part of this research and to those who have contributed to ongoing conversations. I would like to pay tribute to Ben Koralek who died during this study and whose work revolved around transforming spaces with children. My thanks to colleagues at Thomas Coram Research Unit, particularly Peter Moss for his continued interest and encouragement and Nina Wigfall for her hours of transcribing. Particular thanks to my advisory group and to Kate Pahl, Rob Walker, Cathy Burke, Margaret Carr, Julia Brannen and Liz Brooker, as well as to colleagues and students at Roehampton University for ideas shared and to the Open University for time to write. My continued thanks to Jonathan, Anna and Will who have lived through this book too.

An earlier summary of the Living Spaces study was published in 2008 by the Bernard van Leer Foundation, who funded the three-year study. I would like to express my thanks for the support of the Foundation, particularly Rita Swinnen and Marion Flett.

Part I
Finding the tools

1.1 Introduction

> Children and the way they live in places, build relationships, and learn are not always the primary starting point of reference guiding the various phases of school design and construction.
>
> (Vecchi 1998: 128)

Can the design process accommodate the perspectives of the youngest citizens? Can a desire to listen to young children's views and experiences lead to more 'people-centred' (Fielding 2004: 213) learning communities which can provide living spaces for adults and children?

This book sets out to explore how young children can play an active role in the designing, developing and reviewing of early childhood centres and schools. Focusing on children from three to seven years of age, this book describes the adoption of participatory research methods and visual narratives, particularly in real-life building projects. A key objective is to explore how young children's views and experiences can inform both the planning of new provision and the transformation of established provision.

Bringing young children into the frame raises their status from an often invisible object of design to an active, visible presence within this complex process. Seeking ways to make young children's perspectives visible has demanded a search for a common language on which to base this model of dialogue. Photography has been one of the means to make accessible some of the knowledge children hold about their environment. It has become a key tool in extending communication between the different players involved.

Early childhood centres and schools are not exclusively environments for children, but are shared spaces for children and adults. This book explores how other perspectives or voices, including those of practitioners and parents within these institutions, can be given currency throughout the design process.

Rather than begin by looking at hopes for future spaces, this book firmly roots discussions about possible spaces in increasing understandings about children's existing environments. What objects, features and people do young children draw attention to or appear to ignore? What issues may this raise in terms of priorities in design?

Completing a new building or transforming an existing environment only marks a stage in an ongoing dialogue between children and adults. This book examines children's and adults' views and experiences of their new environments using their own visual narratives for a catalyst and point of exchange. This model of dialogue has implications beyond the design process. It implicates wider questions about participation, learning and democracy.

Part I introduces the theoretical and methodological tools which underpin this exploration of involving young children and adults in changes to their learning communities. Chapter 1.2 begins with an introduction to the theoretical approaches. This is followed by an introduction to the research case studies which inform the remaining chapters. This part ends with an introduction to the methods – the Mosaic approach (Clark and Moss 2001; 2005) – which provide the principles and tools for constructing the narratives to facilitate exchange within the design process.

Part II focuses on gathering children's narratives about existing, possible and new spaces. Detailed examples of the methods in action are given. This leads to a discussion of the major themes which emerged about the young children's perspectives of their environment, including some surprising insights about scale and perspective and personal spaces. This part ends with a chapter (Chapter 2.5) on temporal spaces which investigates how young children's narratives about spaces may change over time.

Part III explores facilitating exchange between young children and adults within the design process. Chapter 3.2 examines how making young children's perspectives visible can open up debate within learning communities and among practitioners and parents about shared environments. This includes a detailed account of how a multi-agency team in a children's centre used the Mosaic approach to review the completed building. Chapter 3.3 illustrates direct and indirect engagement between young children, practitioners and architects at different stages of the design process, from initial discussions to post-occupancy reviews.

Part IV discusses possible implications of adopting the model of dialogue described in this book in terms of the design process, learning communities and research with both children and adults. This model of dialogue is underpinned by constructing narratives. Can these ways of communicating across generations and professions contribute to more schools and early childhood institutions becoming living spaces for children and adults, attuned to each person's capabilities and needs? Does a role remain for the researcher?

1.2 Viewfinders

I believe that education, therefore, is a process of living, and not a preparation for future living.

(Dewey 1897: 77)

Introduction

'To picture a world, a variety of worlds'

There is a children's storybook by Hiawyn Oram (1984) entitled *In the Attic*. A young boy is at home and bored. He decides to climb an imaginary ladder into his attic. This leads to the discovery of new spaces and friends. One illustration shows the boy leaning out of a window which has appeared in the sky, gazing onto a new landscape. He is surrounded by other window frames, each of which shows other spaces. The boy continues on his way, carrying one of the frames under his arm. How do young children see their world? What images do they carry round with them in order to make sense of new spaces, people and objects? How equipped are practitioners who work each day with children? How equipped are architects who design learning communities to engage with these perspectives?

The account which follows is not a static narrative, but a series of multiple images and accounts which attempt to reflect the complex reality of the landscapes in which young children spend increasing amounts of time. I have found encouragement to pursue this bringing together of images, both visual and verbal, from several writers. Psychologist Oliver Sacks describes a similar desire in the preface to his book *Awakenings* (1973; 1990). Sacks' account is a narrative about the effects of a new drug treatment on patients suffering from 'sleeping sickness'. He describes how he could have produced a clinical account of the drug trials. However, he did not desire to create a static account. He desired to create a moving image of the lives of the patients:

> The general style of this book – with its alteration of narrative and reflection, its proliferation of images and metaphors, its remarks, repetitions, asides and footnotes – is one which I have been impelled towards by the

very nature of the subject matter. My aim is not to make a system, or to see patients as systems, but to picture a world, a variety of worlds – the landscapes of being in which these patients reside. And the picturing of worlds requires not a static and systematic formulation, but an active exploration of images and views, a continual jumping-about and imaginative *movement*.

(Sacks, Preface to the 1973 edition: xviii; original emphasis)

I am interested, like Sacks, in picturing a world, a variety of worlds – the landscapes of being in which young children reside. This requires 'an active exploration of images and views', as Sacks suggests, and 'a continual jumping-about' between different perspectives and between different research tools. The complex task of picturing these diverse worlds has been shared with young children and adults through the participatory, visual research methods of the Mosaic approach (for example Clark and Moss 2001; 2005), which I have developed with Peter Moss (see Chapter 1.4). Some of the narratives are told through photographs taken by young children of both their existing and newly built learning spaces. Thus this book encompasses both visual and verbal methods of communicating in order to further our understanding of young children's 'ways of seeing'. John Berger (1972) made this phrase common currency in the visual arts field through the book and television series of the same name. His opening sentence explains: 'Seeing comes before words. The child looks and recognizes before it can speak' (1972: 7). Berger explains how photography has contributed new ways of seeing:

> Every image embodies a way of seeing. Even photographs. For photographs are not, as is often assumed, a mechanical record. Every time we look at a photograph, we are aware, however slightly, of the photographer selecting that sight from an infinity of other possible sights.
>
> (Berger 1972: 10)

It is this 'infinity of other possible sights' which I am attempt to explore in relation to young children's perspectives of their early childhood environments. Berger encourages us to think about seeing as more than the mechanical act of viewing an image:

> Yet this seeing which comes before words, and can never be quite covered by them, is not a question of mechanically reacting to stimuli. (It can only be thought of in this way if one isolates the small part of the process which concerns the eye's retina.)
>
> (Berger 1972: 8)

This broad understanding of seeing acknowledges that interpretation is part of the process. This theme of interpretation runs through each of the chapters of this book. Acknowledging the place of interpretation is a recognition of the practice and a necessity of subjectivity. We observe from a variety of professional and personal positions, carrying a series of frames under our arms.

Journeying

Oliver Sacks refers to a description by the philosopher Wittgenstein of 'thoughtscapes', which Wittgenstein created with words and images:

> For this compels us to travel over a wide field of thought which criss-cross in every direction. The . . . remarks in this book are, as it were, a number of sketches of landscapes which were made in the course of these long and involved journeyings.
>
> (Wittgenstein, Preface to *Philosophical Investigation*, quoted in Sacks, 1973: xviii)

My account which follows focuses on a three-year research study which began by aiming to assemble sketches of landscapes, including the individual and shared landscapes of early childhood environments which are in the process of change (see Epilogue for further reflection). The views and experiences of young children are central to this account. However, these landscapes are examined alongside the perspectives of other stakeholders, including practitioners and parents, together with accounts by architects. As researcher, I draw these together. These landscapes have been built up over the course of the research process, moving between, as Sacks describes narrative and reflection, images and metaphors.

The metaphor of research as a journey may particularly apply in the case of a longitudinal study. This has given the opportunity for theoretical and methodological journeying over many months. The subject matter which demanded travelling over a wide field of thought, as Wittgenstein describes, led to some surprising new meeting points, as described in Part IV. This thinking benefited from the several years of research and reflection which had taken place since the original study to develop the Mosaic approach began in January 1999. The travelling has been theoretical, practical and professional. Some of the theoretical explorations are described in the rest of this chapter. The practical element of the travelling has been as a result of the desire to contribute to cross-national exchange and dialogue about young children's involvement in the design process. Examples gained from visits to early childhood practitioners, academics, architects and children in Italy, Norway and Iceland have particularly enriched this journey. The cross-professional dimension to this travel has benefited from meetings and workshops with architects and artists who have in turn introduced new languages for thinking about spaces and communication.

Key themes

Three overarching themes are discussed below: participation, environments and relationships. These are three of the issues which were important way markers at the start of the Living Spaces study. They developed in new directions during the subsequent three years.

Participation

Participation in living

The central idea at the heart of the Living Spaces study has been to involve young children in the design process of learning communities. Involving children in design can be viewed in terms of current debates about children's participation. I begin by discussing participation in decision making before discussing participation in learning. The discourse of children's participation is open to a variety of interpretations (Clark and Percy-Smith 2006; Thomas 2009). When I describe one of my research interests as 'young children's participation', several colleagues have asked 'participation in what?', although those who have a background in community development or children's rights often have an understanding of the phrase. This serves to underline the importance of making understandings about participation explicit, particularly if we are working in a cross-disciplinary or cross-national context.

Children's participation focuses on how children are able to be involved in decision-making processes, whether on a day-to-day basis or on a wider level. This decision making, however, needs a shared means of communication to be established before such participation can be built. Listening is an important part of communication and of participation. Listening, however, may not necessarily lead to action. The following purposes for listening emerged during the compiling of a review on listening to and involving young children in education and childcare settings:

- Everyday listening by those who regularly work with young children, giving opportunities for decision-making in routines and activities, and
- One-off consultation about a particular issue, event or opportunity.

(Clark *et al.* 2003: 5)

Norwegian sociologist Anne Trine Kjørholt remarks how children's participation in relation to their own learning is not a new concept. What is new is a different interpretation of participation:

Children's active participation in learning processes has long been a central theme in progressive education . . . during the last fifteen years the emphasis on children as social and political actors holding special rights in decision-making processes at different levels has been overwhelming.

(Kjørholt 2001: 67, 68)

This trend has continued. One demonstration of the international interest in young children's participation has been the General Comment on early childhood issued by the United Nations Committee on the Rights of the Child (UNCRC) (2006). The General Comment can be seen to support a view of children as acute observers of their environment:

General Comment 7

14. Respect for the views and feelings of the young child

The Committee wishes to emphasize that article 12 applies both to younger and to older children. As holders of rights, even the youngest children are entitled to express their views, which should be 'given due weight in accordance with the age and maturity of the child' (article 12.1).

Young children are acutely sensitive to their surroundings and very rapidly acquire understanding of the people, places and routines in their lives, along with awareness of their own unique identity. They make choices and communicate their feelings, ideas and wishes in numerous ways, long before they are able to communicate through the conventions of spoken or written language.

(United Nations Committee on the Rights of the Child, United Nations Children Fund and the Bernard van Leer Foundation 2006: 40–41)

This understanding is not new, but it has not always been recognised at a strategic level. Children's advocate and writer Leila Berg points to the Peckham Health Centre, established in the 1930s by two doctors, George Scott Williamson and Innes Pearse (Pearse and Crocker 1985). This centre embodied a competent view of young children and families:

So when, for instance, they made the cots for the crèche that would be part of the centre, they made them not with high sides to deliberately imprison the babies and stop them getting out and crawling off, they made them with sides as low as possible so that when the babies felt strong enough, vital enough, to want of their own accord to get out and crawl off, they got out and crawled off. This was empowering babies.

(International Child and Youth Care Network 2005)

Strategies at an international level have been followed by a number of policy initiatives at a national level to promote children's participation. In the United Kingdom, for example, a Children's Commissioner for England was appointed in March 2005 to champion the views and experiences of children and young people. The Childcare Act 2006 places a duty on local authorities to take account young children's views in the development of early childhood provision (McAuliffe *et al.*, 2006). One challenge is making this legal requirement a reality, in view of the range of stakeholder perspectives which need to be taken into account.

In the political rhetoric surrounding participation, little attention has been given to considering listening to young children as part of a listening culture which supports both children and adults (Kirby *et al.* 2003). This was one of the emerging issues from the listening to young children review discussed earlier:

> . . . There is also the need to consider how practitioners are listened to within the early years provision in which they work. An environment which respects and listens to the views of three year olds needs also to respect and listen to the views of sixteen year olds on the staff or people of whatever age.
>
> (Clark *et al.* 2003: 45)

This notion of reciprocal listening is linked to the leadership approach within individual institutions (for example Benson 2006). Anecdotal feedback from practitioners I have met during events promoting methods for increasing young children's participation suggests that this can be a disempowering process if the working culture within the provision is not one which demonstrates how practitioner's own views and experiences are acknowledged and valued (see Chapter 4.3). The Living Spaces study set out to promote young children's participation within the design process. However, the need to increase the opportunities for practitioners to participate, both in thinking about new spaces and in reviewing changes which had been made, quickly became apparent. This has raised the question of whether there is a place for visual participatory methods solely designed for young children or whether such approaches may have a wider applicability.

The participation of children and adults raises wider questions about democratic practice. Mannion argues for a reframing of listening to children and children's participation as 'the study of child-adult relations' (Mannion 2007: 411). I return to this idea in the section below on relationships.

Participation in learning

Children's participation in learning is an important element of participation within learning communities. Here I would like to draw attention to the concepts of meaning making and documentation which have informed the approaches discussed in this book. It would be difficult to embark on participatory projects about the physical environment of schools and early childhood centres without engaging with the wealth of literature about children's involvement in their own learning or meaning making. Gordon Wells (1986) uses the term 'meaning making' in his study of the language development of young children. This view of children as meaning-makers is in keeping with a social constructivist view about learning where children are seen as playing an active role in knowledge construction in a social context (Vygotsky 1978; Rogoff 2003). Jerome Bruner (1990) describes young children's meaning making in relation to language acquisition. He describes how meaning making is not about the act of reporting or describing, but it is about pushing beyond this to find a structure to experience. In describing the conversations of a young child with herself he comments:

> She was not simply reporting, she was trying to make sense of everyday life. She seemed to be in search of her own integral structure that could encompass what she had *done* with what she *felt* with what she believed.
>
> (Bruner 1990: 89; original emphasis)

This introduces the idea of feelings into the task of meaning making. The children who have taken part in the Living Spaces study have not been engaged in clinical tests seeking objective answers. They have been engaged in a messy, open-ended quest in a context which is concrete and specific. This has provided the grounding for their explorations. There have been many opportunities within the case studies for young children to be engaged in making meanings and thinking about thinking. Bruner (1996: 64) describes this process of metacognition as an important part of modern pedagogy. Children and adults who have participated in the case studies have been given time to reflect on the question 'What does it mean to be in this place?'. It is a question which reveals insights into thinking, as well as into the subject matter of the environment.

Pedagogical documentation can play an important role in meaning making (for example Project Zero/Reggio Children 2001; Dahlberg and Moss 2005). Carlina Rinaldi, in her accounts of the practices of the preschools in Reggio Emilia (Rinaldi 2005; 2006), refers to the central role of documentation in making learning visible:

> A broad range of documentation (videos, tape recordings, written notes and so on) produced and used in process (that is, during the experience) offers the following advantages:
>
> - It makes visible (although in a partial way, and thus 'partisan') the nature of the learning processes and strategies used by each child, and makes the subjective and intersubjective processes a common patrimony.
> - It enables reading, revisiting and assessment in time and in space, and these actions become an integral part of the knowledge-building process.
>
> (Rinaldi 2005: 23)

Gathering perspectives about particular spaces is a complex knowledge-building process. A task of this magnitude does not lend itself well to quick methods of data gathering, such as short questionnaires. The difficulties are increased by the range of age groups and different levels of literacy. Documentation offers a way of bringing together a range of different material which is gathered from multiple perspectives using contrasting media. Making understandings explicit or visible can have both a 'subjective' and 'intersubjective' value. New insights can be gained by the individual involved and between individuals. Rinaldi emphasises that knowledge building is viewed as a process rather than an isolated event. Revisiting the documentation is an integral part of this process rather than an unplanned or peripheral activity. Knowledge building about children's spaces can benefit from this way of working.

Throughout the account which follows there are examples of how narratives constructed by young children and by adults have facilitated communication in the design process. This has at times bridged disciplinary, professional and generational boundaries. This theme is explored throughout the book, but particularly in Parts III and IV.

Documentation is one theoretical viewfinder which I have adopted from discussions about the preschools in Reggio Emilia. Another theme to which I refer from this pedagogical tradition is 'the hundred languages of children' (Edwards *et al.* 1998). Malaguzzi, the first pedagogical director of the preschools, drew attention to the multiple ways in which young children use a range of visual, verbal, sensory and kinaesthetic methods of communication. This belief in 'the hundred languages of children' led to a touring exhibition of the same name, the first version of which was launched in 1981 (Vecchi 2001). The Living Spaces study has set out to demonstrate children's competencies by fostering communication through a range of languages, including visual languages. These tools are explained further in Chapter 1.4. Part II illustrates how these tools have been used in practice to further understand children's views and experiences of their schools and centres. Part III discusses how the theory of the hundred languages can also be applied to adults within the context of changes to their physical environment.

Environments

The second overarching theme in this study is the environment, both physical and emotional. This research has taken place in the midst of real-life building projects rather than sitting at an academic distance and discussing theories of design. This has rooted the study in discussions about tangible objects, places and spaces – the material culture of schools and early childhood centres (Lawn and Grosvenor 2005). This fits well with working with young children whose lives are deeply involved in the physical reality of their environments (for example, a particular favourite bike, the feel of paint on their fingers or the struggle of turning off a tap).

Early childhood spaces – whether these are nurseries, preschools or nursery classes within a school – are rich in symbols, rituals and routines, which Cole (1996) may describe as artefacts. Young children are engaged in everyday tasks such as meeting friends, having snacks, finding their pegs, playing on the bikes and listening to stories. It is a world of glue, toilet paper and sand. These

Figure 1.2.1 Tangled-up bikes
Source: Spaces to Play study

objects and others define the day-to-day details of the young children's lives. It is also an environment in which the physical and emotional are bound together. This relationship is acknowledged in the Early Years Foundation Stage principle of 'enabling environments' (DCSFb, 2008: 9), which outlines the importance of the emotional environment for young children from birth to five years old, as well as indoor and outdoor environments.

The initial impetus for this research arose during my first study developing the Mosaic approach (Clark and Moss 2001). I was spending the day in the nursery and being led by small groups of children on a tour of the site. The children were in charge of which route we took, whether we went outside and how the tour was recorded. At one point I was walking along a wide corridor and being shown by a group of three four-year-olds the way to the 'singing room' when we were overtaken by a group of three adults: the head of the nursery and two architects. They were discussing the new building as they went past us. They were carrying out a snagging report to note features which needed further attention. It struck me at the time how the child-led tours could offer professionals such as architects a valuable set of alternative perspectives on the reality of their designed environments.

The child-led tours helped to give another emphasis for my future research: the importance of considering both outdoor and indoor spaces. Many of the children in this first study were quick to identify outdoor spaces as the most important places for them in the nursery, whether these were actual or imaginary landscapes: 'In my cave listening to music. It's magic music from my magic radio' (see Clark 2004: 142). The cave for three-year-old Gary was a curved bench on a patch of grass. The importance of outdoor spaces for young children has been a fundamental feature of nursery provision since Friedrich Froebel developed kindergartens in Germany in the 1830s (Brosterman 1987). The open-air nursery school, founded in 1914 by Rachel and Margaret McMillan in Deptford, East London, focused on the benefits of children's access to the outdoors: 'The nursery is for them a kind of return to the outdoor theatre; it is an open space, a garden, a school. Above all a place of life and movement and action' (McMillan 1919: 30).

This emphasis can still be seen in the present-day nursery school on the same site. A visit to the nursery school reinforced for me how environments could be designed and fine-tuned to the interests, priorities and needs of young children. The buildings or 'shelters', as they were originally called, appear secondary to the outdoor spaces. There is one outdoor space on a roof which is reached by a flight of steps. These felt difficult to walk up until I realised the height of the steps had been designed for small feet rather than for adult strides.

I have drawn on two understandings of children's spaces to act as theoretical viewfinders for thinking about space. The first is the work of Moss and Petrie in articulating the idea of children's spaces rather than children's services (Moss and Petrie 2002; Dahlberg and Moss 2005). The second is understandings of school spaces as coexistent layers of the official, the informal and the physical (Gordon *et al.* 2000). 'Children's spaces' refers not only to physical environments, but also to a range of different contexts for engagement:

> We choose another concept of institutions for children. The concept of 'children's spaces' has a very different rationality to that of 'children's services' – aesthetic and ethical rather than instrumental. The metaphor is the forum or meeting-place, for the concept understands institutions for children as environments where the coming together of children and adults, the being and thinking beside each other, offers many possibilities – cultural and social but also economic, political, ethical, aesthetic, physical.
>
> (Dahlberg and Moss 2005: 28)

The concept of 'meeting-place' conveys children's spaces as sites of exchange where meanings can be articulated and debated. This understanding can also open up possibilities for 'children's spaces' to be given higher status within society and seen as integral to wider discussions. These understandings of space see spaces as named places rather than non-places. The question has been more about searching for the meanings and narratives and enabling young children to be part of these conversations.

Gordon *et al.* (2000) identify physical spaces as an important element in understanding social practices in school, but they also refer to other discourses in their ethnographic study of secondary schools in London and Helsinki of the official and informal.

I refer to this way of understanding learning spaces in more detail in Part II, where I use this viewfinder to consider the official, informal and physical layers revealed by the young children in the Living Spaces study.

Relationships

The third overarching theme which underpins the thinking behind this book is the importance of relationships in understanding children's and adults' perspectives about change. I view listening as part of a discourse about relationships. This view is shared by Kjørholt (for example Kjørholt 2005), who expresses concern that an emphasis on 'listening to young children' driven by a children's rights agenda may promote the individual voices of children at the expense of collaborative dialogue between children and adults. This links to wider understandings about listening as part of democratic practice as promoted in Nordic countries, which respect both adults' and children's views and experiences. This may partly explain the bemused reaction of a group of Danish practitioners to a presentation I gave on a review I carried out with colleagues on listening to and consulting with young children (Clark *et al.* 2003). The discourse of listening, consultation and participation appeared strange, whereas listening as part of everyday relationships between adults and children was taken for granted. This encounter emphasised the importance of seeing 'listening' as a contested term which may hold different meanings, possibilities and challenges according to the cultural and disciplinary lenses applied. This appeared to run counter to a prevailing policy and practice interest in listening to young children in the United Kingdom at the time which had given rise to a host of national and regional conferences and publications (for example Lancaster and Broadbent 2003). This questioning led me to approach academics and practitioners from England, Scotland, New Zealand, Italy, Denmark and Norway to consider their understandings of what we mean by 'listening', how we listen to young children and what risks listening might entail for young children (Clark *et al.* 2005). An important part of the writing process of this book, *Beyond Listening*, was to bring together as many of the authors of the planned chapters as possible to discuss each others' drafts and exchange ideas. One theme which emerged from these discussions, particularly with practitioners, was the importance of seeing listening to young children not as a fact-finding strategy, but as an ethical relationship between children and adults (Dahlberg and Moss 2005).

Another way to think about relationships in the context of everyday spaces is to engage with ideas developed by anthropologists. Clifford Geertz quotes Max Weber when he says man is like 'an animal suspended in webs of significance he himself spins' (Geertz 1973: 5). The phrase 'webs of significance' suggests the connections between objects, places and people which adults and children create in the environments in which they live. Geertz uses this phrase to describe culture. He continues, 'I take culture to be those webs and the analysis of it to be therefore not an experimental science in search of law but an interpretative one in search of meaning' (Geertz 1973: 5).

Webs are a useful metaphor. The word 'web' creates a visual image about connections. A spider creates a web by anchoring one point to another. Geertz, in quoting Weber, draws attention to the agency involved in the process. It is the spider who spins the web. Making webs is an active process. This theme of webs has been taken up by several writers concerned with how children and adults make sense of their world.

Cultural psychologist Michael Cole draws attention to Geertz's reference to 'webs of significance' as one of several images Geertz uses for culture. Cole (1996: 123) reminds us that webs can suggest beautiful patterning. This raises the possibility that children's ways of seeing may reveal patterns of intricate complexity. Cole (1996: 135) explores a concept of thinking which understands context as being 'that which weaves together'. He points out that contextual approaches to thinking have frequently used metaphors of weaving, threads and rope:

> When context is thought of in this way it cannot be reduced to that which surrounds. It is, rather, a qualitative relation between a minimum of two analytical entities (threads) which are two moments in a single process. The boundaries between 'task and its context' are not clear-cut and static but ambiguous and dynamic.
>
> (Cole 1996: 135)

Intersections

The three overarching themes of participation, environment and relationships are closely linked. Mannion (2007), as referred to earlier, emphasises both the relational aspects of participation and the importance of considering the spatial dimension in these interactions between children and adults. He refers to Cockburn, who notes:

> In order to bring this forward attention must be paid to issues of engagement, co-construction and partnership in participation. Adults need to check their own motivations and assess their readiness to work in partnership with children . . . Furthermore children's views must be placed alongside with other adult stakeholders, who may have conflicting agendas.
>
> (Cockburn 2005: 115 quoted in Mannion 2007: 413)

Mannion continues, 'Spaces (inclusive of their practices and objects) too play a role in how intergenerality, and hence "participation" is constructed' (Mannion 2007: 413).

The physical environment includes schools and early childhood centres. They are two types of spaces in which the relationships between children and adults are constructed and reconstructed. Changes to the environment present an opportunity to re-examine these relationships and introduce new possible relationships with adults in different professional roles. These intersections are the central focus of this book, bringing young children's perspectives into the arena of architecture and design. This takes the concept of listening beyond the immediate confines of the early childhood community to other professionals who may have no training in working with children. Architects are one of a number of professions whose work has a direct affect on the day-to-day lives of young children. However, few channels of communication have existed between the two groups. One of the challenges of the Living Spaces study has been to see if a language which enables architects to consider the perspectives of the youngest users of buildings can be found. A series of examples has emerged. Visual, participatory research methods have provided a platform for architects to engage with the perspectives of young children and the views and experiences of adults in these spaces.

Working with architects has in turn opened up new possibilities for improving communication between young children and a range of adults in different roles within early childhood services and beyond. Relationships need common languages in order to grow. One possibility is that combinations of visual and verbal languages, as developed through research, may contribute to deepening communication between young children and adults, whatever their shared environment.

This chapter has introduced the main theoretical viewfinders which have informed this exploration of involving young children and adults in the design process. These underpin the discussions which follow and are examined in more detail. The themes of participation, environments and relationships continue as I introduce the research case studies and methods in the next chapters in Part I.

1.3 Case studies

I find it surprisingly difficult to sum up my impressions of this visit. What a complex, multi-layered, multi-faceted place a school is. Full of contradictions, loaded with meaning.

(Judy Torrington, School of Architecture, Sheffield, personal correspondence)

Introduction

This chapter introduces the two case studies from the Living Spaces study which feature throughout the book. Both are children's spaces which have been engaged in major building work. Each case study is introduced with a brief summary of the phases of the research and the participants.

The first case study, Holly Lodge, is a primary school in an inner-city area in London. This case study follows a major building project in the school, from the early design stage through to a post-occupancy review of the completed facilities. A key focus of the building project was to replace a free-standing nursery class and integrate the classrooms for the youngest children (from the nursery and reception classes) together in the main body of the school. The main participants have been a group of three- and four-year-olds in the existing nursery and reception class, their teachers and parents and the architect. I refer to this as the 'school case study'.

The second, smaller case study is a review of a recently completed children's centre. The Geffrye Children's Centre is in another inner-city area in England. The complex combines an existing nursery and Sure Start team working with children and families. The main actors are a group of three- and four-year-olds, the early years practitioners, parents, Sure Start professionals from a range of disciplines and the architect. I refer to this as the 'children's centre case study'.

The school case study

Selecting the case study

There are several ways in which case studies of this nature could have been selected. One approach could have been to start with a local authority engaged in early childhood building projects in order to identify a possible research site. I decided, however, to prioritise finding an architect's practice which had both a strong track record in early childhood architecture and an openness to participatory approaches and research. Experience gained through the earlier studies and both planned and informal discussions with architects had impressed upon me the importance of finding an architect who was willing to engage with the study. One encounter reinforced this decision. I was attending an opening of a new outdoor play space during the Spaces to Play study. Whilst I was there, I met an architect who was at the opening with his young son. The architect asked me about my research and was surprised to hear I was finding out from three-year-olds about their early childhood environments. He said, 'Well why would you want to do that? Surely if you've found out from one three-year-old you don't need to ask any more?' His response appeared to be linked to a developmental model of childhood (James and Prout 1997) which believes that if you knew the 'age and stage' of the children involved then no further understandings were necessary.

Several meetings with architects led to a meeting with a practice based in central London. The architecture practice chosen had an established portfolio of early childhood projects together with an interest in a participatory approach to design.

The final choice of case study was made after reviewing the early childhood projects which this architecture practice were about to start or were at an early design stage. The next selection criterion was to find a nursery or school which was willing to be engaged in the project. Secondary considerations were for the case study to be located in an area of social disadvantage, which was a stipulation of the research funding body, and in commuting distance of London, due to the extended and frequent fieldwork visits.

Location

Holly Lodge is a primary school in an inner-city area of South London. The school is built on a large plot of land and surrounded on three sides by residential housing. The diversity of this housing from low-rise, council-owned flats to an owner-occupied Georgian terrace is reflected in the intake of the school. The school reflects the ethnic diversity of this part of London. Inspection reports have commented on the harmonious nature of this learning community. The primary school, originally built in the 1960s, has been part of a building project involving its nursery provision.

The school had a nursery class for three- and four-year-olds which had been housed in a 'temporary' free-standing, single-storey building (a portacabin) for thirty-seven years. This was situated in a separate corner of the school grounds. This nursery area was cordoned off from the main school playground by a low-level wooden fence which was painted in primary colours. The only area of grass in the playground was within the nursery area, together with the stump of a tree and a large sandpit. There were a few planted beds, flanked by a row of sycamores, which ran along one boundary to this nursery area.

School building

The school had three entrances. The first was a pedestrian only passage leading from the Georgian close, which passes between two high brick walls and leads past the entrance to the nursery. The second entrance, known as the 'main entrance', was one of the two gates with access to vehicles. The high metal gates include a pedestrian side gate. The third entrance leads from the staff car park and past the kitchens into the school playground.

Walking across the playground at lunchtime, it would be typical to find small and large groups of children busily occupied in their own conversations and games. The head teacher would often be on duty and surrounded by a number of children who were either in conversation or bringing disputes to be settled. The main playground is flanked on one side by the school hall, which also houses two toilets which open onto the playground. The hall contains the school kitchens and the library and has the estate manager's flat on the first floor.

A concrete breezeway links the hall block to the main building. By the entrance to the school is the office. All visitors need to sign in before being admitted through an electronically-controlled door. Immediately facing this entrance is a concrete flight of stairs up to the first-floor classrooms. A narrow corridor to the right leads to a small staff room, the head's office and a larger store room. The infant classrooms are on the ground floor. The school's older students are housed upstairs.

The general feel of the nursery classroom was light and colourful. There was a large surface area of windows out of which the children could see. The main door to the outside had a glass panel in the top and bottom section, which meant the children could see through this to the outside. The main classroom area was dominated by groups of tables with chairs which were arranged with daily activities, including art activities. Several rooms led from the main space. There was a large stock cupboard for resources and equipment. There was a small office for the early childhood practitioners. It was only large enough for a small desk, two chairs and a filing cabinet. This was shared by up to four members of staff, as well as visitors. There was a small food preparation area and toilet for adults and a separate cloakroom and toilet area for the children. This area was showing signs of wear, with ceiling tiles missing in places.

The nursery was surrounded by a large play space with soft and hard surfaces and lined with trees along one side. The play space was divided off from the main school playground by a low fence.

Figure 1.3.1
The nursery class housed
in a temporary classroom

Source: Living Spaces study

Fieldwork

The study began at the start of a new academic year. The plans were for the nursery class to be situated next to the reception class, joined by a shared space or hub, thus bringing alongside each other all the children who were engaged in the Early Years Foundation Stage curriculum. Other elements of the proposed design included a new children's centre, a learning resource centre (library), new administrative facilities and improved external play spaces for the whole school.

The main participants were two groups of children: a nursery class of three- and four-years-olds and a reception class of four- and five-year-olds who have been engaged in the research over a three-year period. This core group were joined by the large group of (approximately 180) children who took part in a whole-school consultation together with the lead architect, the head teacher

Nursery class three- to four-year-olds (15)		Reception class four- to five-year-olds (8)
Architects (6)	**Early design stage**	Whole school consultation (approx. 180)
Parents (8)	Researcher	Practitioners (5)

Figure 1.3.2 Groups involved in the early design stage in the school case study

Table 1.3.1 Timeline of school case study showing children involved

Phase one (2004): autumn term: nursery and reception class	Phase two (2005): summer term: nursery and reception class	2005–2006: building work under way	Phase three (2006–2007): autumn and spring terms: nursery, reception, Year One and Year Two

and myself (see Chapter 2.3). This core group of children were joined in the final year of the study by new occupants of the nursery and reception classes. This wider group of children have taken part in the review of the completed building (see Chapter 2.4).

Involvement in an early childhood building project can be a time-consuming and anxious period for those who are responsible for its success. There are many stakeholders to take into account, including parents, practitioners and the local community, as well as the young users of the provision. The views and experiences of young children have been brought together in this case study with those of adults. The early childhood practitioners included adults in a number of different roles, including the head teacher, teachers, early years professionals and nursery nurses. This complex array of roles reflects the diversity of the early childhood workforce in the UK. Parents' perspectives have been gathered as part of the first year of the case study. An important additional perspective has been given by the lead architect, along with interviews and meetings with her colleagues (see Chapter 3.3 for a detailed account of these discussions).

It can be difficult to maintain a focus on young children throughout the design process from initial consultation through to the completed building. One of the challenges of this case study has been how to keep young children part of the discussions amidst the inevitable complex negotiations which take place during a building project. It has been my goal, however, to make the views and experiences of the youngest children more visible, beginning with gathering their perspectives of their existing environment (see Chapter 2.2).

There were three phases to the fieldwork in the school case study. Phase one and phase two focused on the early design stage. These phases were carried out over a nine-month period. A post-occupancy evaluation took place during phase three, which focused on children's and adults' views of the completed building.

The children's centre case study

Selecting the case study

The second case study in the Living Spaces study was chosen because it presents an example of a review of a recently completed children's centre. This centre, in keeping with others in the country, combines a refurbishment project with new build elements.

I decided to organise the selection of the second case study in a different way from the first case study. Rather than prioritising the choice of architects' practice, I decided to focus on finding a local authority, head teacher or head of centre and practitioners who were interested in taking part in such a project. The centre was identified by the Head of Early Years in the London borough concerned as a potential partnership where the practitioners and architects would be interested in a project which centred on listening to young children. The centre had already been engaged in several projects and training days which involved gathering children's perspectives. This prioritising of the early childhood institution in the choice of the second case study reflected my concern with the school case study in which, whilst the head teacher and the architects had been interested and engaged in the study, it was harder to involve the practitioners in discussions about the research (see Chapter 3.2). The architects' practice for the second case study had an established reputation for both its innovative early childhood provision and its consultative approach to the communities with which it works. There had been considerable consultation between different users and the architects at earlier stages in the design process, before the research began. This was a time-consuming commitment on the part of the architects as this was partly a refurbishment of premises which housed many different community groups and was partly funded by a government-funded regeneration grant which involved additional consultative procedures.

The architect had run a design workshop with a group of young children in the existing nursery school. Children's play with boxes was one element which was translated into the final design of the new build component of the project.

Location

The children's centre case study is in area of social disadvantage in North London, in a borough which has one of the highest numbers of nationalities represented in a local authority in the country. Several high-rise blocks of flats are in the surrounding area of the children's centre. There is limited open space nearby.

The building project involved creating a children's centre to include facilities for young children and their families. The children's centre incorporates an existing nursery school for children from three to five years old, with new office facilities for a multi-disciplinary Sure Start team and facilities for children under three. Additional community facilities on the site have been refurbished. There have subsequently been changes to a courtyard and other outdoor space.

There has been an increasing number of new build and refurbishment projects involving early childhood provision in the UK since the Labour government was elected in 1997. This has included government-funded initiatives including the Sure Start programme and Children's Centres. Despite the scale of the building programme, there have been few documented post-occupancy reviews of such provision (CABE 2008). At the time of writing, there have been very few, if any, published examples of reviews which have included young children's perspectives.

Building

The children's centre has two entrances, each of which faces a different street. The main entrance leads past the community garden, into the new part of the building. The rear entrance, where the majority of families going to the nursery enter the building, leads into a small courtyard which is open to the sky. The buildings on several sides of the courtyard have been clad in wood as part of the new building work. This gives a warm feel to the space. The courtyard leads to the different sections of the children's centre. Once through into the nursery rooms, there is a sense of light. The new wing contains the rooms for the youngest children, from six months old to almost three years old. The windows reach to the floor. The furthest room is carpeted, has a lower ceiling and has several cots. The philosophy of the centre is for free-flow access between the inside and the outside and between age groups. This has resulted in the rooms being designed so the youngest children may start off in their own safe space and then, when they feel confident, start to move out into other rooms where there is access to resources such as wet play and creative materials.

Figure 1.3.3 External view of the new children's centre

Source: David Spero

This new wing is sandwiched between two existing buildings. On one side is an old Victorian board school building where the whole of the nursery school used to be housed in part of the ground floor. Two of the legacies of this period of school design are the high windows and ceilings. This part of the children's centre is where the three- and four-year-olds are now based. There are two main rooms and a wide corridor which leads to the toilets and other small rooms, including the parents' room. The main classroom is carpeted and not dominated by tables. A key feature of this room is a large block play area.

A lift had been installed to lead up to the Sure Start offices. A new reception desk and waiting area were created. A floor-to-ceiling window gives a view across the community garden to the high-rise flats beyond. The Sure Start rooms included a meeting room, an open plan office, a staff room with kitchen and small offices for meetings with parents and practitioners. Downstairs, a rabbit warren of passageways leads from the courtyard to the original community centre facilities. This houses a large hall, a community café and other community rooms used by Sure Start groups and others.

Fieldwork

The fieldwork took place over a nine-month period. There were five groups of participants: young children, nursery practitioners, Sure Start practitioners, parents and architects (see Figure 1.3.4). The children who took part were between three and four years old. This group included those in their first few months of being in the centre and older four-year-old children, some of whom left to start school during the research.

Three- and four-year-olds in the nursery school (over 30 children)		Architects (8)
	Participants in the children's centre case study	Sure Start practitioners (10)
Parents using the children's centre (6)	Researcher	Nursery school practitioners (19)

Figure 1.3.4 Participants in the children's centre case study

Table 1.3.2 Timeline of the children's centre case study showing participant groups

Phase one (2006): spring term: nursery practitioners	Phase two (2006): summer term: Sure Start practitioners parents and nursery children	Phase three (2006): autumn term: whole-staff workshop nursery children

Each participant group – adults and children – represented a range of experience. The nursery school practitioners included a group of three women who had recently joined the centre and others who had worked in the original nursery school for over ten years. The review process for this last group of practitioners involved an element of comparison with the past environment. The Sure Start practitioners were representative of the multi-agency composition of this staff group. Participants in this group included crèche workers, a social worker, a speech and language therapist and a midwife. All the practitioners were female.

The two main architects involved were the lead architect with responsibility for the design and the senior partner in the practice. There were, however, other architects in the practice who took part in seminars about the research. Similarly, in addition to the core group of practitioners involved, there were others who took part in workshops. This rises the total of those involved in this case study to approximately eighty adults and children.

There were three phases to this review. The first phase of three months focused on preparing for and gathering the views of practitioners in the nursery school. The second, four-month phase focused on working with children, Sure Start practitioners and parents. The third phase, during the final three months of the case study, involved children and adults in workshops about the outdoor play space.

This chapter has given a brief introduction to the case studies. Engaging with these two learning communities has rooted the discussions which follow in the complex day-to-day interactions which take place between young children, adults and their shared environments.

1.4 The Mosaic approach

How am I supposed to talk to a group of three year olds?
(Architect discussing a post-occupancy evaluation)

Introduction

Involving children in changes to their current environment requires tools which enable both children and adults to understand these spaces in more detail. These tools need to be accessible to a diverse group of individuals, including those from different professional backgrounds, to people of different ages and with a range of skills and interests. These tools also need to be able to explore beyond the physical bricks and mortar to consider the culture which has been established there.

It is important to understand how tools are intended to be used before beginning to work with them. This chapter explains how the Mosaic approach, a set of narrative tools, was developed and adapted to use with young children. This chapter begins by discussing the wider theoretical context of these research methods before describing each tool in detail.

Insider accounts

This study is one of a growing number of research studies undertaken in the sociology of childhood to adopt an ethnographic approach. As James and Prout comment:

> It allows children a more direct voice in the production of sociological data than is usually possible through experimental or survey style of research. Similarly, fieldwork-based research encourages researchers to focus on the ongoing roles which children play and the meanings they themselves attach to their lives.
>
> (James and Prout 1997: 4–5)

This 'more direct voice' is referred to by Hammersley and Atkinson (1995) as 'insider accounts'. They list several reasons why such accounts have a place within ethnography, starting with Burgess (1985), who describes such insider views as providing a check on data obtained from observation and at times providing information when observation is not possible. Hammersley and Atkinson highlight a more active role for insider views:

> Accounts are also important, though for what they may be able to tell us about those who produced them. We can use what people say as evidence about their perspectives, and perhaps about the larger subcultures and cultures to which they belong.
>
> (Hammersley and Atkinson 1995: 125)

It is these perspectives, in keeping with James and Prout's standpoint, which are of central importance to this study. The insider views and experiences are not a minor addition to observation; they lead the direction of the research. Emond describes this rearranging of research priorities and roles in her choice of ethnographic methods with children:

> Children become the instructors and we as researchers, become the pupils. We may have 'hunches' or ideas about the ways in which this world works but in the course of our instruction these ideas may be thrown aside or adapted.
>
> (Emond 2005: 124)

Researcher's voice

Ethnography can make explicit the voice of the researcher as well as the voices of research participants. The term 'voice' is not limited here to the written or spoken word. It is shorthand for whatever form the researcher chooses to explore and articulate his or her interpretations. An ethnographic study can enable a researcher to be acknowledged as a meaning-maker within the research process rather than an invisible hand or pair of eyes. This visibility can allow the researcher to reflect on their role, and confront this in the analysis of the data. This acknowledgement implies that the researcher is not there just as a recorder to document the forms of culture they are studying; 'ethnographers are themselves constructing the social world through their interpretations of it' (Hammersley and Atkinson 1995: 11) This understanding of ethnography has enabled me to reflect on my role within each stage of the research process (see Chapter 4.4). This can be seen as 'articulating experience' (Gray 2003), both in my own experience and in creating the opportunities for others to express their experiences. Describing ethnographic methods in cultural studies, Gray critiques the term 'experience': 'It attracts with notions of obviousness and simplicity, of authenticity and a democratic ethos' (Gray 2003: 25).

  Both Gray (2003) and Probyn (1993) challenge the notion that experience is beyond question but at the same time see experience as playing an important part in the research process:

Experience can be understood as a discursive site of articulation upon and through which subjectivities and identities are shaped and constructed. This involves both how we are positioned in the world and how we reflexively find our place in the world. Thus experience is not an authentic and original source of our being, but part of the process through which we articulate a sense of identity.

(Gray 2003: 25–26)

An ethnographic framework recognises the experience of the children and adults involved in a study, as well as those of the researcher. My intention has been to create discursive sites of articulation where young children and adults can reflect on what it means to be themselves in this place and, in so doing, understand how their identities are shaped and constructed.

'Giving us the world back'

Creating, reviewing, sharing or reflecting on images can provide new ways of engaging with a research topic: 'Images provide researchers with a different order of data and more importantly an alternative to the way we have perceived data in the past' (Prosser 1998: 1). Prosser and Schwartz discuss the sometimes subtle details which may be brought to the surface through using images:

Through our use of photographs we can discover and demonstrate relationships which may be subtle or easily overlooked. We can communicate the feeling or suggest the emotion imparted by activities, environments, and interactions. And we can provide a degree of tangible detail, a sense of being there and a way of knowing that may not readily translate into other symbolic modes of communication.

(Prosser and Schwartz 1998: 116)

The exploring of experiences of space can lend itself to visual research methods. This statement draws attention to the ability of image-based research to explore emotions about spaces and the physical elements of those environments.

Prosser and Schwartz are discussing here the role of research-generated photography. This is one of many different ways in which photographs and film can be used to explore experience and space (for example Walker 1993; Banks 2001; Pink 2001; 2006). Images can be taken by the researcher or the research participant. There is a growing body of research in which children and young people have generated their own images in the process of participatory research (Burke 2007; Thomson 2008).

Photography is a visual medium designed to reveal individual perspectives. Enabling others to take their own photographs can, in a literal sense, help others to see these perspectives. This can be the case when the photographer is a young child. Their short stature results in their field of view being very different from that of an adult of average height. One example of this occurred in the Spaces to Play study (Clark and Moss 2005), which involved children's perspective of their outdoor play area. Several children took photographs of the perimeter fence. I had noticed the fence as an observer in the space, but the children's photographs conveyed the intrusive, cage-like feel of the play area when taken from the height of a three-year-old (Clark 2005c).

However, there are other reasons for including photography as a participatory research tool. As Sontag explains, 'photographs are evidence not only of what's there but of what an individual sees, not just a record but an evaluation of the world' (Sontag 1979: 88).

Artist Bill Viola uses both still and moving images in his work which investigates perception (Viola and Violette 1995). He describes cameras and video cameras as being more than technical devices:

> They are machines that produce content that have as their product the direct imprints of the outside world. They give us the world back and for this they are much more profound and mysterious than people realize. By nature they are instruments not primarily of vision, but of philosophy.
>
> (Viola and Violette 1995: 256)

Photographs are one way to 'give us the world back'. They therefore enable both children and adults to reflect on or evaluate what is going on. This fits well within a constructivist paradigm, where photography can be part of a search for meaning from multiple perspectives (Wertsch 1991; Dockett and Perry 1996; Fasoli 2003). Children's photographs can bring the important details of the context of their everyday lives into the classroom and provide a visible platform for creating and exchanging meanings. Photographs are tools for reflection and interpretation. They are about meaning making not fact finding. Photography can be a 'thinking device' (Walker 1993). This definition fits neatly with Sontag and Viola's descriptions of photographs being a way to evaluate the world. A thinking device indicates that photographs and the act of taking photographs can be an active process of making sense of what we see. This has particular resonance when placed in the hands of young children. The act of taking photographs and looking at photographs can provide another way for children to think about who they are and the objects, places and people who are important. This relates to Gray's aforementioned discussion about experience, through which children shape and construct their identities (Gray 2003: 25–26).

Understood in this way, photography can be about knowledge construction rather than knowledge extraction. Tolfree and Woodhead echo this concern:

> It's not so much a matter of eliciting children's preformed ideas and opinions, it's much more a question of enabling them to explore the ways

in which they perceive the world and communicate their ideas in a way that is meaningful to them.

(Tolfree and Woodhead 1999: 21)

Photography appears to offer children a way to explore their ways of seeing which is valued by the children themselves. A young child who takes her own photographs may be able to play an active rather than a passive role in the research. It can be a participatory tool, particularly when used within a theoretical framework of the competent child (or adult). This is perhaps of particular importance when the research participants are young children, who are therefore in a less powerful position than older children or adults (Clark 2009).

This search for gaining children's perspectives has been one element in developing new research methods for listening to children (for example Lewis *et al*. 2004 and Greene and Hogan 2005). Photography – with both the use of still and moving images – is one of a range of research tools employed within the sociology of childhood to give status to children's perspectives (for example Kaplan 2008). This in turn has led to studies with young children exploring the potential of photography to provide a visual starting point for describing experience. One important example is research by Sue Dockett and colleagues in the Starting School Research project (Dockett and Simpson 2003; Dockett and Perry 2005). This has demonstrated the important contributions that children's photographs and drawings can make to current debates about education and childhood.

The Mosaic approach

The Mosaic approach is a research framework which aims to play to the strengths of research participants, drawing on expressive languages to facilitate thinking about experience and communicating these ideas with others. I developed this approach with my colleague, Peter Moss, beginning with the original study which started in 1999. The focus of this first study was to find a way of including young children's voices in the review of provision for children and families. The Living Spaces study has been the first in which I have adapted this approach to include adult perspectives as well as those of children. The account which follows will describe the initial development of the participatory approach with young children.

Observation and interviewing sit alongside participatory tools, including children's use of cameras, child-led tours and map making, in which children play an active role in gathering and discussing the research material. The name 'mosaic' was chosen in order to convey the construction of an image of an individual or a group or an organisation using a variety of research pieces. This is designed to be an active research process where meanings are constructed from a variety of sources and by different individuals in order to compile a picture or series of pictures. I can remember one of my first school trips whilst at infant school was to Fishbourne Palace near Chichester in Southern England. This Roman site is renowned for its series of intricate mosaics. Standing close to the mosaics reveals the huge number of individual pieces which make up the images. It is sometimes only in standing back from the mosaics that the viewer can understand the whole picture. In a similar way, the Mosaic approach sets out to bring together details of children's everyday lives. Each method can form one piece of an overall image. There can be a value in examining one piece; for example, interviews with children may reveal important insights into their experiences. However, a more detailed image can be gained from drawing on a number of different methods or pieces. These pieces can be brought together to compose an image of an individual child, a group of children or a larger mosaic of a particular school or centre or organisation.

This next section outlines the individual pieces or tools which can be used in the Mosaic approach, beginning with the traditional research methods of observation and interviews.

Observation

The aim is that each research method or tool in the Mosaic approach contributes to increasing understandings of the participant's ways of seeing. Observation has been used extensively in early childhood research and practice to understand the details of children's lives (Drummond 1998; Warming 2005). When promoting 'enabling environments', the Early Years Foundation Stage guidance underlines the importance of observation:

> Babies and young children are individuals first, each with a unique profile of abilities. Schedules and routines should flow with the child's needs. All planning starts with observing children in order to understand and consider their current interests, development and learning.
>
> (DCSF 2008b: 3.1)

Time spent observing in a setting can be a way to immerse oneself in a new environment or to reconsider a familiar landscape in a different way.

The relationship between the researcher and the researched is linked to the type of observation which is chosen, in particular whether it is non-participant or participant observation. Non-participant observation enables the researcher to take on a role of passive observer, not actively engaged in the daily activities but engaged as a bystander. This non-participant observation is recorded in a qualitative rather than a quantitative way by writing narrative accounts. One such use of this technique to understand young children's lives has been the Nursery Stories developed by Elfer and Selleck in their three-year study of children under three years old in daycare (Elfer and Selleck 1999). It is a case study approach to observation, following in detail the lives of particular children and expressing these accounts in narrative or story form rather than as a checklist of activities carried out. The episodes described by the researcher become 'snap shots' which can be discussed with children, practitioners and parents. Interpretations from the observations can also be included at the analysis stage, alongside information from the different research methods.

I have begun each study using the Mosaic approach with a period of non-participant observation based around one key question: What does it mean to be in this place? Each half-day observation focuses on a different child. This question is then taken up in the participatory methods, enabling the children to explore the question for themselves. This marks a change in the relationship with the children who become co-researchers with the adult researcher.

The intention is for the researcher to change from passive bystander, in the initial days of the study, to interested adult or 'authentic novice' (Clark and Moss 2005: 97). This role aims to provide a platform for continuing relationships with both children and adults in the research setting (see Chapter 4.4).

In reality, the visibility of the researcher is influenced by the reaction of the children to the researcher. It is very difficult to remain an invisible person in a class of inquisitive three-year-olds. Greene and Hill (2005) discuss this issue of visibility in relation to the role of researchers in the research process: 'We disagree with the view, still apparently fostered in some schools of thought, that researchers can be like flies on the wall or in some way neutralize themselves' (Greene and Hill 2005: 11).

Participant observation can be an effective method of learning more about young children's ways of seeing (Fine and Sandstrom 1988). This has been demonstrated by research in early childhood settings, including William Corsaro's studies of peer culture in preschools (for example Corsaro 1985; Corsaro and Molinari 2008). Hanne Warming (2005), in her study of preschool culture in Denmark, argues how participant observation can be a powerful tool for listening to the hundreds and thousands of languages of young children:

> Participating in children's everyday lives may not only allow one to listen closely to what the children say in words and through body language, it might further one's learning about children's cultures and one's familiarization with children's life worlds, allow one to ask better questions, as well as to interpret what the children say and do.
>
> (Warming 2005: 65)

The Mosaic approach seeks to enable children and adults to be active participants in the research rather than depend on the researcher becoming an active participant in the research participants' lives.

Interviews

Interviewing children is a complex task. It is made potentially more difficult if the children are young (Delfos 2001). In this study, the children were five years old or younger. The power differences between adults and children are accentuated in an interview situation, where the adult is in control of the location, the timing, the questions and the close of the interview. Margaret Carr (2000: 45) refers to a number of researchers who have been honest enough to discuss examples of unsuccessful interviews with preschool children. Hatch (1990) asks a young child: 'What do you like doing best in the housekeeping corner?' The girl's responses imply she is trying to second guess the answer: 'Play dress-up', 'Is it computer?' This example shows that children's responses can be linked to the role the child expects the researcher to be playing.

The power differential in an interview situation can be decreased by a careful choice of location. The differences between the adult researcher and the child will not be removed, but young children can be made to feel more at ease and given some control over the process. Interviews can, for example be carried out outdoors, in an environment more familiar to young children than a head teacher's office. Interviews can also be carried out on the move so children can talk and play at the same time. This can lead to an interview answer turning into a role-play game before the child signals they are ready for another question.

There is also a possible difficulty with the language used in questioning young children. The interpretation of the exact wording of questions has been partly responsible for challenges to Piaget's description of young children as 'pre-operational' (for example Donaldson 1979). Donaldson and her colleagues demonstrate how it was the wording used in a question rather than children's lack of competency which rendered the children unable to carry out the task.

These potential dangers point to the need to pilot interview questions carefully. Interviews in my earlier studies suggested that asking a three- or four-year-old a question beginning with 'why' often leads to a surprising answer or a refusal to answer the question, whereas a question beginning with 'tell me about' can lead to detailed observations from a child. One of the boys I interviewed in my first study (Clark and Moss 2001; Clark 2004) responded to my opening interview question, 'Why do you come to nursery?', by carefully explaining to me how he came by bike.

Interviewers of young children need to be sensitive to the interests and skills of the individual children involved. Some children will only respond to interview questions if asked in a group session, whilst others will only answer if asked in a one-to-one situation. Flexibility is key.

Children's interview responses can provide the opportunity for children to revisit their answers. This has become an important element in the Mosaic approach, which seeks to provide numerous opportunities for children to reflect and reconsider as they construct meanings. One way to do this with an interview is to present the interview in a booklet form, with one question per page, so the children can add their own drawings and writing, depending on their interests and abilities. The children can then revisit their answers at a later date and add supplementary comments. There may be some children who do not have the verbal skills or inclination to answer the questions. This highlights the importance of having a range of research methods available to enable as many children as possible to make a contribution to the study. Children, for example, whose speech and language delay may prevent them from giving their own responses in an interview may respond to being read the comments of their peers.

Interviews with adults can also form a part of the Mosaic approach. Practitioners who know the children well and parents may add their own perspectives to the details of the children's lives. Children's responses, whether in verbal or visual form, may be a springboard for adults' own reflections. Parents can bring their own insights on how they perceive their children's lives in the early childhood institution.

The tools described so far provide possible ways in for exploring young children's perspectives of their physical environment. The following part of this chapter looks in detail at the visual tools brought together in the Mosaic approach.

Book making

This tool provides the opportunity for children to explore their own perspectives of their environment through photography. This can include reflections on their particular place within the institutions in which they spend increasing amounts of time: 'by giving cameras to children we tried to capture more directly both their ways of looking at the world and their physical social positing in it' (Orellana 1999: 74).

Book making as adopted in the Mosaic approach is a form of children-authored books based on children's own photographic narratives. Books made in this way can form an individual record or piece of the mosaic. This is intended to complement other visual methods (see below) which emphasise shared understandings. It is important that a research strategy which aims to capture young children's ways of seeing makes space for individual as well as collective interpretations or narratives.

This tool may provide a useful introduction for children who are unfamiliar with using cameras. A wide range of cameras, including disposable, single-use cameras and digital cameras (see Chapter 2.2), can be used with young children. Young children do not need to be limited to cameras designed by toy manufacturers. The aim of the research activity is for each child to take photographs of important things in their environment. The activity is structured in such a way that only one child uses a camera at any one time, even if other children accompany the child photographer. The intention is that the researcher is able to listen to and carefully observe the child as she selects the images to take. It is important that the researcher adopts a passive role during the process, making a deliberate effort to not suggest what the child photographer should be taking.

The initial photography session is closely followed by a book-making session. The short length of time between the children taking photographs and the book making is designed to make it easier for the young children to discuss the photographs. Children are asked to select what they think are the most important images from their photographs to make into an individual book of their environment. This book-making provides an opportunity for discussion and reflection in a similar way to reviewing interview responses discussed earlier. However, some young children who have participated in earlier studies have demonstrated a particular interest in reviewing their own photographs. This is perhaps linked to the camera's ability to fix everyday experience, which prevents it from floating by, as Benjamin, writing about photography and film describes:

> The photographic or film image recorded moments of everyday experience but at the same time re-presented the moment through the image, it decontextualised it and thereby allowed the viewer to look into the world as well as at the world and thus give meaning beyond the event shown. It made analyzable things which had heretofore floated along unnoticed in the broad stream of perception.
>
> (Benjamin 1979: 237)

Tours

This tool in the Mosaic approach is designed to enable young children to guide adults around an environment, indicating important features from the children's perspectives. Researchers can never experience the world in exactly the same ways as others, but this method may provide some opportunity to edge closer in this direction. Children's photographs taken on a child-led tour enable other children and adults to discuss these possibly different ways of seeing through the documentation produced.

This method starts from the premise that the children have local knowledge about their environment. They can articulate this in a physical, verbal and visual way by walking through a space, talking about their experiences and recording in images. Local knowledge is an important component of anthropological studies (for example Geertz 1983), where attention is given to studying local practices and routines in order to construct wider understandings about society. French philosopher Foucault (1972) also refers to the importance of power being recognised in local knowledge rather than in global structures. Perhaps it is not unconnected to this claim that a global bank adopted the following advertising campaign in 2005: 'Never underestimate the importance of local knowledge.' If status is given to local knowledge by businesses, politicians or researchers then there is a shift in power from these more powerful representatives to individuals. The individual may be the customer of a global bank or a three-year-old attending a nursery. If local knowledge is recognised then there is a change in the power imbalance between the individual and the organisation.

Tours as a method have their root in International Development, where 'transect walks' are used in Participatory Rural Appraisal to enable non-literate communities to share their local knowledge (Hart 1997). There is a parallel here with using tours with young children. In a similar way to these rural communities, young children would be unable to share their expert knowledge if the research method was based on a written questionnaire. The use of child-led tours privileges the ways that young children communicate in active, visual ways. This method does not rely on verbal communication as children can point out features, but rich conversations may be triggered by children walking through their environment. Langsted (1994) adopted this method in the BASUN project, a study of the everyday lives of young children in Scandinavia. Five-year-olds took the Danish researcher on a 'walking interview' through their day. He explains how the walking tours enabled temporal and spatial issues to be addressed:

> We asked what the children did on a specific day from morning to evening, so the cyclical progress of a day provided the structure for the interviews. Five-year-olds find it difficult to sit still and be interviewed and it is often a help and a support for the child (and the interviewer) to conduct the interview in the environment which is being discussed. So conversations about the flow of events from morning to evening took place in the child's home. The daily routine takes a child from the bedroom where he/she wakes up; to the bathroom and getting dressed; to the kitchen and breakfast. The interview took the same route, with the child taking the interviewer on a sightseeing trip of his/her daily life.
>
> (Langsted 1994: 35)

Child-led tours in the Mosaic approach may be conducted by individual children, in pairs or in small groups. The exact composition of the group may depend on the particular children involved; for example, a shy child may only feel comfortable taking part in a tour if accompanied by a friend.

The researcher's role is intended to be one of interested adult. The intention is not to draw attention to places the researcher might want to include, but to remain attentive to where each member of the group chooses to go. The children are the main documenters of the tour, using digital or single-use cameras together with a tape recorder and supplemented by drawings if they wish. The adult researcher supports these records with on-the-spot notes of places on the tour and conversations held. The results of the tours are again discussed with the children through two further research activities: slide shows and map making (see below).

Slide shows

This tool was added to the Mosaic approach during the second study, Spaces to Play (Clark and Moss 2005) This study involved seeking young children's views about a future play space. It therefore required opportunities for children to think about alternative spaces. Described as the 'magic carpet' in the Spaces to Play study, a slide projector was used to show children images of other playgrounds and community spaces, as well as some of their own photographs (Clark and Moss 2005: 43–45). Digital technology has increased the opportunity for children to reflect on their own or other images. Children are able to review their own photographs taken on a tour on the same day or shortly afterwards through a computer or television, which will appear as a slide show or sequence of images. The method of viewing, whether through a television or computer, will depend on such factors as the size of group and the type of resources available. A review of a set of images to a whole class would work better through a television screen or whiteboard, if available. A laptop computer may provide an unobtrusive way of reviewing photographs with a small group of children in an environment in which the children feel comfortable. This could be outside, on the floor or in the home corner.

This slide show format may also provide the opportunity to discuss other environments with children. This may include photographs of their local environment beyond the school gate or other early childhood institutions in other parts of the world. The researcher's role is to observe the children's reactions to the images and to record the conversations which may be provoked by these encounters. Christine Parker (2001) used a slide show format as an early years' practitioner to discuss a visit to Reggio Emilia, in northern Italy. She uses the term 'magic carpet' to describe this activity, conveying the idea that the children are taken on an imaginary journey to a far away place. This tool could be supplemented by taking children on visits to alternatives spaces. This firsthand experience can be an invaluable way of extending children's ideas of the possible in terms of design (Ryder-Richardson 2006; Sorrell and Sorrell 2005).

The primary audience for the children's images are the children themselves and the researcher. A secondary audience are practitioners and parents. This visual method may provide a useful catalyst for interviews with adults who know the children well. The children's images may provide a concrete starting point for discussing different perspectives and understandings.

A selection of images from these slide shows can form visual narratives for communicating different ways of seeing to a tertiary audience. In the case of a building project, this may include architects and the funders or client (see Chapters 3.3 and 4.2). This raises a number of ethical issues about the appropriate audience for children's material, which is discussed further in Part IV.

Map making

Map making is an important piece of the Mosaic approach, providing children and adults with the opportunity to provide a visual narrative of their environment using their own photographs and drawings. There are myriad types of maps created for a range of social and artistic purposes (Harmon 2004). A map can be a way of anchoring memories and reinforcing identity as well as an aid to travel. Maps produced by children can be interpreted in terms of children's spatial cognition and mapping abilities (for example Blades *et al.*, 1998; Matthews 1995). Holloway and Valentine discuss different ways of interpreting children's map making, based on an understanding of children as social actors (Holloway and Valentine 2000). Maps can hold information and associations about the past as well as the present. They can represent events as well as geographical locations and time and space. It is these understandings of maps involving memory which have been incorporated in the Mosaic approach.

Harmon (2004), in her book *Personal Geographies*, includes several authors' accounts of memory maps, including Fulford (Harmon 2004: 131), who describes how personal map making can become a shared source of local knowledge across generations. Fulford depicts the personal landmarks he remembers from his daily route to school. These include a stone wall ('always walk on top'), the greatest tree house and a doctor's house ('Dr Coomb's = vaccinations = ouch!'). His nieces, who now use the same route to school, have added their own individual markers to the map. Banks refers to examples of maps which are mementos or records of past events, but which set different rules for displaying this visual information:

> For example, the Plains Indians of North America used animal hides as a canvas on which to paint maps of space and time, recording the successful hunts and harsh winters of previous years, or the personal war records of warriors . . . This 'map' does not conform to the topographical conventions of European mapping, but it does document a 'where' and a 'when' of past events of significance that could be read by its makers.
>
> (Banks 2001: 37–38)

Map making in the Mosaic approach contains several similarities to the maps described above. The maps are first produced by the children for themselves (and for the researcher). The children's maps can contain spatial and temporal information. Children may include the 'where' of present objects, people and places. Some children choose to add a further layer by including the 'when' of past events. In this way, they can be seen to be maps of time and space. Fulford in Harmon (2004) comments about one young child's approach to map making:

> My three-year-old daughter . . . can generate map after map . . . each with an elaborate verbal narrative in place of a key. She has learned about maps in pre-school but not to the extent that she thinks there is any 'right' way to draw them. Three-year-olds are born cartographers, eager to claim their own territories and impose order on surroundings that are widening and becoming more complex by the day.
>
> (Fulford in Harmon 2004: 11)

One of the important features of the map making in the Mosaic approach is that this is map making with no right or wrong answers. This is not map making in order to gain accurate topographical records, but the purpose is to enable the map makers to identify places of significance. Previous studies using the Mosaic approach have included map making as a way for young children to make a visual record of their tours of their environment (for example Clark and Moss 2001: 28–31; Clark and Moss 2005: 39–43). The tour may stand alone as a method, but a map creates a more permanent record of the event. This can offer further opportunities for the children involved to think about their environment and for others to discuss their perspectives illustrated by the map. The map turns a momentary experience into an artefact. Children who are interested in making a map are offered the choice of making a shared or individual map. The following example is taken from the first study using the Mosaic approach:

> Cathy and Clare worked together on a map following their tour together. The spaces they chose to represent their institution were: the cook and the kitchen, the receptionist and the office, the staffroom, Cathy's key room where her key group meets and the view out of the back window, 'the fruit table' in the conservatory and a table in another key group room. Clare also chose a photo of her 'glitter picture' from her portfolio of work which she included on her tour.
>
> (Clark and Moss 2001: 29)

The map-making process can provoke discussion. Further conversations with a wider group of people may result from displaying the maps. Displaying maps in a classroom may enable children to discuss the outcome with their peers and practitioners. The maps may also be displayed in a cloakroom area in order for parents to be part of the discussions. In a similar way to the slide shows, the maps may provide a platform for discussion with a tertiary audience of researchers, policy-makers or other professionals, including architects: 'The process of map making is visible listening at a group level, which opens out into listening at an organisational level by displaying the maps for practitioners, parents, and other children and visitors to engage with' (Clark 2005b: 42).

These possibilities have been extended through the Living Spaces study and are the focus of Part III.

Gathering parents' and practitioners' perspectives

Listening to the views and experiences of adults about their children has been an important element of developing the Mosaic approach (Clark 2005b: 38–42). The intention has been to include adults who know children well in dialogue about these young children, whilst focusing on the views and experiences of the children themselves. The combination of visual and verbal material has enabled conversations with practitioners and with parents to begin from different starting points. Discussions with practitioners in the Spaces to Play study included a debate about the function of a playhouse in the outdoor area (see Clark and Moss 2005: 60–61; Clark 2005b: 40). This revealed differences about how the play space was perceived by the majority of the children and the practitioners. Children's accounts and photographs demonstrated the importance of this space as a social gathering point and for the imagination, which was supported by one of the parent's accounts. However, practitioners expressed concern about the behaviour in the playhouse and difficulties of supervising this area. Drawing together these different perspectives and making them visible enabled the discussion to focus on finding a way to extend the play children enjoyed there.

Several adaptations have been made to the Mosaic approach as the study has progressed. A series of new tools has been added to support young children's reflections on possible spaces (see Chapter 2.3). A major new development has been giving the research tools to practitioners and to parents to explore their own views and experiences about an environment. This has been in addition to adults' commentaries on material gathered by children (see Chapters 3.2 and 3.3).

Different stages of the research process

Applied research rarely divides into neatly definable stages. A researcher may identify a particular aim for an encounter with children or adults, which, in reality, may take on another purpose. I have identified, however, a number of broad stages which feature in studies using the Mosaic approach to act as a guide. The first stage involves children and adults gathering material. During this stage participants use a number of the visual and verbal tools described above. The more tools adopted may increase the opportunity to build up a more detailed image of children and adult's lives.

The second stage involves a review of the material gathered or 'piecing together information for dialogue, reflection and interpretation' (Clark and Moss 2001: 37). This review draws on narratives and images from the activities and opens up discussion with adults and children to discuss meanings and look for consensus and disagreement.

The third stage refers to decision making. There were only two stages – gathering and discussing – in the first research study, *Listening to Young Children*:

> Stage One: children and adults gather documentation
>
> Stage Two: piecing together information for dialogue, reflection and interpretation.
>
> (Clark and Moss 2001: 11)

However, in order to emphasise the desire to go beyond listening to children to promote changes in attitude and action, a third stage was made explicit.

Stage One: gathering children's and adult's perspectives

Stage Two: discussing (reviewing) the material

Stage Three: deciding on areas of continuity and change.

(Clark 2005b: 33)

This third stage acts as an important reminder of the practical context of the listening which takes place in projects focusing on change. Participation in this context seeks to contribute to tangible developments in practice.

The research analysis: different waves of interpretation

This framework for participatory research seeks to promote the use of tools for reflection. This has an impact on the analysis of data. The intention is not to keep the analysis locked behind closed doors for the whole process, but to enable children and adults involved in the data construction to discuss their meanings and contribute to this analysis. This theoretical underpinning leads to analysis being an ongoing feature of the research. There has been a practical impetus for this as well. The study has been real-world research (Robson 2002) taking part within the time constraints of building projects. This has led to the need for initial reporting on material gathered, often occurring within weeks of fieldwork taking place in order to be part of the design process.

This cycle of analysis continued over the next two years, aided by frequent presentations of the data and emerging themes to a range of audiences. These included meetings at a school or centre level and with external bodies: the team of architects and, in the school case study, with the local authority representatives responsible for asset management. The purpose of each of these encounters was to facilitate discussion rather than to present a finished script. Subsequent analysis was informed by these ongoing encounters between people and the research material. The role of the researcher in the research process is returned to in Chapter 4.4.

1.5 Conclusion

This opening part of the book has introduced the main theoretical and methodological tools which underpin this exploration of involving young children and adults in the design of learning environments. Chapter 1.2 is based on the three overarching themes of participation, environments and relationships. Within each of these themes I have identified my theoretical frames or viewfinders through which I seek to view children's and adults' perspectives and to facilitate exchange through the design process. I return to and explore these concepts in the chapters which follow. My hope is that their brief introduction in this opening section guides readers through the text.

The first overarching theme involves young children in changes to their physical environment and raises questions about children's participation in decision making. This leads to wider questions about democracy in an early childhood context. Listening to children about their views can challenge assumptions about their capabilities and raise their status within the organisations they inhabit. Examples of such changes are documented in the chapters which follow. A further theoretical thread about participation has introduced ideas about young children's participation in learning. Here two theoretical viewfinders have been theories about 'documentation' (Rinaldi 2005) and 'the hundred languages of children' (Edwards et al. 1998) as discussed by those engaged in the preschools of Reggio Emilia in northern Italy. Both concepts provide helpful ways to articulate how to promote dialogue between children and adults. This dialogue focuses on the people, spaces and objects which are identified as holding meaning.

The second overarching theme is environments, acknowledging the practical context for listening to young children discussed here. 'Children's spaces', as discussed by Moss and Petrie (2002), Dahlberg and Moss (2005) provide a way to reflect on children's environments which encompasses the physical but is not limited to this interpretation. Children's spaces can take a variety of forms, including virtual, imaginary or social functions, but they are not limited to adult-imposed reasoning. I have also drawn on the work of Gordon et al. (2000) to begin to investigate the layers of meaning attached to learning spaces. Grosvenor and Lawn refer to this type of task as 'an archaeology of the school . . . to see the layers of change over time, the sedimentation

or routines and the changing contours of schooling and work practices'
(Grosvenor and Lawn 2001: 67).

The third overarching theme is relationships. The learning communities
under discussion here are complex organisations which cross professional and
lay boundaries and raise inter-generational and inter-professional differences.
This raises the importance of listening, both in terms of self-reflection and
listening to others. This theme is explored in more detail in Part III. Listening
to young children is not seen in this book as an alternative to listening to
adults, but it is seen as part of a search for more democratic practices.

These theoretical viewfinders have been set against a brief introduction to
the two case studies which feature in this account: a primary school planning
a new nursery and a recently completed children's centre. The origins of
the methodological tools have been explained before demonstrating, in the
following part, their adoption in gathering young children's perspectives of
their existing, possible, new and temporal spaces.

Part II

Gathering children's perspectives

2.1 Introduction

Jerome Bruner (2006: 176), in a reflection on pedagogy in schools, commented how rare it is in educational debates to hear meanings made explicit about everyday experiences. It is particularly rare to hear the local knowledge of the youngest members in a school community given currency. These sometimes overlooked views and experiences may provide insights into present environments which can inform future change.

Part II explores examples of gathering young children's perspectives through the design process. This is not a clinical, abstract set of exercises, but a series of in-depth encounters gathered amidst the ongoing pressures of design deadlines, building schedules and everyday life in the institutions. A central question throughout has been 'What does it mean to be in this place?' or, at times, 'What does it mean to be me in this place?'. This emphasis on shared and individual meanings has revealed different layers of understanding about the purpose of a school or children's centre. Gordon, Holland and Lahelma (2000) discuss such layers of meaning in their ethnographic study of secondary schools in London and Helsinki. They describe in their study, *Making Spaces*:

> Within the school we distinguish between three layers: (1) official school, (2) the informal school and (3) the physical school. These layers are in practice entwined but making distinctions between them allows us to analyse aspects of school which often remain invisible.
>
> (Gordon *et al*. 2000: 5)

The following chapters each reveal insights into how these three dimensions of the official, the informal and the physical are articulated by the young children involved through their own images and words. These sometimes invisible layers reveal some surprising perspectives when seen through the lens of some of the youngest children in a school community. The official layer will relate to teaching and learning and to the practices and objects associated with these structures, from whiteboards and book bags to classroom rules. The informal layer will relate to the social and personal connections which exist below the surface of the official school. Gordon *et al*. (2000) describe these alternative ways of seeing school as not in opposition to the official school but in dialogue with it:

> While we have chosen the term 'informal' to avoid a binary opposition between 'official' and 'unofficial' school, and draw attention to the separate lived meanings inherent in the informal school, it should be noted that the informal school exists in relation to the official.
>
> (Gordon *et al*. 2000: 102)

The lived meanings explored by young children involved in the Living Spaces study reveal this interconnectedness between the official and the informal, concentrating on the physical school, both current and future, which has helped to make these different layers visible.

Chapter 2.2 begins by focusing on children's views and experiences of their present environment. This is a deliberate attempt to root discussions about change in children's understandings of the present rather than in their dreams for the future. Building on these understandings, Chapter 2.3 looks at young children's perspectives on possible spaces. Here issues are raised about the inherent difficulties of discussing abstract future possibilities with young children. Following on through the design process, Chapter 2.4 illustrates ways in which young children have played an active role in the review of new spaces. Different methods are investigated for creating opportunities for children to compose narratives about their experiences of new buildings and transformed spaces. Part II ends with a reflection on the relationship between time and space in Chapter 2.5, which has emerged through this longitudinal study with young children.

2.2 Existing spaces

Introduction

This chapter sets out to give a detailed account of how young children involved in this study chose to document their current space as the context for thinking about changes to the physical environment. This chapter examines some of the individual and shared narratives revealed by the children involved in the school case study. What knowledge did the young children reveal about this adult-led environment? What themes were raised and had implications for future design and pedagogy?

The chapter begins by detailing the process of assembling material with young children using visual participatory methods. This is followed by an individual case study of a four-year-old boy to illustrate the bringing together of these methods. This chapter then discusses findings about the spaces identified by the children. Links are made with other research into young children's perspectives (for example Einarsdottir 2005) and studies involving older children's perspectives of learning environments (for example Burke and Grosvenor 2003).

Gathering material about existing spaces

Observation

Observation gives the opportunity for adults to begin to tune in to the way in which young children use their physical environment. This began in the school case study by carrying out two half-day narrative observations (for example Harding and Meldon-Smith 2000). The observations focused on two four-year-olds, a girl and a boy who were among the older children and were familiar with the setting. The decision to initially focus on children who appeared to be at ease in their environment was deliberate as it avoided encountering the risk of making less-settled children feel more anxious (see Chapter 1.4 for more detailed discussion of methods).

Afternoon observation: dry, cloudy with some sunshine

12.40 The nursery children are going outside after lunch. Sally finds the Spacehoppers (inflatable ball large enough to sit on). She is joined by another girl. They bounce on the Spacehoppers across the large play area over to the short boundary fence of the nursery. This is adjacent to the main school playground. Sally and her friend bounce up to the older children who are looking over the fence. There is now playful screaming and bouncing as the girls bounce up to the fence and away again.

12.52 There are three girls including Sally on the Spacehoppers chatting to the older children over the fence. This continues for a few minutes until it is time for the nursery children to 'line up' for the start of the afternoon session.

(Fieldnotes, October 2004)

This extract shows that the current location of the nursery had advantages as it enabled interaction between the nursery children and the older members of the school. (I subsequently found out that Sally had a sibling, who was probably among the group to whom she was talking, in the school.)

Observations carried out inside the nursery pinpointed certain places in which children spent a significant amount of time, sometimes of their own choosing and on other occasions because of classroom routines. This latter category of places included the carpet. Each morning and afternoon session began with a class discussion and learning activity, with the children sitting in a circle on a carpeted area of the nursery classroom. This could take forty minutes, so it was one of the areas of the classroom with which the children became familiar from their first day at nursery. Other features of the classroom included a home corner, which was used for role play and as a quiet area with cushions and books. Another area of carpet was used for construction play with a range of big building blocks and smaller construction toys. There was a small water tray in the classroom.

The study could have concentrated on building up observational accounts of how the children were using the current environment. However, the aim was not to rely solely on adult observations, but to give young children many different opportunities and tools with which to picture their world during a time of change.

Photo books

This stage of the study began with two linked activities: introducing disposable cameras to a group of nursery children and making individual photo books of children's chosen images. These children had not used cameras in nursery, so the study was an opportunity for the children to explore photography as a means of expression. This began with disposable cameras in this research activity, but they were subsequently replaced with digital cameras for the greater flexibility which digital photography offered (see tours below). Working with nine children in total, one child at a time had the opportunity to photograph important things in the nursery. Children expressed delight when they felt they had taken the photograph of their choice. One of the girls exclaimed, after taking a photograph, 'I camera-ed him!'. The children could choose whether we went outdoors or stayed inside. However, at times rainy weather meant that children were limited to indoor images, even though they might have preferred to take outdoor images. The intention was for each child to take approximately twelve photos; one disposable camera could be shared between two children. Some of the children were happy to take a few photos and then hand back the camera. One of the boys continued until he had taken the full film of twenty-seven images.

Once the children had taken their photographs, I arranged for these to be developed quickly so the follow up activity could take place within a few days of the photographs being taken. I met with the children to talk about their photographs and to decide which images the children wanted to be placed in their own individual book of the nursery. Talking to the children was an important part of the process, as they took the photographs and as they reviewed their images. The photographs became a focal point for the co-construction of meanings. Great care was needed to ensure that my interpretation of the images did not overrule the meanings offered by the children. Rather than remark 'Oh that's a lovely photograph of . . .', for example, I would wait for children to give their own explanations and captions to their photographs (see Table 2.2.1). My focus was on recording the interactions which took place around the selection of photographs. I did this by taking notes and tape-recording the session. This turned into a group activity as one child selected their own photographs whilst talking to their peers. The final product was a series of A4-size booklets with approximately six colour photographs – one to a page – each with a caption written by the child or dictated to me by the child. The primary audience was intended to be the child author, their peers, their family and their practitioner. The secondary audience to whom permission was granted were the architects.

These visual records of the nursery revealed personal and shared meanings attached to different places, people and things. Most of the nine children who took part in this activity included photographs of other children. One of the boys included children in seven of his chosen eight images in his photo book. He even managed to include himself by turning the camera around and photographing himself! Only one child included an image of a practitioner, in this case a close-up of the teaching assistant's legs. Photographs taken of me by children as the study progressed emphasised the different perspectives children had of adults, often showing legs or chins and noses as this was the view from their height.

Example of a photo book

Natalie chose to include a record of herself in her book of the nursery by including her name card. This nursery had a visual class register. On arrival, each child was given their duck – a name card in a duck shape which the children placed on a display board. There were different coloured ducks according to whether the children were full-time or part-time members of the nursery. Children consistently chose to photograph these name cards, emphasising the importance of their name cards to belonging to the nursery.

Natalie's photos emphasised activities which took place in the space, such as the sand and water tray. The class pet hamster was a popular choice. Natalie's image of the hamster's cage prompted an interesting conversation about colour. The cage stood by a radiator which was covered by wooden panels to prevent the children from touching the hot pipes. This radiator cover was painted bright blue. When Natalie and Jules saw their images of the hamster cage they looked at the radiator cover in the photo and exclaimed, 'It looks different.' They ran off to compare the image with the actual object. It seemed from their conversation that the photo had made the radiator look a different shade of blue. Once the children had made their photo books of the nursery, they were placed on the bookshelves so the rest of the class could share these records. In this way, the personal narrative could become a shared narrative. The photo books served as an important reference point in the final phase of the fieldwork after the completion of the building work (see Chapters 2.4 and 2.5).

The book making was followed by a pair of related activities: tours and map making.

Tours

Ten children worked in pairs to lead a tour of the physical environment and to document the event by making a map with their photographs and drawings. This time the children used a digital camera. My initial hesitancy in using

Table 2.2.1 Description of a photo book by Natalie

Page	Child's description	Researcher's description and comments
Cover	M, S and C.	Three children with a close-up of a boy (C), but Natalie indicated he was not the intended focus of this photo.
2	My name.	Registration board with close-up of duck shape showing child's name.
3	The hamster's thing. Amy is in her house.	A close-up of the class pet hamster (Amy) and her exercise ball.
4	This is the water.	The water tray.
5	There is the sand.	The sand tray.
6	The bookshelf.	Bookshelves at children's height.

digital cameras with young children was more a reflection of my lack of confidence rather than the children's lack of competency in handling the technology. The children adapted quickly to the use of a digital camera. This tool enabled the children to review their images instantly on the built-in screen, and assess whether they were satisfied with the image they had taken. This added another layer of reflection into the research process. The children were asked to begin the tour from where they came into school in the morning and then continue to walk around the site, showing me what was important. Thus, as discussed in Chapter 1.4, there was a temporal and spatial dimension to this activity as children were walking through different parts of their day. Within the parameters set for the activity, the children showed variations in the tours, which lasted between fifteen and forty-five minutes.

The aim was to allow the children as much freedom as possible to direct the tour as they wished, providing their safety was not compromised. Most of the children chose to remain within close proximity of the nursery classroom, which was in keeping with the majority of their spatial use of the site during their time in nursery. However, one boy was keen to take me to the school hall, where he had recently seen an assembly about Goldilocks and the Three Bears.

Map making

The aim of the map making was twofold: for the children to make a visual record of the nursery in the context of the school and to give the young children the opportunity to discuss and reflect on their experiences of being in this place or, as discussed earlier, creating a context where the children's thinking could continue to evolve.

An important next step in the process was allowing the children to review their images. This provided an opportunity for more discussion about the children's interests and priorities. There were several possibilities presented by working with digital photography for reviewing the tour photographs before making maps. It would not have been possible to use all of the children's photographs on each map due to the number of images taken – in some cases more than forty images. The children reviewed their images on a computer or using an index card which showed thumbnail-sized images of each of their photographs in sequence. The children had little difficulty in recognising their own photographs in miniature; they expressed delight at seeing their images displayed in this way. The next task was for the children to decide which images they thought were the most important ones to be printed out to go on their maps. The children then placed these photographs on their maps. A further layer was added to the maps by children adding their own drawings:

Researcher: Okay. So tell me . . . this is the cushion and this is the door and this is Milly and where's . . .we need to find out . . . Nicholas, can you just tell me who your pictures are of and then I'll write them on [the map].

Nicholas:	He's my brother.
Researcher:	Nicholas' brother with lovely hair okay.
Nicholas:	The door.
Researcher:	Which door?
Nicholas:	That one.
Researcher:	And this one here?
Nicholas:	Window.
Researcher:	Window . . . and the tyre . . . no?
Nicholas:	Tiger.

Two of the children chose to make individual maps of the nursery whilst the remaining children worked in pairs or threes to make three shared maps. The individual maps were made of small rectangles or circles of card. The aim was to give children a choice as to how they represented their images and to increase the opportunity to provide their own interpretation of the space. The group maps were assembled on large circles, which were one metre in diameter, enabling different children to work on one map at the same time.

The maps showed a range of personal and shared meanings about the nursery and its environment (discussed in the second part of this chapter), reinforcing the impressions gained from reviewing the children's photo books.

Interviews

Visual methods open up many different avenues for communicating, but interviewing children can help to reinforce understandings gained by other methods or present opportunities to discuss unclear issues. The exact wording of the questions can be problematic when consulting three- and four-year-olds (for example Clark and Moss 2005: 101–102). I adapted an interview schedule which I had developed to talk to children of a similar age about their outdoor provision (Clark and Moss 2005). The questions chosen for the Living Spaces study were designed to help children express their feelings about being in a particular physical environment, for example: If you want to be with your friends at nursery where do you like to go?; If you want to be by yourself at nursery where could you go? This last question provoked unexpected responses. Several of the children replied they would go home to be by themselves. These following responses are by three- and four-year-olds in the nursery class:

Researcher:	If you want to be by yourself at nursery where could you go?
Chrissie:	At my mum's house.
Helen:	In the play dough.
Julie:	I'd go back home.
Jules:	Outside place.
Nicholas:	I go with my Mum and Dad. I was sitting over there when I saw you.

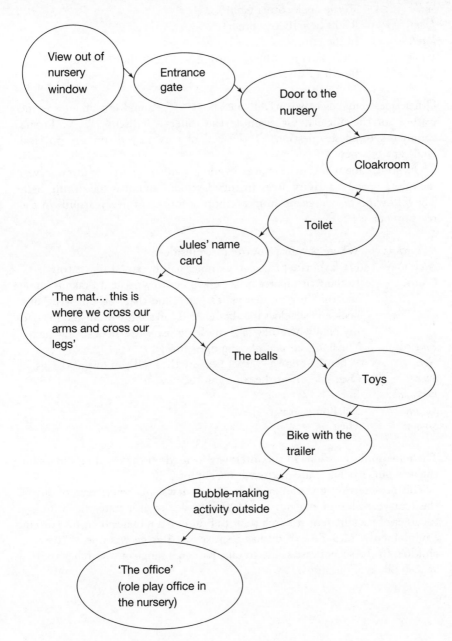

Figure 2.2.1 Example of a template recording a child-led tour

Sally: To the book corner (shhh).
John: Right here [book corner].
Paul: In the rain.
Victor: I like staying at home with myself in the home corner.
Natalie: Be with Sally.

Other questions began with 'Tell me about . . .' to find out about specific features of the nursery, for example the toilets. (I discuss the children's comments to these questions at the end of this chapter on the physical landscape of school.)

Questions about favourite places inside provided a range of alternatives, including specific activity areas in the classroom and also the dining hall. The following responses are from a group of four- and five-year-olds in the reception class.

Researcher: Where is your favourite place inside?
Alex: My favourite place is the dinner hall because I like eating.
Claire: In the writing area because you get to write and I take it home and then my mum says it's good, and that you can write in a book and she does it at home . . . I can see my mum and my dad my Nan when they take my little sister to school – I say hello.
Kate: The home corner, playing dress ups.
Neil: When I sit on the carpet because they tell you lots of things.
Yusuf: Over here [near the train] on the mat.
Fernando: In the book corner.
Susan: The home corner.
Shaun: The cars.

The remaining questions in the interview focused on the children's ideas for the new nursery. These are discussed in Chapter 2.3.

This next section gives an example of the views and experiences of one of the four-year-olds in the nursery class in order to illustrate the bringing together of the different research tools to build up a mosaic about his current environment. Jules' case study has been selected as he was one of the core children in the school case study to take part in a range of research activities at each phase of the study.

Individual case study: Jules

Jules was four years and two months old when he was first involved in the study. He was the second youngest in a family of four children and spoke English as his second language. He was in his final term in the nursery before moving to the reception class after Christmas. He had two older siblings who attended the same school. He had been attending the nursery class for one year when I first met him. He was a popular child in his class and appeared, from my initial observations, to be at ease in the nursery environment.

Book making		Map making
	Jules (age four)	Child-led tour
Review	Interview	

Figure 2.2.2 Research activities undertaken by Jules in the first phase of fieldwork

Book making

Jules began by using a disposable camera to take photographs of objects, people and places he considered to be important in the nursery. He then chose the photographs he wanted to include in his book about the nursery.

Three of the six chosen images were of close-up images of children – both girls and boys – in the nursery. Jules chose a clear image of the home corner. This was in keeping with my observations of Jules in the nursery as one of the boys who enjoyed playing in this part of the classroom. As well as physical spaces, Jules drew attention to imaginative spaces (which I discuss later in this chapter).

Table 2.2.2 Description of a photo book by Jules

Page	Jules's description	Researcher's description and comments
Cover	J.'s photo of the forest.	Close-up image of a model mountain for play figures.
1	This is O. and this is the teddy bear.	A close-up photograph of one of the girls outside with a small teddy motif showing on a second girl's coat.
2	The home corner.	The home corner showing equipment and furnishings.
3	This is A.	A close-up of one of the boys taken outside.
4	J.	A close-up image of one of the boys.
5	The water and the boat.	A purple shiny tablecloth with a white glue stick.

Tours

Jules took me on a tour of the nursery with one of his peers, Helen, who was also four years old. The children were in charge of taking photographs to record the walk. This time Jules used a digital camera and reviewed his photographs as they were taken. I took notes of where we stopped on the tour, using a 'stepping stone' template to help me document the places in each photograph and any comments made (see Figure 2.2.1). This was a quick running record which needed to keep pace with the swift speed with which the children carried out the tour. Helen and Jules also carried a digital recorder, which enabled a transcript to be made of the conversations. The tour lasted fifteen minutes.

The first images taken were to check that Jules and Helen understood how to operate the camera. I suggested they take a photograph of the toy bear which I brought on each research visit and then a photograph of each other to check they were familiar with how to take and review an image.

Jules carried on by taking a photograph looking out of the nursery into the playground, revealing the tops of buildings and the sky. I suggested the children start by taking me to where they come into school in the morning, thus introducing a temporal and spatial dimension to the tour (as discussed in Chapter 1.4). Photographs taken by Helen and Jules – at the height of a four-year-old – on this section of the walk revealed the towering walls of the brick passageway to the side gate of the school.

Next, the children took me to the nursery entrance door and through into the cloakroom and the toilet. (They would have included a photograph of the toilet, but it was in use.) Helen chose to leave the activity at this point. Jules continued by showing me his duck – his name on the visual class register – and taking a photograph. He walked over to the carpeted area – 'the mat' – where the rest of the class were sitting. He explained quietly, 'This is where we cross our arms and cross our legs.'

The next sequence of photographs on the tour was taken outside. Jules showed me the barrel of large balls in the middle of the outdoor space. There were several activities laid out for the day, including a construction toy and an activity with water and a bubble maker, which Jules photographed. He was also keen to take me over to the bikes which were lined up against the wall of the nursery. Jules ended by taking me back inside to photograph the home corner, which was arranged as an office with a toy typewriter and paper. There was an absence of people in the photographs Jules took on the tour. This was in contrast to the many images of children he took when he first used the camera. This was mainly a reflection of the time of day in which the tour was taking place. The rest of the class were on the mat with their teacher whilst the tour took place. This highlights the importance of being aware of the context in which children are researching and the need to give children more than one opportunity, if possible, to document their views and experiences.

Map making

Jules chose to make an individual map of the nursery. Working on rectangular card, he chose six of his photographs and one of Helen's photographs. There were five outdoor images: the nursery door, the bubble activity, the bikes with the trailer, the barrel of balls and the construction activity. The two remaining indoor images were about Jules himself; the first was a photograph of himself taken by Helen to test the camera and the second was the image of his name card in the shape of a duck. Jules' map was displayed on a low display board in the block play area, where he and other children could easily see his photographs.

Interview

Jules' photo book and map emphasised the outdoor play space and the home corner. Jules' interview responses reinforced this impression.

Researcher: If you want to be with your friends at nursery where do you like to go?
Milly: Go and find them – go and play in the home corner.
Jules: In the home corner.
Researcher: If you want to be by yourself at nursery where could you go?
Jules: Outside place.
Researcher: If you are feeling tired at nursery where could you go?
Milly: In the home corner to sleep.

Jules:	Bed [in home corner].
Researcher:	Tell me about the toilets.
Milly:	Putting the seats up – they are dirty.
Jules:	And flush the toilets.
Researcher:	What do you like about nursery?
Milly:	Home corner and reading the books.
Jules:	Playing with the car – the blue car [inside].
Researcher:	What don't you like about being here?
Milly:	[No reply.]
Jules:	[No reply.]
Researcher:	Where is your favourite place inside?
Jules:	Outside!
Researcher:	Where don't you like inside?
Milly:	[No reply.]
Jules:	[No reply.]
Researcher:	Where is your favourite place outside?
Milly:	The bikes.
Jules:	The balls.
Researcher:	Where don't you like outside?
Milly:	The storm – a thunderstorm.
Jules:	Not playing with the bubbles.
Researcher:	When there is a new nursery, what should it be like?
Milly and Jules:	Play with your friends.
Jules:	and with the cars.

It was surprising to note that Jules described his favourite inside place as 'outside', a response which was echoed by one of the boys in the children's centre case study. Jules also described an outside place as a place to be 'by yourself'.

Review

Jules had several opportunities to review his initial thoughts about the nursery over the next two years. The first opportunity came six months after our initial meeting. Jules had moved to the reception class (in the same school) with the older members of the nursery class. The purpose of my return visit was to give Jules and his peers the opportunity to reflect on their earlier responses and to think about changes to the outdoor space. I made the children's interview responses into individual books for them to read with me with the aim of giving status to their comments and providing a catalyst for further discussion. Jules added further responses to some of his earlier answers, for example:

Reseacher:	If you want to be with your friends at nursery where do you like to go?
Jules, November 2004:	In the home corner.
Jules, May 2005:	Playing scooters.
Researcher:	If you want to be by yourself at nursery where could you go?
Jules, November 2004:	Outside place.
Jules, May 2005:	To the slide.
Researcher:	What do you like about nursery?
Jules, November 2004:	Playing with the car – the blue car [inside].
Jules, May 2005:	Ladders outside [the climbing ladders].

These later comments suggested that playing outdoors had become an even more important feature of Jules' feelings about the nursery now that he was reflecting back on his time there. As a member of the reception class, Jules would not have access to scooters, but he would be able to play on a slide in the outdoor space shared with the new nursery class. The review was extended by leaving a book of the children's photographs and interview responses in the nursery and reception classes for children to look at together (see Chapter 2.5 for further details).

Parent's interview

Jules' mother was one of the small group of parents I interviewed to discuss their children's experiences of being in the nursery or reception class and of taking part in the research. His mother confirmed his love of imaginative play and physical activities outside, including water play and playing with cars.

Researcher:	What does he enjoy doing at home inside or outside?
Mother:	Cars, kitchen corner with his little sister, cycling and running, football, cartwheels on the sofa, pole jump with a broom.
Researcher:	What do you think would be a good day for him at nursery?
Mother:	Dancing, cycling and sports. Photographs.

Jules had taken his photo book home and had talked about using the camera. His mother reflected on this process:

Researcher: What did you learn about from the photographs and other activities he has taken part in?

Mother: He can take photographs [this] confirms his interest: cycling, balls, home corner and water games.

Practitioner's interview

Jules' nursery teacher reviewed a slideshow of his tour together with photographs taken by other children. She was surprised by the children's ability to offer articulate insights into their current environment: 'I guess you knew that they could do all the visualising, remembering and vocalising?' She felt the documentation produced by Jules and his peers during this phase of the study provided a useful pedagogical window: 'To know what they are thinking now is very important.'

Jules' teacher kept a summary of Jules' responses in his profile book so there was an individual record of his views and experiences before leaving the nursery class the following month to move to the reception class.

Drawing the pieces together

A recurring theme through each of the methods used by Jules was his love of being outside. He had taken photographs of outdoor spaces and equipment. He included them in his book and on his map. In the interview, he was able to articulate that being outside was preferable to being inside. Jules identified the outside as his private space to be by himself. This desire to be engaged in physical activities such as cycling and sport outdoors was echoed by his mother. Another priority appeared to be social spaces to engage with friends. Jules indicated the importance of having traces of himself in the nursery by pointing out his name card and placing a photograph of himself on his map. Another strand was

Table 2.2.3 Matrix of Jules' perspectives on the existing environment using the Mosaic approach

Jules	Book making	Interview	Tour	Map	Review	Parent
Personal spaces	✓		✓	✓		
Outdoor spaces	✓	✓	✓	✓	✓	✓
Private spaces		✓			✓	
Imaginary spaces	✓	✓		✓		✓
Social spaces	✓	✓	✓		✓	✓
Controlled spaces		✓				

spaces for the imagination, whether through role play in the home corner, which he described on his map and in the interview, or through his use of photographs to convey imaginary worlds. Whilst the outside and the home corner represented spaces to play, the carpeted area was a controlled space where children sat as a class on the carpet and needed to 'cross your arms and cross your legs'.

The next section of this chapter looks at emerging themes identified by the young children about their current environment.

Official, informal and physical school

Listening to the young children through their use of the research tools revealed important spaces in their shared environment. These spaces and the activities which were associated with them can be seen to relate to the different layers identified in school by Gordon *et al.* (2000) (see 2.1, Introduction). The young children involved in the school case study in the Living Spaces study revealed insights about the informal school, but they revealed less about the formal school aspects of teaching and learning. However, the physical school of specific places, objects and senses seemed to provide a powerful catalyst for creating ongoing narratives about being in this place.

Official school

Controlled spaces

The interviews with children together with the child-led tours and map making revealed insights into the importance of rules. Jules' comment about the carpet – 'this is where we cross our arms and cross our legs' – showed this association between a space and the behaviour which was expected there. Other children seemed to regard rules as important information to tell an enquiring adult:

Researcher: Is there anything else I need to know about your school?
Sophie: Never go in the drawers.

Each child in the reception class had their own tray or drawer which was identified by their name card. One of the rules in this class was to prevent children taking things from anyone else's drawer. Sophie was also keen to see this order preserved in a new nursery. When asked 'What should the new nursery be like?' Sophie replied, 'Don't forget your book bag' (Reception class interview). Map making gave children another opportunity to indicate how their knowledge of rules and behaviour influenced their description of the

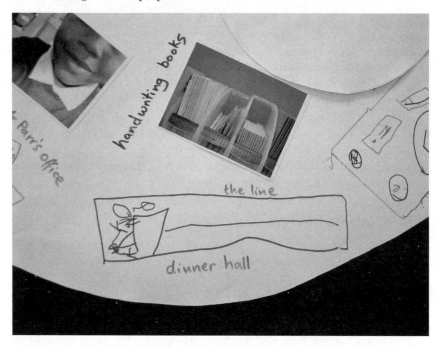

Figure 2.2.3 Detail of a map showing the dinner hall

Source: Living Spaces study

space. Alex's map illustrated lunchtime with a queue where children needed to wait to collect their lunch. Alex labelled this drawing 'the line'.

'Tidy up time' occurred several times during the school day when children were expected to each contribute to tidying the classroom. This routine was identified by two of the boys in the reception class as a time in the day they did not enjoy:

Researcher:	Where don't you like inside?
Neil and Fernando:	When we have to tidy up and it's a bit long.

This comment was echoed by some of the four-year-olds interviewed by Cousins (1999) in her study based on observing and listening to young children about their early childhood environments. Cousins discusses the frustration children expressed not only about the length of time tidying up took, but also about the need to stop working on a particular construction or activity. One of the boys in her study, Sonnyboy, commented: 'That don't make no sense . . . I just got to the interesting bit. I don't care about the time, that's plain stupid . . . time's as long as it takes' (Cousins 1999: 36).

There were more mentions of rules and behaviour by children in the reception class in the school case study than in the nursery. This may indicate both an increase in the expected norms of behaviour as the children moved to this class and a greater ability to articulate these expectations. Gordon *et al.* (2000) put forward the idea of the 'professional pupil', who has acquired the skills needed to negotiate a school day:

> To become 'professional pupils', secondary-school students need first to learn appropriate behaviour in and outside the classroom. They have to learn the basic features of the pedagogic process, the hierarchical relations within the school, and the possibilities and spaces for, as well as limits of, student agency.
>
> (Gordon *et al.* 2000: 72)

The children in the nursery and reception class in the school case study exhibited some of the elements described as being a 'professional pupil'. The attention paid to the rules indicates how some of the youngest members of the school community were acutely aware of what was seen as appropriate behaviour both inside and outside the classroom. Certain spaces and times of day were identified as having particular demands placed on conforming.

Langsted (1994), in the study of childhood in five Nordic countries, asked five-year-olds children directly about the difference between rules at home and in their early childhood institution:

Interviewer:	Is there a big difference between home and your daycare centre?
Child:	Yes! Very, very, big.
Interviewer:	What are the differences? Can you decide more at home?
Child:	Yes. Eating rules – at home I can decide where to sit when I eat lunch. And . . . and when we go out I'm allowed to decide at home. And when we eat . . . when I want something to eat like a carrot or apple, I can help myself at home from the fridge, but when I'm at the centre I can only have fruit and stuff . . .

(Langsted 1994: 39–40)

The five-year-old in this Nordic study was able to articulate his feelings about 'eating rules' at his nursery, which restricted the place, time and content of meals and snacks.

Adults in school

Teaching and learning are central features of what can be seen as the official school. There were many opportunities in this study for children to draw attention to their teachers or numerous other practitioners working in the school and to features of the curriculum through photographs and conversations involved in the different research tools. However, there were very few references to adults engaged in teaching or learning-related activities. One exception was one of the boys who took a photograph of a climbing frame and included the legs of an adult (who was a temporary member of staff). The photographer needed to ask the name of this adult, but the children were equally hesitant about the names of permanent members of staff and other members of the nursery. These photo books were made during the second month of the autumn term, when some children were still re-acclimatising themselves to the nursery after the holidays: 'It feels like the children are still getting used to everyone – each other's names, adults' names, the hamster's name' (Fieldwork notes). Other adults not involved in teaching had attention drawn to them in the children's photographs. The estate manager (or caretaker) had a flat on the school premises. Several children took photographs of this flat and were aware of who lived there. The estate manager was over six feet tall and had a visible presence around the school. Children's tour photographs also drew attention to the adults who were involved in administration at the school. One of the girls in the reception class walked to the entrance hall on her tour and took photographs of two administrators in the main school office.

Curriculum spaces

It was a noticeable feature of the child-led tours, particularly by the youngest children in the school, that they draw attention to the in-between and informal spaces rather than focusing on what might be described as curriculum spaces, which have a formal learning focus. This is illustrated by numerous photographs of pathways, shrubbery and fences, as well as cloakroom areas and toilets. Specific toys or objects were signalled out. Anna, one of the youngest three-year-olds, chose to take a photograph of a My Little Pony bag in the home corner which she chose for her map: 'I like playing with that.' Bikes were another frequently chosen item (discussed below).

There were few examples of literacy activities chosen by the nursery children on their tours. However, a number of the maps made by children in the reception class showed exercise books and reading books. These areas of the classroom were also chosen for their association with people (see Chapter 3.2). There were more photographs taken by children in the reception class showing the class computer, although there was a computer in the nursery too. Yusuf, one of the five-year-old boys in the reception class, took photographs of equipment around the school and chose to make a small map showing two computers, a tape recorder and a mechanical stair lift. Another boy in this group identified the 'carpet' as a place of learning:

Interviewer: Where is your favourite place inside?
Neil: When I sit on the carpet because they tell you lots of things.

This was too small a sample to draw conclusions about gendered differences between the type of learning spaces identified by boys and girls. However, the inclusion of visual methods did appear to enable less articulate boys to reveal individual priorities within the environment.

Informal school

The children's narratives of their existing environment draw more attention to the informal school practices than to the official school practices. These informal layers of school can be explored in terms of personal spaces, private spaces, social spaces, imaginary spaces and caring spaces.

Personal spaces: self-identity

Children's self-identity is inextricably linked to their sense of place identity. Proshansky and Fabian indicate that the establishment of a distinct self is supported by interacting with 'real objects, spaces and places':

> Children learn to view themselves as distinct from the physical environ-
> ment as well as from other people and do so by learning their relationships
> to various objects, spaces and places including ownership, exclusion,
> limited access and so on . . .
>
> (Proshansky and Fabian 1987: 21–40)

Early childhood institutions will be among the first public 'spaces and places' in which many young children begin to establish these relationships. It is therefore important in design terms and as educators to try to understand more from young children's perspectives about how this process takes place and what practice and design features may support or hinder this process. Young children across the three studies carried out using the Mosaic approach have identified spaces as important because of their association with themselves, their family members and friends.

Young children have found ingenious ways in which to document the importance of recording themselves in this complex exploration of 'what does it mean to be me' in this space? This has included taking self-portraits and identifying name cards, records of work and examples of art.

Clare, one of the four-year-olds in the Listening to Young Children study (Clark and Moss 2001) found another way to emphasise a personal connection with the space. On her tour, she led me to her portfolio book, which had been built up over her time in the nursery. These personal records can hold particular significance for young children (see Driscoll and Rudge 2005). Clare took a photograph of her 'glitter picture' from this portfolio book and included it on her group map of the nursery (Clark and Moss 2001: 29). (The role of portfolios as personal markers for young children is discussed in detail in Chapter 4.3.)

During the Spaces to Play study (Clark and Moss 2005), one of the boys was keen to make sure that a photograph of himself appeared on his map of the outdoor space:

> *Jim* (three years old): Can I have me on there? (*pointing to the map*)
> *Researcher*: Oh. You. Yes, we'd better have you on the map. That's very important.
> *Jim*: (laughs) . . . because I like me.
>
> (Clark and Moss 2005: 43)

In the first phase of the Living Spaces study, I asked one of the girls in the nursery what was the most important place in the nursery and she replied, 'The most important place is "My name is Fiona,"' pointing to her name card. Many children, including Jules, whose case study was discussed earlier, took photographs of their duck-shaped name card and peg on their tours and identified these as significant personal markers in their early childhood landscape. Photographs taken of the cloakroom are one example of these recordings of personal markers. Children on each of the tours stopped to take specific photographs of their peg and photograph. Nicholas, one of the four-year-olds, exclaimed about what he was taking, 'the cloakroom . . . On my name.' This school did not have a child-held record, so there were fewer traces of the children's work in the classroom than had been the case in my original study (see Chapter 4.3).

Einarsdottir (2005) notes young children's attention to their own name in her Icelandic study, which adapted the Mosaic approach. The four-, five- and six-year-old children in her study in a preschool in Reykjavik took photographs of birthday charts and other planning or organisation charts which featured the children's names (Einarsdottir 2005: 535) Children's own names seem to hold particular significance for young children. It is as if the letters are not only a representation of themselves, but are in some ways part of themselves. Pahl makes a similar observation in her ethnographic study of children's literacy development in a nursery: 'Drawing and writing are both symbolising activities; ways in which children express their world. Their names are intensely symbolic to children; they represent them, and can "stand" for them' (Pahl 1999: 63).

Personal spaces: family members

Personal spaces can represent links between places and family members. This first example is taken from the Listening to Young Children study (Clark and Moss 2001; Clark 2004). Gary was one of the first three-year-olds to take me on a tour of his recently completed nursery. The nursery was divided into two wings, one for the under-threes and one for the older children. Both wings of the building could be reached through the front door by passing through the entrance hall. Gary, camera in hand, took me to the water tray and then straight away led me to the front door of the nursery. He showed me the toys he liked to play with in the entrance hall and then showed me the way to the under-threes' wing of the nursery to find his younger brother. Gary then took great pleasure in taking his brother's photograph and a photograph of the mattress on which his brother, Robin, had his sleep each day. In fact, Robin appeared to be delighted to see his brother and to be the centre of this exchange. When I had developed these photographs, Gary chose these two images of his brother and his brother's mattress to have a prominent place on the map he designed of his nursery.

The child-led tours in the Living Spaces school case study emphasised the personal markers relating to siblings and parents around the school. Sally was one of the four-year-olds who was first involved in the study whilst she was in the nursery. Sally and Nicholas took me on a tour of the school. I asked the pair to start the tour where they came into school in the morning. The school had three entrances. Sally commented, 'I've got two homes: sometimes I come in from this gate and sometimes from that gate.' Sally stopped to take photographs of a classroom door and a bench. She explained that the bench was where she waited with her older sister and mother in the morning before school started. The close-up of the door was her sister's classroom door. Sally chose both these photographs to be on the map that Sally and Nicholas made of their school. Nicholas added a drawing of his brother to the map.

This child-led approach revealed personal links between the physical environment and individual children which might not have become apparent from interviews alone. A further unexpected connection is discussed in Chapter 2.5, where Samina, a four-year-old, reveals why she took a photograph of an aeroplane to represent home.

This theme of personal markers relating to family members reoccurred when children reviewed the completed building (see Chapters 2.4 and 4.3). Interviewing the children in this study reinforced the importance of siblings to several of the children. This sense of belonging and well-being in the space seemed to be of particular importance at playtime, but this may have been

Figure 2.2.4 A close-up of Sally's sister's classroom door

Source: Sally, Living Spaces study

because this was often the only time when the children would have been able to meet.

Researcher:	What is your favourite place outside?
Sophie:	Playground – the big playground. I like playing with Kirsten [older sister].
Shaun:	Big playground playing with my brother. [He's in] Year One.

Siblings were strong personal markers for some of the children across these studies. However, my encounter with one child has led me to consider whether this may only be the case when siblings like each other. One of the youngest girls in the school case study, Anna, had an older sister in the school. Anna was involved in each phase of the research. She led me on a tour during both phases, with an interval of two years between them (see Chapter 2.5 for her case study). Anna made no reference to her sister during either tour or the subsequent documentation which followed. I interviewed Anna's mother after her first tour. The interview took place in Anna's home, with Anna playing in the background. Her mother made a passing reference to how much Anna disliked her older sister. It is perhaps unsurprising that Anna did not identify objects or places associated with her sister as personal markers within the space, unlike other children. It was not part of her narrative about the space which she wanted to share.

Personal spaces: friends

Friends acted as personal markers in the existing environment for several of the children in the Living Spaces study. Children identified places with the people they played with there, particularly if these locations were outdoors. This links with the above comments from children who linked the playground with playing with siblings. This may be because playtime gave more opportunity to play in friendship groups than lesson time, for example:

Researcher:	Where is your favourite place outside?
Neil:	Playground – both of them, with Fernando.
Fernando:	In the big playground with Neil.

The link between spaces and friends will be discussed further in this chapter when I discuss social spaces.

Personal spaces: practitioners

I had been surprised to find a clear example in the Listening to Young Children study in which a young child had identified a photograph of a practitioner as a personal marker (Clark and Moss 2001: 49–50). Cathy was one of the shyest children to take part in this study. She took part in a tour with two of her friends and adopted the role of artist as we walked around the nursery. She made sketches of the different rooms the girls chose to show me. She asked her friends to take her photograph whilst she was standing by the noticeboard, showing photographs of the staff, next to a photograph of a female practitioner. This practitioner had been Cathy's key worker, but she was currently on maternity leave. Cathy made it apparent how important this adult was to her sense of belonging to the nursery even in the practitioner's extended absence. The photograph on the noticeboard of staff acted as a personal marker.

As commented earlier, the children in the Living Spaces school case study did not draw attention to teachers or teaching assistants in this personal way either through the tours, map making or interviews. Further study is necessary to establish whether participatory methods can reveal more about children's perspectives about the practitioners who work with them.

Some personal markers, such as the links with siblings on the same site, may be known to adults working with young children. However, other personal markers may remain more hidden. The research process has made visible some of these meanings, but other connections remain unknown.

Private spaces

Private spaces may exist among the informal layers of school, but they are rarely part of the design. Young children may succeed in finding such private spaces outdoors, whether as part of natural environments or in pieces of commercial play equipment. One three-year-old in the Listening to Young Children study photographed an important play space. It was a scrubby piece of ground under the 'tall dark trees' and along the base of a hedge (Clark and Moss 2001: 25). Boys on the tour in the Spaces to Play study took a photograph inside the play tunnel, revealing it to be a cavernous space where no adults could fit. Children could feel connected to the activities happening around them, but at the same time they could feel separate.

Private spaces were harder to detect in the review of the existing environment in the Living Spaces school case study. Such 'places of retreat' appeared far harder to find in this setting (see Thomson 2003). Children identified indoor private spaces as the book corner and the home corner. When asked in the interview, 'If you wanted to be by yourself in nursery where would you go?', several children answered they would go home to their parents or outside with friends. Alex, in the reception class, was unusually articulate. He responded, 'Out on the seats – in the other playground or my nice inside self [on the mat].'

Alex was able to convey that his private space in a reception class was internalised rather than a physical reality, whether inside or outside. This contrasts with young children in Einarsdottir's study, based in Iceland, in which the children of a similar age took many of their photographs (without an adult present) in the children-only room in the playschool. This is a room where children can close the door and be unsupervised. One of the children's explanations for this was that they liked to be left alone (Einarsdottir 2005;

536). This is an example of how opportunities for privacy can be a design feature of early childhood environments in different cultural contexts. Wagner (2004), an American academic, discusses 'pillow rooms', which are designed as child-only spaces in Danish nurseries: 'My Nordic colleagues explain that children create rich and expressive cultures of their own when they have space and time without stifling adult intervention' (Wagner 2004: 57).

Hart describes 'places of retreat' to look out upon the world from a place of one's own as places for experimenting with ways of putting together and as locales for hide and seek with other people or with the environment (Hart 1979: 211). Hart's places of retreat are similar to Titman's (1994) observations of school grounds. She outlines four types of places children looked for in the outdoor environment: a place for doing, a place for thinking, a place for feeling and a place for being (Titman 1994: 58). She describes this last type, a place for being: 'which allowed (the children) to "be" themselves, which recognised their individuality, their need to have a private persona in a public place, for privacy, for being alone and with friends, for being quiet in noise, for being a child' (Titman 1994: 58).

These observations are important as they acknowledge that a private place might be somewhere to be alone or with friends. Places to be 'quiet in noise' enable children to be observers, as well as actors, in a space. These images also highlight an ethical consideration; adults are privileged if children reveal their private spaces. There is a need to exercise responsibility as to how this information is applied. There is a danger that private spaces could become overmanaged once adults know of their existence.

This section focuses on children's perspectives of their existing environment. However, the need for privacy applies to both adults and children within learning spaces. This is discussed further in the review of new environments in Chapter 2.4.

Social spaces

Social spaces as well as private spaces may be more readily found outdoors in an early childhood environment. The playhouse in the Spaces to Play study (Clark and Moss 2005) was one example of such a space. This was donated by a local building firm. This playhouse, in effect a small shed, was furnished with plastic furniture and had two windows which overlooked different parts of the play area. The children's photos, tours and interviews revealed this to be a popular social place which was an arena for an array of different practices:

> We play doctors, we play vets, see this – you put the chair there and you lay down on it. This is where we play and talk and cook. It's got a table and chairs and a roof. Hide and seek because you can hide under the table. You bump your head.
>
> (Clark and Moss 2005: 61)

Children's interviews in the nursery in the Living Spaces study revealed a range of outdoor and indoor spaces for meeting with friends.

Researcher:	If you want to be with your friends at nursery where do you like to go?
Bee:	There [the home corner].
Chrissie:	My brother's class.
Helen:	Outside and inside.
Julie:	For a little run [outside].
Milly:	Go and find them – go and play in the home corner.
Jules:	In the home corner.
Nicholas:	I like to go with Jules and Milly. I like to be playing on the train set [outside thing].
Sally:	On the scooters and bikes.
John:	In the Harry Potter door with the big boys [Ben]. My sister Kate.
Victor:	With the dentist with my dad. Outside.
Natalie:	With Mummy at home.

Sally identified the scooters and bikes as places to go to be with friends. Her friend, Natalie, described 'with Sally on the bikes' as her favourite place outside. These interview responses were supported by observations made in the nursery which showed that this equipment gave important opportunities to be with friends. Several of the children in the nursery also took photographs of the bikes and scooters on their tours. There was a close link made among this group of young children between being with friends and being with siblings and parents. John's response of 'In the Harry Potter door with the big boys [Ben]. My sister Kate' referred to the main door to the school, which led to the older children's classrooms.

Children drew attention to the home corner as a social space through interview comments and on their tours. The sand tray was another social space which was photographed, whether it was positioned inside or outside, usually surrounded by children. There was a large outdoor sandpit by the nursery which remained covered up for most of the year. Two of the nursery children photographed the cover of this sandpit on their tour. The sandpit was a special social feature of the preschool in the Spaces to Play study. This sandpit, made by a group of parents, was large enough for a group of children to sit inside. One of the boys included his photograph of this inside sandpit in his photo book of outdoors at the preschool (Clark and Moss 2005: 65).

The children interviewed in the reception class in the Living Spaces school case study included the playground, the home corner and the book corner as places to be with their friends:

Researcher:	If you want to be with your friends at school where do you like to go?

Alex: Into the little playground.
Claire: In the little playground to skip.
Kate: In the home corner.
Neil: I like to be in the home corner.
Yusuf: In the train.
Fernando: In the book corner with my friend.
Sophie: Into the playground.
Shaun: In the classroom.

Shaun was unusual in identifying the classroom as the space he would go to be with his friends. He identified playing with cars as his favourite place inside the school, which may in turn have been linked to playing with others.

Imaginary spaces

Children's imaginary spaces may be among the informal layers of school which are the most surprising to adults. These narratives appear to be far removed from the official narratives. In the first of the Mosaic approach studies, in July, one of the three-year-olds, Gary, described his favourite place in the nursery as an alternative world: 'Going in my cave, near the big, dark, trees.' He expanded on this description when I talked to him in November: 'In my cave listening to music. It's magic music from my magic radio' (Clark 2004: 150). Several years later, I still recall the shock at hearing this explanation. The richness of the account was far removed from the expected response of identifying perhaps a piece of play equipment or area of the classroom. Gary was an unusually articulate child. Other children have conveyed their imaginary spaces through visual images. Jim, another three-year-old who took part in the Spaces to Play study, used his photographs of the caterpillar-shaped play tunnel to reveal his narrative about trains in the outdoor play space (Clark and Moss 2005: 60). Each of the brightly coloured segments of the play tunnel became carriages: 'the blue carriage' or 'the red carriage'. He linked them to the Thomas the Tank Engine children's books. The case study of Jules (see earlier in this chapter) showed several examples of imaginary spaces. Jules' photograph in his book of the 'water and the boat', as represented by a glue stick on a shiny tablecloth, gives a hint of the imaginary narratives that young children can weave around mundane objects. The home corner is one area of the nursery classroom which was popular as a social space and at the same time gave children the opportunity to create other worlds. This formal imaginary space seemed to continue to have significance in the reception class, perhaps as there were fewer opportunities within the timetable to play. Enabling stories to grow is another way of helping children to gain a sense of belonging to a place. Michel de Certeau describes the role of stories in helping people to feel connected to a city or conversely to feel cast adrift, 'where stories are disappearing there is a loss of space' (de Certeau 1988: 123).

This sense of loss of belonging appeared to be the case in a school I visited in Switzerland during the Living Spaces study. The school building was recently opened, but it was not originally designed for infants. There were now, however, classes for five- and six-year-olds. Their classrooms were on the first floor of the building. Access to the outdoor space was via steep concrete steps down a poorly lit stairwell. Once outside, I was greeted with the sight of a sea of bark chippings with isolated play equipment. The group of five-year-olds were a little daunted by my question: 'Can you show me what is important here?' I had been told by the practitioners that there were problems at playtimes with fights and unhappy children. The children showed me the swing and another flight of concrete steps which marked the edge of the football pitch, bushes and an impromptu slide. But I remember one space more than others: a muddy pit by the edge of the space (which was not covered in bark). One of the boys enthusiastically explained that this was for Star Wars. This was the only space I had been shown which was rich in stories in this whole site.

Caring spaces?

An important informal layer in school may refer to the ways in which children feel that their needs are taken care of. What happens when children are sick, fall over in the playground or feel tired during the day? This type of care may be associated with a particular person or perhaps with a specific routine or room. One of the young children in the nursery hinted at the importance of this level of care in his interview:

Researcher: Where is your favourite place inside?
Paul: Sitting on the chairs when you've hurt yourself.

There was a specific chair in the nursery which was close to the door to the playground. Children were led here when they had fallen over outside. They were then looked after by one of the practitioners, either the teacher or a teaching assistant. This chair was photographed by one of the children assembling their photo books. One interpretation of Paul's comment is that the discomfort of having hurt oneself was outweighed by the special attention received. Nursery children with minor injuries were attended to in the nursery instead of going to the main school building. Young children may experience a range of different routines and environments if they need medical attention in school. This was one of the aspects of school life investigated by Mayall *et al.* (1996) in their study of children's health in primary schools. The research involved a survey and six in-depth case studies, detailing the different approaches to health care, accidents and illness within the schools. In one of the case studies, North School, the secretaries' room acted as the first aid space:

As in most schools (90 per cent [of 620]), there was no designated first-aid room – children were cared for in the (very cramped) secretaries' room, and if need be they sat in the corridor nearby and waited for parents to pick them up.

(Mayall *et al.* 1996: 125)

This is a reminder that being sick in school often involves waiting. The physical environment can become intensely important in such situations. One of my students showed me a photograph that one of the children in her reception class had taken of things he did not like in the school. It was a close up of the so-called 'welfare chair'. This leather chair was where children waited in the office when they were sick and needed to go home. This boy associated the chair with being unhappy as his mother had been cross when she collected him on one occasion.

What if young children become tired in school? A question on this was included in the interview to see if particular spaces were associated with being able to rest. The responses from the children in the nursery class were divided between those who suggested the book corner or home corner as a place to rest and those who advocated going home.

Researcher:	If you are feeling tired at nursery where could you go?
Helen:	Home.
Julie:	To bed.
Milly:	In the home corner to sleep.
Jules:	Bed [in home corner].
Sophie:	If you're tired you can sleep over here.
Nicholas:	The book corner.
John:	Over there.
Victor:	I would like to go home and sleep.
Natalie:	Stay in the home corner.

Similarly, the reception class respondents suggested the home corner or the book corner or removing oneself from the school environment altogether. As Shaun succinctly described it, 'Just leave.'

Physical landscape of school

Listening to young children in the context of a design project focuses interest on their implicit or explicit views about the physical environment. I was interested to see what understandings could be gained about young children's perceptions of design qualities such as light, colour and texture, as well as information about specific physical spaces and features. This learning journey for me continued as I worked with children on their ideas for possible spaces (see Chapter 2.3) and reviewed the newly completed spaces (see Chapter 2.4). During the first phase of fieldwork in the school case study in which the young children were considering their existing environment, the following main themes emerged: outdoor spaces; lights, ceilings and floors; and beauty and colour and legibility.

Outdoor spaces

The young children demonstrated, through their photographs, conversation and actions, that the outdoors was an important space, though it was often controlled by adults. An illustration of this occurred during one of the first book-making activities in the Living Spaces study, with children in the nursery class. It was a rainy day and the children were not allowed access to the outside. Undeterred, while I was asking one of the four-year-old boys, Nicholas, to photograph what was important in the nursery, he took a photograph through the glass door to the outdoor space beyond. He was able to convey his priorities through his choice of subject, finding a means of bringing the outdoors into his narrative (Clark 2007).

Outdoor spaces in this study were associated with the play equipment which was available to the children. Children in the nursery drew attention to the importance of the bikes and scooters and several named these objects as the favourite part of being outside (see Figure 1.2.1). They were also important social spaces for being with friends, as discussed earlier in this chapter. There are strong similarities between the priorities expressed by many of the children in this case study and the reactions of children who were involved in my earlier studies. Two boys took me on a tour of their preschool on a cloudy day. The class did not have access to the outdoors that day due to the unsettled weather. Therefore, when the boys took me outside, the toys and equipment were not in place. They, however, were not daunted by this; they galloped around the space, pretending to be riding and shouted to me, 'We're on the bikes!'. This mime conveyed both their enthusiasm for being outside and their favourite play equipment (Clark 2007: 352–356).

There were some differences, however, with the young children's responses to the importance of being outdoors in the Living Spaces study. This was the first time I had involved children in a reception class in research about their physical environment. The children in this class did not have regular access to play equipment in their own designated space, as children in the nursery did. (This was later changed as a result of adaptations made to the outdoors during the building process.) For the reception class children, being outdoors was therefore associated more with the people with whom you could play than with what play equipment was available.

Lights, ceilings and floors

The youngest children's maps, in particular, contained close-up images of a range of indoor and outdoor ground-level surfaces. This included photographs of wooden ramps in the playground for buggies to be pushed up a kerb. These images also drew attention to the sycamore seeds which had accumulated in the crevices nearby. Indoor flooring included photographs of the lino covering in the toilets and the carpeted area. These details were in keeping with the observation made by Colin Ward in his ground-breaking book, *The Child in the City*:

> Obviously the younger the child the closer his eye level to the ground, and this is one of the reasons why the floorscape – the texture and subdivisions of flooring and paving, as well as changes of level in steps and curves is much more significant for the young.
>
> (Ward 1978: 22)

What was perhaps more surprising was the number of images taken on the youngest children's tours, some of which were included on their maps, of the sky and ceilings. Children in the nursery class, for example, took photographs of a mobile on the ceiling and of the strip lighting and a skylight in their Porta-kabin. Similar observations had been noted in the earlier studies using the Mosaic approach. Young children continued to photograph the sky and ceilings at each stage of the research process and in both case studies (see Chapter 2.5).

Beauty and colour

Children's records of the physical characteristics of their school included references to qualities about colour and beauty. These insights would not necessarily have been deduced by interviewing the children alone. However, some of their images particularly drew attention to the aesthetic features of the school.

One example of this occurred during a tour of the school led by two of the four-year-olds, Sally and Nicholas. The children were walking on the pathway around the main school building when Nicholas, who was holding the camera, happened to glance up and spot a reflection of the nearby trees and chimney pots in a window on a sloping roof. He quickly took a photograph before moving on.

I referred earlier to an incident that happened while making photo books with the children in the nursery. Natalie and Jules expressed surprise and annoyance that the shade of blue in their photograph of a radiator cover was a slightly different blue from the object itself. This draws attention to a more sophisticated understanding of colour than that for which young children may be given credit in design projects.

Burke and Grosvenor (2003) draw attention to historical perspectives on children's perceptions of such qualities:

Figure 2.2.5 A reflection in a skylight

Source: Nicholas, Living Spaces study

Children are particularly susceptible of surrounding influences, and their daily familiarisations with beauty and form, or colour in the simplest and most ordinary objects cannot fail to assist in fostering the seeds of taste . . .
(Moss 1874: 360 quoted in Burke and Grosvenor 2003: 135)

It is interesting that this quote is written in the nineteenth century and is not a contemporary observation. Early childhood pioneer Maria Montessori encouraged the development of young children's sense of colour. This included an exercise in sorting variations of up to sixty-three different hues of colour. Montessori describes one five-year-old she encountered who was able to do this task almost perfectly (whilst he still had difficulty naming colours) (Montessori 2004: 193). Margaret McMillan describes the use of the variation of shades of colour in the nursery garden to extend young children's knowledge of colours (McMillan 1919: 102).

Legibility

Lynch, in talking about a city, refers to legibility as '. . . the ease with which its parts can be recognised and can be organised into a coherent pattern' (Lynch 1960: 2–3). Adults and children in schools and early childhood environments share this need to understand the patterns by which the constituent parts fit together. The maps constructed by the four- and five-year-olds who were in the reception class conveyed their knowledge about what parts made up the school. Two of these children, for example, chose a large wooden rectangular block to draw round on their map to represent the school. They then added numbers (1 to 6) to represent the different year groups in the school. They added a separate picture to indicate a child going to the nursery class in the playground. The numbering seemed one way of the children naming their school and, in so doing, defining what happened where. The authors of this map also included other physical features through their drawings and photographs, including the head teacher in his office, the dining hall and the queue (discussed earlier in this chapter) and the entrances and exits of the school.

Another map by another group of four- and five-year-olds included careful attention to the upstairs floor of the school. They took a photograph of the stairs and added their own staircases to their map. At the same time, they drew on the upstairs classrooms. My interpretation of these details was that this older group had worked out a sophisticated place knowledge.

The maps produced by the younger children in the nursery did not contain such a widespread knowledge of the school site. Their way markers were, on the whole, contained in the nursery classroom and the surrounding nursery play space. Drawings added to their maps contained references to doors and windows, for example, and to family and friends, but not to identifying other classrooms. The exception to this was Sally, who included the photograph of her sister's classroom door (discussed earlier in this chapter.)

Toilets

Toilets were a recurring theme across the different phases of the study. This is in keeping with several other studies involving older children's perspectives of school environments (for example Mayall, Bendelow, Barker, Storey and Veltman 1996; Burke and Grosvenor 2003; Sorrell and Sorrell 2005). Children in both the nursery and reception classes added photographs and drawings of the inside and outdoor toilets. The young children were quick to point out the differences between these sets of toilets in school and between school toilets and those with which they were familiar at home. Several children commented about the pleasant smell of the inside toilets, whilst expressing strong reactions against the outside toilets in the school playground: 'The inside toilets smell nice. The outside ones stink!' Comparisons with toilets at home included reference to the size of nursery toilets, with children asking me why they were small. The toilets in the nursery had been fitted with curtains which the children interviewed found perplexing as other toilets they encountered elsewhere had doors.

These discussions about the toilets serve as a reminder that children as young as three years old (and younger) bring their knowledge and experience of other spaces to their learning environments; they are not oblivious to design features.

The implications of some of these perceptions of the physical characteristics of the school landscape are continued in Chapter 2.3.

Discussion

Invisible connections

I have been struck by the importance of the personal in institutional spaces for young children. Children have indicated through their photographs, conversations and map making how their immediate environment contains connections with people, objects and places which provide guides or way markers. These connections may be particularly intricate where a child has siblings or other older and younger friends in the school or setting, or where there are numerous objects or places which relate to themselves. The imaginary city, Ersilia, described by the Italian writer Italo Calvino, is one in which the invisible connections between people and places are made visible:

> In Ersilia, to establish the relationships that sustain the city's life, the inhabitants stretch strings from the corners of the houses, white or black or grey or black-and-white according to whether they mark a relationship of blood, trade, authority, agency. When the strings become too numerous that they can no longer pass among them they leave: the houses are dismantled; only the strings and their supports remain . . .
>
> (Calvino 1997: 76)

What would learning communities look like if these relationships were made visible? Would a primary school environment look very different from a secondary school if viewed in this way?

Foregrounding the informal

The invisible connections children demonstrated drew attention to the importance of the informal landscape in the layers of meaning associated with the school. The study by Gordon, Holland and Lahelma (2000) was carried out in secondary schools. They discuss the powerful influence of the official layer of school, in the cross-national sites in their study, alongside which an informal layer of school of children's culture existed.

The school case study of under investigation in this chapter is a primary school rather than a secondary school. It therefore represents a different form of learning community. I have been seeking to understand the different layers in this school from the perspectives of some of its youngest members. What has emerged is a complex set of views of the official, the informal and the physical dimensions of the school. These characteristics are entwined. However, it seems from looking at this initial phase of the fieldwork when the focus was on the existing environment that the informal layers of school were already strongly developed for these young children. We have seen this in the details revealed about the range of different spaces which co-existed within the physical shell of the buildings and grounds. The importance of personal spaces was brought sharply into focus, for example, through the research tools. This is one area where there may exist a wide gap between adult assumptions about what is important in a learning environment and young children's views and experiences.

Tools and time

This chapter has deliberately been a detailed account of young children's perspectives of their learning environment. I have both discussed the process of listening in this visual, participatory way and begun to untangle some of the themes which have emerged. This provides the foundation for the subsequent investigations of possible spaces, as well as the reviews of completed building projects. It is important, having established that it is possible to gather young children's perspectives of spaces they know well, to spend time looking through the microscope with children to see what they draw attention to in the complex patterns they see. This can be a lengthy process as listening in this way requires repeated discussions rather than gathering ready-made answers. These answers, in contrast, are under construction. Adults and children are working together to construct meanings. Further reflection on this topic continues in the following chapters and particularly in Part IV.

2.3 Possible spaces

Introduction

How can adults and children be involved in discussions about future spaces? Having discussed young children's understandings of existing spaces in Chapter 2.2, this chapter considers young children's involvement in considering new environments. This task, by its very nature, involves dealing with abstract rather than concrete concepts. It is this abstract nature of thinking about future spaces which makes this a difficult topic to approach with young children. Adults can also find this a complex challenge. Architects wishing to engage stakeholders' views on future spaces have explored different ways of capturing these ideas.

Consulting with adults or children can involve a wish-list approach. This relies on those being consulted producing ideas of what they would like. This can be a fairly straightforward exercise to accomplish. It can be seen as enabling people to have a voice. However, there are several drawbacks to this way of consulting, perhaps particularly when working with young children. One difficulty is the tendency to attract impossible suggestions which may raise expectations which cannot be fulfilled. Another drawback is the reliance on people knowing what they would like or how things could be different. This requires adults and children to have had the opportunity to reflect on their current circumstances.

Will Alsop is one of a number of architects to explore creative methods with potential users of a building to feed into the design process. Alsop is an artist and an architect for whom drawing and painting are important parts of design (Powell 2001: 206). It is these means of expression which he has opened up to future users of some of his new building projects by asking people to draw or paint their ideas.

Such an approach is one strategy for bringing a more playful, creative set of possibilities into the sometimes barren landscape of consultation. Ways of fostering creativity has been the focus of the 'Joinedupdesign for schools' initiative (Sorrell and Sorrell 2005). Set up by the Sorrell Foundation, this approach brings together teams of designers and children to produce design solutions. The aim is to enable schools and designers to work together on a design brief to answer the key question: How can good design improve the school's quality of life? The process is described as having four parts: the challenge, the brief, the conversation and the solution. Children and young people have focused on such issues as redesigning toilet facilities, reception and storage areas, and creating social spaces indoors and outdoors. The majority of these innovative projects, however, have been with secondary schools or with older children in primary schools. Overall, children's involvement in the design of specific buildings is an under-researched area:

> There has been little research that has started from the child's view of their own world now – what is important to them in the present as well as feelings about the past and the future, what makes them feel happy and secure, what meanings do they attach to the physical spaces they inhabit and to the people and activities in their lives?
>
> (Clark and Statham 2005: 46)

Documenting possible spaces: indoor environments

It was a deliberate feature of the Living Spaces study to begin by providing time for young children to think about their existing nursery in order to consider a new space. Each of the research activities were designed to give children opportunities to step back and reflect on where they were and what they thought. These activities provided the grounding for exploring ideas about a future space.

This was the first step in making discussion about an invisible future environment less abstract as the children had gained practice in considering what was important to them in their existing setting. The children had placed their nursery under the microscope or behind the lens and honed in on those features which were of particular significance. They had talked about this with their peers and with an interested adult. Discussions about a future nursery were set against this background of heightened awareness.

I was intrigued by what local knowledge of other spaces and experiences children would bring to thinking about what a nursery could be like. I have been challenged on many occasions when presenting my research studies and whether it is appropriate to seek young children's views of future spaces or whether outdoor spaces or indoor environments are appropriate. The reluctance in my questioners seems to stem from an uncertainty about the range of experience which young children can or cannot call upon in future-orientated discussions.

This question of future spaces was a central issue in the Spaces to Play study as the purpose was to involve young children in the redesign of their play area. This was approached in several ways with the children (see Clark and Moss 2005: 43–51): first, through interviews which included questions about features to include in a future space; second by using slide shows of other spaces; and third, by reflecting on documentation gathered about the existing

Interviews with children in the nursery	Slide show of current nursery and different spaces	Model making with small bricks and blocks	Children's review of documentation
Drawing activities	Children's involvement in discussions about future spaces		Initial workshop with architect prior to the research
Interviews with children in the reception class	Whole-school consultation with the architect	Story-based activity	School Council workshops and visits to play spaces

Figure 2.3.1 Children's involvement in discussions about future spaces in the school case study

play area. The slide shows (described in Chapter 1.4) were an attempt to bring into the conversation a range of other environments, some of which would be familiar to the children and others of which might introduce different features. I was keen to enable children to bring to the research their local knowledge of the wider environment, including the shopping centre, the castle and the park. The visual images on the slides acted as a catalyst to help children construct a shared narrative about what an outdoor play area could be like.

Children in the Living Spaces study had several opportunities to express their views about future spaces as part of the research and during earlier discussions with the architects which took place in both case studies before the research began. Figure 2.3.1 illustrates the range of opportunities that were created for the children to participate in this aspect of the design process. These activities took place during one academic year, with activities concentrated in the autumn and summer terms.

Before the research study began, the lead architect in the school case study, Jennifer Singer, had organised a workshop to gather children's thoughts about the new possibilities for the site. Children's ideas were gathered in the form of a wish list of features which they would like to see included in changes to their school. This list included the addition of a tree house. Spaces in which to look out and observe others was one of the ideas carried forward into the designs.

Interviews with children in the nursery and reception class

Asking young children direct questions may contribute valuable insights in to their ways of seeing (for example Smith, Duncan and Marshall 2005; Dockett and Perry 2005). Research by Jacqui Cousins (1999) is one well-documented example of entering into conversations with four-year-olds in order to understand more about their views and experiences. Interviews can provide a structured way to enter into discussion with young children, but some children will be unable to decide or will decide to not offer their thoughts if addressed in this formal way (see discussion in Chapter 1.4 on methods).

Building on the work around the existing environment (described in Chapter 2.2), I decided to ask a number of questions about the new nursery. I remember feeling a level of trepidation. It was difficult to gauge how to phrase the questions in order to give young children the maximum opportunity to share their ideas. Experience gathered during the Spaces to Play study had highlighted how a question which might appear straightforward to an adult could be interpreted in very different ways by a group of three- and four-year-olds. One question demonstrated this problem. Whilst interviewing the children outside about their outdoor space I asked the children, 'What is missing outside at [your preschool]?' (Clark and Moss 2005: 50–51). I intended this question to tap into children's knowledge of the resources already provided and their experiences at home and in other environments. One of the children interpreted the question in the way I had envisaged. Jim replied, 'Another bike because the tangled-up bikes are missing. We took a picture of them.' The 'tangled-up bikes' had been placed by the adults behind a fence and were no longer available for riding. Jim thus saw the bikes as missing and worked out that they could be replaced. However, other children interpreted this question in another way. When asked what was missing, Mollie, Alice and Bob replied, 'the windows.' I had asked the children this question whilst sitting outside in the playhouse, which no longer had a window pane as the plastic sheet had been cracked by vandals. This was a sensible, context-specific response to my question; it highlighted the complexity of involving young children in discussions about future spaces.

I began my questions about future spaces with an open-ended enquiry: 'When there is a new nursery what should it be like?' The intention was to allow children as much scope as possible to give their point of view. The two subsidiary questions were 'What colours should it have?' and 'What about the floors?'. They were chosen in order to explore whether specific adult-led questions about colour and furnishings would be an effective way of involving young children:

Researcher:	When there is a new nursery, what should it be like?
Responses from children in the nursery	
Anna:	I don't know yet.
Helen:	Playdough, sand, teddy bear.
Milly and Jules:	Play with your friends.
Jules:	And with the car.
Sally:	A playground.
Victor:	A sandcastle.
Natalie:	Pictures of Maire and Morgan.

Responses from children in the Reception class

Alex:	Some slides outside because it's not really fun. I like sports.
Yusuf:	Cars and bikes and 'blades' and the train.
Sophie:	Don't forget your book bag and computers.

Some of the children were honest and said they didn't know what the nursery should be like. Anna, one of the younger three-year-olds answered, 'I don't know yet.' This was her response to many of the interview questions, although her photographs built up a clearer picture of what she enjoyed about her present environment (see Chapter 2.5). Other children associated a new nursery with objects with which they enjoyed playing, for example the sand tray and train set. 'Blades' referred to a toy craze linked to a cartoon programme which was popular at the time. Other children wanted a new nursery to be associated with people who were important to them. Natalie's response of 'pictures of Maire and Morgan' reinforces the importance of personal markers for young children (see Chapter 2.2).

There was a practical design dimension to other children's responses:

Nursery children

Nicholas:	Make it hot when you come from outside and tidy up and then go to the carpet and then have fruit. Make it warm yes.
Paul:	Build it properly – build the lights.

Reception children

Fernando:	Bricks and paint it and put everything back . . . Put new boards up for my pictures.
Alex:	Decorations to make it look nice and take the lights off and put sparkle lights. (They've got them in the Argos catalogue.)

Nicholas, in the nursery, referred to the importance of a new nursery being a warm place. This maybe reflected the fact that the interviews were first conducted in November and December (in the United Kingdom). The free-standing building (Portakabin) in which the nursery had been based for over thirty years was not well insulated. This perhaps added to children's awareness of the importance of temperature. There was a strong sense that the job needed to be done properly and tidied up afterwards. Children returned to this sense of the need to restore order several times during the course of the building process (see Chapter 2.5). Jules said to me on a subsequent visit after the old nursery had been demolished, 'The builders broke it.'

It is interesting that these comments about the physical qualities of the space were made by boys. However, during other activities, the girls who were part of the study offered perceptive insights into their learning environment (for example see the account of Sophie's model making later in this chapter and the case study of Anna in Chapter 2.5). This underlines the importance of giving young children – boys and girls – the opportunity to express their ideas using a range of languages.

Choosing colours can be a contentious issue in consultations about design. It is a subject which can highlight differences of opinion and present architects with dilemmas of how to reach a final decision. It can be the only area in which future users of a space are allowed to express an opinion. If this is the case then the subject can be fraught with tension, which may be more a result of frustration over a lack of opportunity to contribute a view than a passionate commitment to a particular colour scheme – more a question of power than interior design.

I was interested to see how the young children responded to a direct question about colour whilst being aware that this information may raise more questions than answers. The responses covered a spectrum of colours, with more girls in this small sample suggesting purples and pinks than the boys. Nicholas was aware that he would like the colours to blend with the other furnishings. Colour schemes were equally varied for the floors. For example, Alex suggested blue, green, yellow and black. Fernando introduced the subject of patterned flooring, which he apparently had a strong aversion to: 'I hate patterns.' This raises the question of what assumptions are made about designing interiors for young children. Perhaps more recognition could be given to the breadth of opinions young children may hold about the sight and feel of their immediate environment, enabling different ways for children to interact and change these features. An infant school in Milan, for example, enables children starting school to dress their empty classroom, by moving cupboards and shelves and choosing displays for the walls, with the help of adults (Children in Europe 2005: 21).

Model making

Interviewing children provides one mode of expression about future spaces, but it seems an inadequate language to rely upon for young children to explore their experiences about their environment. The three-dimensional nature of the subject matter fits more easily with modes of expression which are three-dimensional. Roger Hart, in his book *Children's Experience of Place*, describes how the children in his New England study made models in the dirt to illustrate their local neighbourhood (Hart 1979; 1997: 167). Hart describes small-scale modelling as a useful tool for facilitating exchange between designers and children:

> It is surprising that planners and designers have not made more attempts to work with children using toys and models, for toys are the tools of language between children in their everyday play with each other. Children are most familiar with this medium and most eager to use it.
>
> (Hart 1997: 169–170)

Block play is one of the 'tools of language between children in their everyday play' which Hart discusses. In the Living Spaces study, block play was one of the activities which children in the nursery in the school case study were familiar. The blocks were stored in a carpeted area and appeared to be one of the favourite indoor occupations for boys and girls, although children seemed to choose to work in gendered groups. This familiarity and popularity seemed a good starting point for basing a design activity about the new nursery on block play.

Working in two groups, I asked seven children to build a new nursery. I made available a variety of different textured material which the children could choose or not choose to combine with the blocks. I deliberately did not offer any further instructions. I attempted to create an opportunity for the children to exercise their imagination.

Each group approached the activity with enthusiasm. They created a kaleidoscope of rooms which constantly changed as new features were added or reinterpreted. The first group, with three girls and a boy, were keen to include windows and doors and chose to use drapes as soft surfaces for the floor and walls. A piece of green artificial grass became the roof. Height was another important feature with a tower structure incorporated into the building and a 'sandpit house'.

The second group, with three girls, started by building a chair which grew into a flight of stairs. The girls added a stage with curtains made out of the drapes of material I had provided and cushions. The girls made a carpet area in the nursery, where they first placed the bear and one of the girls. The group then arranged a series of planks to make the floor, which swiftly became a sandpit, then a swimming pool followed by a double bed. At each stage, the girls extended the activity by role-playing different characters and incorporating dolls and a bear into their game.

Photographs were taken of the block play, which became the focus of a slide show with the children. However, the interest in this activity appeared to be in the moment rather than in the recall of the event. This activity was about the process for the children and perhaps for myself as researcher too. The design message was not so much about a final product or image. It was related more to the demonstration of the young children's flexibility and resourcefulness in creating a myriad of play environments.

I approached the model-making activity with children in the reception

Figure 2.3.2 The 'Harry Potter tower' made by Year Two children during model making

Source: Living Spaces study

class on a different scale. The class did not use block play on a regular basis, but they did have access to small wooden blocks. I therefore decided to use these small blocks in this activity for this age group as I wanted to find resources with which the children would be familiar. This would maybe enable the children to concentrate on communicating their ideas instead of exploring a new medium.

The six children chose whether to work in groups or individually. The children were given large circles of card on which to place their models. The models quickly became both three-dimensional and two-dimensional artworks. A sequence emerged whereby the children concentrated on using the blocks to build a new nursery, giving a commentary as they progressed. This was followed by reviewing the structure with me. I used sticky notes to label different features described by the children. The children and I then photographed them. Finally, children drew around some of the blocks and added more drawings; composite three-dimensional maps emerged.

The children each decided to place a new nursery within the context of their existing environment. There were references made to specific features, such as the playground and toilets. Structures of different heights were added including a Harry Potter tower inspired by the popular children's books by J. K. Rowling. The following excerpt below from my fieldnotes illustrates the complex layers which some of the children conveyed through their model making:

> Sophie approached the activity in a purposeful manner. She had joined the school in the reception class so she did not have experience of the nursery class but she had taken part with me in a tour, interview and map making with her peers and so had heard about the 'old nursery' and reflected on what nurseries were like.
>
> Sophie chose to set the new nursery within a garden next to a playground. She paid close attention to the outdoor features of the nursery. These included a 'bumpy roof' and chimney. Equal attention was given to the interior features. Sophie built a tap which appeared on a giant scale compared with the rest of her building.
>
> Sophie's drawing added another layer of understanding about her future environment. She drew bikes for the nursery playground, a comfy corner inside and a place for displaying name cards. Sophie had heard many mentions of these 'talismatic' symbols and decided to include them in a future nursery.
>
> (Fieldnotes of model making with Sophie
> (four years old), school case study)

Documenting possible spaces: outdoor environments

Environments for young children do not necessarily neatly divide into indoor or outdoor spaces but are best thought of as a whole. This was in keeping with

Children reviewing tours and map making		Children reviewing interview responses
	Research activities about the outdoor play space	
Story-based activity		Drawing activity

Figure 2.3.3 Research activities with young children about the outdoor play space

the reactions of the children participating in the study. Their views and experiences of being both indoors and outside were woven together in their documentation – in their photo books, maps and interviews. There was the opportunity, however, to focus some of the discussion in the second phase of fieldwork in the school case study (see Figure 2.3.3) on changes to the nursery outdoor environment. The relocation of the nursery to within the main school building had implications for the outdoor spaces to which the young children would have access. Their new space would be smaller and would change from a square to a rectilinear shape. This new area was to be a shared resource for the nursery and reception class: a Foundation Stage outdoor area.

Discussions about the possible outdoor space began with a review of the documentation the children had produced in the first phase of the study, six months earlier. This was followed by a story-based activity and a drawing workshop.

Reviewing

Small groups of children within the nursery and reception class began by reviewing their conversations with me about the outdoor area and reflecting on their photographs, interviews and maps. The children's photographs from their tours were shown to the children as a slide show on a laptop computer. The review was arranged in an informal way, with the children and researcher sitting on the floor with the computer. The children were in charge of the slide show of photographs so they could decide when to linger on a particular photograph and when to move on. If this technology had not been available, children could have been given the same level of control of the exercise if the children reviewed an album of their own photographs with a researcher.

Some of these children had since moved from the nursery class to reception and so had a different perspective on the space. Sally, for example, had said in the nursery how she did not like going on the circular climbing bars. But when reviewing her thoughts, having moved now to the reception class, she commented, 'But now I can do the ones without the big circles but I can't do the ones with circles.'

Story

One of the challenges was how to harness the children's imagination to think about alternative outdoor spaces. Stories offer ways into other worlds for adults and children, so they presented possibilities for this task. Children listened to a children's story called *In The Attic* by Hiawyn Oram (see Chapter 1.2). The story features a small boy who finds his way to an imaginary attic by climbing a pretend ladder. He goes to many places, including climbing in a spider's web, finding a 'cool, quiet, place to rest and think' and meeting a friendly tiger. This story was the catalyst for thinking about the future outdoor space.

Some of the children had already illustrated how they used their imagination to create different environments within the existing nursery space (see Chapter 2.2). This was a reminder that young children are not necessarily limited by the physical restraints and possibilities of a particular site; they come with knowledge of a range of imaginary spaces gathered from their own cultures.

Drawing

The final activity drew together the children's work to decide on which elements of their old playground should be kept, if possible, which should be replaced and which should be added. Drawing was chosen as the medium. This is in keeping with the principles behind the Mosaic approach; tools which play to young children's strengths were used.

The following themes emerged as important features for the new play area. This included thinking about equipment as well as social and aesthetic spaces:

- places to climb and slide;
- places to sit and wait with parents and siblings;
- quiet places;
- places to 'run around and do things';
- things to keep, including the bikes and balls;
- things to replace, including the tunnel, plants, the playhouse and the sandpit.

The play space which was established alongside the new nursery set out to include these features. Popular toys from the old nursery were transferred to the new space. These were supplemented by expenditure on new pieces of play equipment, including a large climbing structure and a sandpit with a cover.

There were plans to incorporate children's designs from the drawing activity in the soft play surface, but unfortunately budget cuts resulted in these features not being added. A grassy area under trees was maintained. It could provide opportunities for quieter activities. The climbing structure has a hideaway space big enough for a couple of children to hide in together.

The architect's final designs for the exterior of the building included alcoves for groups of children and adults to be together. This feature has been identified by practitioners and children as a popular addition to the school.

Reviewing possible spaces

Dialogue with older children

The participatory research with the youngest children in the school supported the ongoing consultative process with the older children and the rest of the school community. The head teacher, the practitioners and architect had discussions with the older children in the school about their hopes for the new build. The maps produced by the young children after their tours of the school were used to promote more discussion with older children about the future. These maps were on display during a whole-school consultation day, organised by the architect and the school. Each class in turn came to the school hall to see the young children's maps and to review the architect's plans and model. This session was led by the ten- and eleven-year-olds, who were the oldest children in the school. Later in the day, the consultation was opened up to parents and members of the local community for their comments.

Older children were also involved in planning ideas for the playgrounds around the school. These large tarmac areas were separate from the nursery and reception outdoor areas. Members of the school council, from five to eleven years old, spearheaded this project. The young children's maps, made during the Living Spaces study, provided the starting point for this older group to think about their existing playground. This was followed by a series of visits to local outdoor spaces in schools and youth centres before they undertook an audit of their own playgrounds.

Dialogue with practitioners

The primary aim of this study is to involve young children in the design process. However, the contexts for the case studies are learning communities that are shared environments for children and the adults who work in these spaces. This highlights the twofold reason for dialogue with practitioners. It was important to review the material produced by the children with practitioners in terms of understandings about the environment and individual children's current interests and priorities. It was also essential to discuss practitioners' own views on the new building project. A slide show was compiled of children's images taken on the tours. This was shown individually to the early years' practitioners in charge of the nursery and the reception class, together with individual records of the children involved.

Both practitioners were surprised by the level of competence displayed by the children (see Chapter 2.2). This reinforces the value of listening to young children's perspectives in ongoing pedagogical practice as well as for future-orientated research (Kinney 2005; Carr *et al*. 2005; Driskoll and Rudge 2005).

Dialogue with parents

Slide shows of the children's images facilitated exchanges with parents. The children's photographs provided an immediate and concrete way into discussions about the children and the parents' insights into their children's views and experiences of the nursery and reception class. Several of these discussions took place in school, but on one occasion the interview took place with a mother and her nursery child in their home. Parents may experience frustration and seldom receive an informative reply when trying to find out from children of all ages what they did in school on a particular day. The children's photographs provided another way into such a conversation.

One of the benefits of talking to parents was to hear their own experiences of the school environment. One father commented that a particular walkway was difficult to pass through in the morning as the gap between the classroom and fence was very narrow. This useful piece of information was prompted by an image of this passageway taken by his daughter. It is possible that without this visual catalyst he would not have thought to share this information.

Dialogue with architects

Dialogue with the lead architect, Jennifer Singer, took place through the different phases of the case study. This included discussions at the school and specific workshops based on the children's documentation at the architects' office with other colleagues. (These interactions are explained in detail in Chapter 3.3.) Reflection on the children's material led to a debate among the architects about specific aspects of the design changes to the school in the Living Spaces study, as well as wider aspects of the design process. The general reaction from the architects was one of surprise at the environmental competency expressed by the children. The material produce by the young children demonstrated that they had built up layers of knowledge about their immediate surroundings, including how the nursery was part of a detailed cognitive map of the site which the children had assembled.

Emerging design themes

There were four main themes which were discussed: personal markers, scale and perspective, legibility and privacy. (Each of these themes have been discussed in Chapter 2.3.) This summary draws attention to the design implications of these themes, which influenced the design changes.

Personal markers

The young participants in the school case study showed how their feelings about the space were linked to their own sense of identity. First, this was demonstrated by children drawing attention to any detail which made reference to themselves (see Chapter 2.2). Children photographed their own photographs on their coat pegs and any other references to their name in the classroom. In some cases this included photographs of artwork on display. Second, children identified features which they linked with members of their family, whether parents or siblings. Some of the children were keen on the tours, for example, to point out places where they sat with their parents at the start of the day. Several children photographed their siblings' classrooms.

This material reinforced the importance of ways of identifying particular space for individual children within the nursery. One early design idea was to create cubbyholes for each child in the cloakroom area. This design question links to one of the challenges taken up in the Joinedupdesignforschools initiative (Sorrell and Sorrell 2005). A group of nine- and ten-year-olds asked for somewhere to keep their own things in school. The children suggested some innovative ideas, for example, 'How about having chairs with cushioned seats that have a fabric locker on the back for your bag and coat; it could have your name on it' (Amy, age ten, in Sorrell and Sorrell 2005: 140). The final design in this Joinedupdesignforschools initiative, developed with designer William Warren, involved personalised lockers, each of which had a different front door design which could be customised by the children with different handles and plaques.

Scale and perspective

The children's images raised questions about scale. There were examples where the environment could be seen to disadvantage young children. They stretched up to take a photograph over the top of the counter into the school office. The entrance way to the school, down a passageway surrounded by high brick walls, appeared daunting from the perspective of a three-year-old.

A different sense of perspective was conveyed by children's attention to the sky, ceilings and the ground. One of the messages seemed to be that designing for young children needs to take into account this attention to close-up details and far away spaces (see Chapter 2.2). Seamus Heaney (2002), the Irish poet, draws attention to the ability for people to be drawn to fine details and the wider horizon. He uses as an illustration the Roman god of boundaries, Terminus. The statue in the temple of Jupiter was rooted to the ground and was open to the sky:

> And it is this double capacity that we possess as human beings – the capacity to be attracted at one and the same time to the security of what is intimately known and the challenges and entrancements of what is beyond us – it is this double capacity that poetry springs from and addresses.
>
> (Heaney 2002: 48)

There have been examples in this study of this double capacity in young children to seek the security of what is intimately known and relish acres of blue sky. Perhaps this duality has been overlooked, to some extent, in designing for young children. There are echoes of this idea in the Scotland Street Primary School in Glasgow, designed by Charles Rennie Mackintosh. The outside and inside of the school are enhanced by two glass spiral staircases. Walking up the stairwell, children and adults can look through the square glass tiles to the sky before approaching lowered ceilings with a different sense of scale.

In response to the photographs of the sky, ceiling and floor surfaces in the Living Spaces study, the architects designed island-like floor patterns and a unique ceiling with a swiss cheese pattern and floating clouds to mimic the sky. The architects worked closely with the engineers to create a special lighting scheme to enhance the ceiling design. There were also several skylights in the new sections of the building to open up the sky to both children and adults. The final designs included a variety of platforms to create different scales of spaces for teaching, drama and play. All the joinery was designed with the scale of the nursery child in mind; the lower shelves and cupboards were accessible primarily to the children and the upper storage cupboards were accessible only to the teachers.

Legibility

Children demonstrated the importance of feeling connected with other parts of the site, including the outdoor spaces. Low windows and glass panels in doors enabled children to remain in touch with the places which were important to them, to see family members or to connect with adults, such as the school administrators, in the school. Trancik and Evans (1995) identify legibility as an important design criterion in promoting young children's competency in early childhood provision: 'Legible environments inform the user of their orientation in space, easing their movement through a building' (Trancik and Evans 1995: 52).

A key feature of the final design in the school case study was the foundation hub. This room forms the link between the reception and nursery classes, providing the main point of transition into the nursery. The aim has been to help children and adults to feel connected to the main body of the school and to its surroundings. The foundation hub features a transparent roof and large folding doors to open it up to the outside. This room extends into the covered play space, allowing the children to enjoy the outdoors as much as possible, even in inclement weather. In addition, the new nursery features a big bay window which allows the children to see out onto their play space and towards the entrance gate, where their parents and siblings come to meet them at the end of the day.

Privacy

A private space may be somewhere to go to be alone or to withdraw with friends (see Chapter 2.2). Altman (1975 quoted in Trancik and Evans 1995) describes privacy as the ability to regulate social interaction. This inter-pretation places an emphasis on the agency of the individual to control the desired level of contact with others. Play spaces which provided privacy had been identified as important places by young children in my two previous studies (see Clark 2004 and Clark and Moss 2005). Initial observations in the nursery in the Living Spaces study raised the question of how few oppor-tunities the environment appeared to offer for children to withdraw.

The architects debated how privacy could be provided within the parameters of an early childhood environment, where the ability to observe children at all times is seen, in the United Kingdom, as an important con-sideration. This led to a discussion about how to make explicit the values on which early childhood practice is based. It is far easier for architects to work with clients who are explicit about how they see children and childhood. Reflecting on projects undertaken, the architects in this discussion group felt that, in the majority of cases, the clients' values had remained implicit, which made the task of design more difficult.

The final designs included alcoves around the school building for parents and children to sit together before school or for groups of children to gather away from the thoroughfare of the playground.

Discussion

Creating contexts for thinking about design

This chapter has described how participatory research methods may provide one way of involving young children in the early stages of the design process. Rather than beginning by asking children for a wish list, the research approach has been to create a context where children can explore their existing envi-ronment and share these understandings with adults. The design themes which have emerged, such as privacy, legibility and the importance of personal markers, are not new concepts in the field of early childhood design. What is more unusual, however, is having these design issues reinforced by material gathered by young children, thus bringing to life the reality of living in such environments for young users.

The original aim of the Living Spaces study was to involve young children in the design process. One of the methodological questions raised after the first year of the study was on how practitioners could be supported in reflecting on their working environment. Discussions with practitioners and architects had underlined how complex a task it was for practitioners – whether they were new to their role or experienced in it – to make their implicit feelings about an existing environment or desires for a future space explicit. This question is explored in the next chapter by involving both adults and young children in a post-occupancy evaluation.

There appears to be a tension in consultations about design. Should consulting children about design be about grasping ready-made answers to design questions? This could be seen as a technocratic response based on a managerial style of listening. Relying on a wish-list method as the only source of information from children could be interpreted in this way. One alternative to this approach is to see consulting children about design as part of a pedagogical enquiry. This latter approach is more subtle. It will not necessarily produce a list of neat solutions, but this way of working may open up new possibilities. A pedagogical approach can make room for adults to learn more from children about how they respond to different environments and resources. This tension between a technocratic and a pedagogical approach mirrors wider tensions within debates about participation, which I return to in Part IV.

I am reminded of a conversation with an architect student who was having difficulty with his assignment. He had been asked to construct a new infant school. His problem did not rest with the design challenge but with the second part of his assignment: 'Explain your new building to a class of five-year-olds.' His question to me was: 'How can I explain my ideas in a way which will make sense to the children?' I reassured him that his audience would bring something very important to the discussion: their imagination. If he could capitalise on this, through for example storytelling, then he would be dealing with a potentially more receptive audience than a room of adults as young children will not be limited to a repertoire of buildings they have already seen.

I referred at the beginning of this chapter to the potential difficulty of involving young children in thinking about future spaces due to the apparent abstract nature of this enquiry. One of the challenges of this area of work is how to make the abstract notion of a future space into a real experience for young children to explore. At this point, it is important to grasp the potential of the hundred languages young children represent. Answering questions devised by adults about colour and space are unlikely to lead to a rich source of new understanding. However, conversations with young children in tandem with storytelling, model making and exploration of real materials, sound and light may enable more young children to contribute to new possibilities in design.

2.4 New spaces

From the moment it is conceived through its design, production, use, continuous reconstruction in response to changing use, until its final demolition, the building is a developing story, traces of which are always present.

(Markus 1993: 5)

Introduction

This chapter explores how young children's narratives about completed buildings can be included in discussions following changes to indoor and outdoor environments. This discussion will be continued in the following chapters, where I investigate how practitioners and parents can be part of this process. This chapter looks at the new spaces created in the school case study, followed by the children's centre case study.

Gathering children's perspectives of new spaces can be problematic. Some of these difficulties rest with adult assumptions about the kinds of narratives we expect to hear about completed building projects. These dangers are illustrated in an encounter between a Chief Education Officer (CEO) and a nine-year-old boy (East Riding of Yorkshire (England) Education Committee 1967). The boy is described in this account as a 'client'. His school has changed from a two-roomed school into a new school which amalgamated three small schools:

> CEO: How do you like your new school?
> John: Smashing.
> CEO: What do you like best of all about your new school?
> John: The dinners.
> CEO: But what else do you like? Are you learning new things?
> John: Yes, I like those French bairns on the film.
> CEO: Is there anything else you don't like about the new school. For instance, don't you find it too big?
> John: Mister, I likes it all. It's just like being in heaven.

CEO: Splendid. Goodbye, John.
John: Au revoir.

(East Riding of Yorkshire (England)
Education Committee 1967: 16)

This short conversation reveals the differences between the expected narratives about the new school and those proposed by John. He declares that the dinners are the best feature of the new school. The CEO's disappointment in this response is almost palpable. The senior official is concerned to hear about the official school of curriculum and learning. The CEO has another expectation based on his adult perspectives of the new school relating to scale. John seems to sense the required answer and manages to draw this embarrassing encounter to a close. It is unlikely that a short conversation between an adult in such a position and a child would elicit much understanding about the reality of being in the new school. However, there may be other ways for children to establish what they think about being in a new space and for adults to engage with these perspectives. This chapter seeks to explore how visual, participatory narratives may enable children to think about what it means to be in a changed environment.

Children's narratives of new spaces: school case study

Following the building work, the nursery class in the school case study was now situated in the centre of the primary school rather than in an isolated corner of the playground. The nursery class and reception class were now next to each other, joined by a shared space or hub. This was designed as a cloakroom area and a play space for wet or sand play or large-scale construction activities. The area had skylights and opened with sliding doors along one side into the outdoor play space. The original design plans were to include a large cubbyhole for each child in the nursery. Practical difficulties resulted in this idea being replaced with pegs and small shelving for children to store their belongings. Working with the children about the existing environment had highlighted the importance of giving attention to the ceilings and floors. The new nursery ceiling included variations in texture. Lighting had been included in several cloud-shaped forms. There were wooden, carpeted and vinyl floor surfaces. Changes in texture and colour were used to indicate different areas of the classrooms.

A walkway had been removed during the building process to make way for the new rooms. This walkway had led to the main entrance to the school. Attention was drawn to the new entrance by alcoves. This is part of seating which follows the line of the new learning resource centre. This well-lit space with low windows – bays on the inside and alcoves on the outside – is the first part of the school seen by visitors. There is a small reception area with space for adults and children to sit and for displays. The counter to the office is low enough for young children to see in easily. Children and visitors walk through the learning resource centre to the rest of the school. It has a light, welcoming feel. Deep, warm colours are used for the cupboards and shelving which contains accessible shelves for children and storage space for adults.

The nursery is designed with this dual purpose in mind; it is a learning space for young children and a work environment for an increasing number of adults. There is a large open-plan area to prepare food. A carpeted area includes steps to a small stage. This contains a bay window through which children can look out onto the play space. The toilets lead off from the main nursery room. Built-in cupboards provide storage as well as display space.

The outdoor play area includes several new pieces of play equipment, including a slide and climbing structure. A store has been built which is surrounded by built-in seating. The play space is easily accessible by both the nursery and reception classes. A grass area (with trees and plants) has been preserved so the children do not need to be limited to playing on the artificial play surface.

One of the challenges of conducting research with young children during real building projects is dealing with the length of time involved from early designs to completion. Young children who were three and four years old (in the nursery) when the school case study began were six and or seven years old when the new parts of the school were ready for occupation. This adds a further complication to the notion of involving young children in the design process. It is not a simple question of gathering their perspectives, bringing these understandings to the design, building and evaluating the final product with the users. In the case of members of a nursery or nursery class, changes other than very minor ones are unlikely to be completed whilst the child is still a member of the nursery. The new users will not have been involved in the original consultation. The children who were originally consulted will have moved on and are unlikely to be familiar with the new changes. This dilemma may be confronted with adults and older children involved in consultations. However, the problem is magnified when those consulted are very young.

Despite these difficulties, I was interested in investigating ways of enabling young children to reflect on new spaces. I was looking to see what the children would identify as important in the new environments and whether this would bear any resemblance to themes which had emerged about their existing environment. I drew on two broad groups of children in the school case study: an older group of students (currently in Year One or Year Two classes) who had been involved in the first and second phase of the study and a new group of children who were current members of the nursery and reception classes. Twenty-nine children from three to seven years old were involved in this phase of the study (see Figure 2.4.1).

The aim of involving children in the post-occupancy review was to see what insights the children's perspectives would add to an understanding of the life of the buildings after completion. Insights gained from gathering children's views and experiences of their existing environment suggested that such a

New nursery children three- and four-year-olds (6)		Children in Year One five- and six-year-olds (6)
Reception class children four- and five-year-olds (6)	Children's groups involved in the review of the school case study	Children in Year Two six- and seven-year-olds (11)

Figure 2.4.1 Children's groups involved in the review of the completed building in the school case study

review using participatory, visual methods would give some insights into the physical changes. The question remained whether children would also reveal their views and experiences about the official and informal landscapes of school. This following section discusses the children's maps about the finished building in the school case study.

Twenty-nine children were involved in leading tours of the completed building, taking photographs and assembling maps. The eleven children in the oldest group had each taken part in the earlier phases of the study, as had five of the six participants in Year One. The twelve children from the reception class and nursery class were taking part in the study for the first time.

The tours and map making created a wealth of data. There were 551 digital photographs taken, of which the children selected 206 photographs to be displayed on the eighteen maps. The maps also contained the children's captions and some drawings, which added further insights into the significance of the images which had been selected. The Year Two maps were made on large circular card that was over one metre in diameter. This format echoed the

Table 2.4.1 Children's maps about the finished building in the school case study

Class	Children involved	Photographs taken on the tours	Photographs chosen by the children for the maps	Maps produced
Year Two	11	163	87	5
Year One	6	124	37	4
Reception	6	148	33	3
Nursery	6	116	49	6
Totals	29	551	206	18

design of some of the original shared maps made by this group. A smaller format on rectangular card was chosen for the remaining maps. The larger maps provided a useful format for discussing with wider groups of children. The completed maps were displayed on the windows of the new learning resource centre, where children could look at the maps from the playground. A maximum of ten to twelve photographs could be displayed on the smaller maps, in contrast to eighteen or more on the large maps. This smaller number focused the children's attention on choosing the most important images and placed a necessary limit on a data-gathering activity which could have become overwhelming for the children and the researcher.

Physical landscape

The maps, both directly and indirectly, drew attention to certain features in the physical environment. There were specific images and captions which highlighted particular spaces. These photographs had a particular focus which was clarified by the captions chosen. Other photographs gave insights into different parts of the school buildings by the scale and perspective indicated. A further category of photographs added to understandings about the new features by capturing the school in an everyday mode with groups of children engaged in official or informal activities. These images of living spaces are in contrast to many taken by architects on completion of new buildings. These are often taken before the building is occupied; as such, they have a ghostly quality, with no children or adults present.

Alcoves

The bays created around the learning resource centre or library, in the heart of the new part of the school, featured on many of the maps, particularly those made by the older children. These alcoves provided spaces for small groups of children to gather or for an adult to sit with one or two children during playtime. One of the oldest children commented on his map: 'This is a nice place to sit down if you are sad' (Alex, Year Two). Several children photographed each other standing in the alcoves on their child-led tours of the school. Another image, labelled 'the way to the office' revealed a small group of boys busily engaged in swapping cards whilst two girls sat together looking out at the playground. These spaces appeared to provide an element of privacy amidst the hectic activity of playtime. They also appeared to act as way markers, indicating entrances into the school.

Lights, ceilings and floors

Particular attention had been given to the ceiling surfaces in the new nursery. This included the selection of textured ceiling board to vary the view of the ceiling from the children's perspective and to provide a surface to which objects could be attached. Different light sources were introduced to create a range of lighting effects. Several of the maps made by children in Year Two drew attention to these features. Nicholas, for example, took a close-up of the spotlights in the hub which joined the nursery and reception class. His caption read: 'The light is shiny.' Another Year Two map included a close-up of the patterned ceiling: 'The ceiling looks like cheese.'

Sometimes the angle of children's photographs revealed details about the effect of a design feature. A wooden floor which was in contrast to the floor coverings in the rest of the school had been fitted in the learning resource centre. One of the photographs taken by a girl in the reception class showed an expanse of shiny wooden floor surrounded by new pink shelving.

Transparency

The maps revealed how children could feel connected with the outside whilst inside or be connected to friends or siblings inside if they were outside. Children chose, for example, to take photographs of the playground through the glass doors in one of the corridors: 'I can see the trees' (Year Two map). These connections with the outdoor environment led to some photographs which emphasised the aesthetic qualities of the surroundings. A Year One map included a photograph of the sun shining through the surrounding trees: 'The sun. It looks nice like a star.'

One of the maps made by a girl in the Year One class included a photograph she had taken from the playground, looking into the new learning resource area. There was a group of children listening to a story at the time. She labelled the photograph 'the reception children in the library'. The low windows meant that she could easily see in and the children could see out, even when sitting on the floor. Another such space was evident in another photograph of the new nursery. It was taken by a member of the reception class and showed a group of children sitting in the bay window which overlooked the outdoor play area.

Absent spaces

Several of the children chose to photograph where the old nursery had stood on their maps. This was illustrated by close-ups of the tarmac where the Portakabin used to be or of old play equipment which had been left in the surrounding borders. Another change which was photographed was depicted by a metal gate. The children's narratives which followed were not about this gate; they were about a wooden gate, in the same position, which had been a temporary feature during the building work. The wooden gate had presented an enjoyable challenge, which several children commented on and included on their maps. Nicholas commented, 'I can see a gate. When we had the wood gate everyone liked going under the gate' (Year Two map). It is interesting to see how children could use photography to indicate past and present experiences of the landscape. These temporal spaces are discussed in detail in Chapter 2.5.

These observations indicate how the children's maps of the completed building did provide some insights into how the physical changes to the site were perceived by the children. However, in a similar way to the explorations of the existing environment, children's map making revealed how these insights into the physical dimensions of the building were inextricably linked to the official and informal aspects of school.

Informal landscape

Children's perspectives on their existing environment had revealed complex layers of understanding which drew particular attention to the informal landscape of personal, private, social, imaginary and caring spaces. Each group of maps constructed about the

Figure 2.4.2 Year Two map of the new space in the school case study

Source: Living Spaces study

new spaces contained a similar range of insights into these informal landscapes, which existed alongside the official landscape of the curriculum, teaching and learning and the physical environment.

Personal spaces

Children across the age range of three to seven years who were involved in making the maps of the new space found different ways of highlighting personal markers. These included self-portraits. One of the boys in the reception class, for example, included an image of himself with the camera in the reflection of a mirror. The different classes involved each had a number of practices for identifying children's belongings within the space. The nursery class had maintained the use of the duck-shaped name cards to register children. Two of the six children in the nursery who made individual maps of the new space included the duck name cards. One of these maps was made by a boy who had recently joined the nursery and had not yet spoken. He chose a photograph of the duck name cards to be on his map. The cloakroom area included large photographs of each child by their peg. He also took a photograph of this portrait of himself by his peg to go on his map. The name cards were also selected by older children who included the new nursery on their tour.

The older children had trays in their classrooms to keep their books and belongings. Several children photographed the trays, taking great care to include within the frame a close-up of their names. Trays and pegs were chosen by children to indicate personal markers relating to siblings around the school. Two of the Year Two children included an image taken in the nursery cloakroom area: 'A. is my sister. She goes to nursery in the morning.' Older children's classrooms, furniture and trays were identified by some of the children who had older siblings in the school. Two girls who were in Year One made sure their tour of the completed site included the first floor of the school, which had not featured on any tour before. They took me into an empty classroom which was one of the girls' sister's classroom. They quickly identified her wooden chair and took a close-up of the back of the chair and then photographed her drawer which she had decorated with her name.

The children across the age groups did not express a connection between the images they included on the maps and their parents. However, several of the children included photographs of books which they commented could be taken home. These included, for example, a close-up of the reading scheme books with the caption: 'you can go next door and take a book home' (Year One map).

Private or social spaces?

Children's maps of their existing environment had drawn attention to the few opportunities for private spaces within the school environment. The few spaces which were identified, such as the playhouse in the nursery garden, acted as both private and social spaces, offering the chance to be in a small group away from the whole class and from adults. A few spaces which could offer this dual function were identified on the children's maps of the new environment. The alcoves around the learning resource centre discussed earlier were examples of how a feature of the school building could offer the chance for privacy and to be with friends. Two new pieces of play equipment in the Foundation Stage outdoor play area provided this opportunity. The new slide and climbing structure had three interlinked towers, each with a hiding space in their base. Children were quick to point out these hidden spaces on the tours of the new environment, and several maps included close-up photographs of this equipment. A shelter provided a similar space where small groups of children could play with construction toys and watch what was happening in other parts of the play space.

Indoor private spaces were less apparent than these outdoor spaces in the children's photographs of the new building. One such private space had been created in the book corner of the new nursery. Soft furnishings and tent-like, brightly coloured drapes had been added. This was designed as a quiet area for reading alone or in small groups. This space was included on maps made by children in the nursery and in Year One: 'It's like a princess chair' (Year One map).

Imaginary spaces

The maps made by the youngest children showed more examples of imaginary spaces than the maps made by six- and seven-year-olds. A boy and a girl in the reception class chose, for example to include three photographs on their map, each of which appeared to be a close-up of a plain wall of colour: bright pink, bright green and bright blue. The images were in fact close-up shots of different surfaces. The captions declared that the bright pink image was 'the kingdom', the bright blue image was 'the pond' and the bright green image was 'the grass'. The blue and green photographs in fact showed close-ups of different coloured soft play surfaces in the outdoor play area. These were isolated islands of colour designed to break up the play area. The naming of these spaces by the children were indications, perhaps, of imaginative narratives which had begun to be built up around these features.

The maps made by the nursery children of the new environment featured several examples of games which were in progress at the time of being involved in the research activity. This was the case in one of the youngest boys' map. He was three years old. His map seemed to take the observer right up to and then within the role-play games he was absorbed in. The camera angle was so close that it feels as though the viewer is entering the imaginary world of the child. The scale of objects is altered by the perspective, so suddenly peering inside a toy microwave oven appears to be like looking into a garage where an egg cup has grown to the size of an office chair (see Figure 2.4.3).

There is a similarity here with some of the earlier photographs taken by children who were three and four years old at the time of the start of the research. Jules (see Chapter 2.2) took a close-up image of a toy island which was designed to be played with small figures. His photograph takes the viewer inside the tunnel entrance.

It is interesting that these examples of imaginary spaces have been created by the children using toys which are commercially produced. Perhaps young

Figure 2.4.3
A play cooker

Source: Henry,
Living Spaces
study

children who had access to a more varied set of resources, including natural materials, would reveal a wider range of imaginary landscapes.

'Official' landscape

Work and learning

The maps included several references to work – whether children or adults engaged in work. This included descriptions by children in the youngest class. One of the girls in the nursery took a photograph of a teacher and group of children engaged in an activity at a table. She included it on her map with the caption 'they are doing work'. A comment by one of the girls in Year One contrasts the discourse of work with that of play: 'We do computers for typing not just playing.'

Narratives about learning took different forms. References to literacy included photographs of both reading scheme books and stories in the book corners and in the library. A boy in Year Two was unusual in drawing attention to numeracy activities. He took a close-up photograph of a large number six on a floor tile in the nursery: 'I like the number six and I like Maths and it's my age.' This comment suggests that the photograph represents learning and acts as a personal marker about his identity as a six-year-old.

Rules and order

Objects which conveyed school routines of control were photographed around the school. A boy in the reception class took a photograph of the hand bell which was rung at the end of playtime. The nursery class had a system of giving stickers as rewards. A close-up of the sticker box was included on one of the nursery maps: 'The sticker box for eating your dinners.' Certain spaces were associated with good behaviour: 'You should read quietly in the library' (Year One map). Forbidden spaces included the old outdoor sandpit: 'We should never go in the sand' (Year One map). Anna's map (discussed in detail in Chapter 2.5) named a specific function with a description of the expected behaviour for each area she photographed. This sense of order was perhaps of more importance to some children than to others.

Practitioners

There were more adults depicted in photographs on the maps of the new spaces than of the existing environment. Each of the reception maps, for example, contained references to teachers. This may have been because children's tours of the new environment took them throughout the school and more adults were encountered. The teachers and teaching assistants showed pleasure in being photographed; these smiling photographs were chosen to be shown on several of the maps.

Food

There had been very few references to food on the maps of the existing school. One of the girls had drawn attention to waiting for lunch, but this was an isolated example. This may be because food did not have a high profile within the old nursery. Lunches were delivered on trolley from the school kitchen. Snacks were prepared in a small kitchen within the old Portakabin but out of sight of the children. The new nursery contained a large food preparation area in the main body of the nursery. Photographs of this area were added to several of the maps of the new space, including one showing an adult preparing food and a stylistic photograph of iced pink and white biscuits displayed along the pink counter: 'Nursery made the cakes' (Year One map).

Displays

The new learning environment was rich in displays in the corridors and in the classrooms. These objects were part of the physical landscape and were representations of the official and informal discourses about school. A new display area had been created by one of the entrances to the playground. At the time of the children's tours of the new building, the board showed a map of the world which had been covered in individual portrait photographs of each child in the school. Each class was positioned on one area of the map together. Several of the children in Year Two took close-up photographs of this display and included these photographs on their maps: 'This is a map of everybody in the school' and 'My brother and his friends and my teacher'. The display could be seen as part of the official landscape by being about geography, but it seemed to act as a strong personal marker in the school for the children involved in the tours. The markers showed traces of siblings, friends and self-identity. Displays may be one of the elements of the school environment which exist in the intersection or borderland between the official, the physical and the informal.

Children's narratives of new spaces: children's centre case study

The next section of this chapter discusses carrying out a review with young children of a different type of building: a children's centre (see Chapter 1.3). This centre brings together a nursery school, which had been expanded to include provision for children under three years old, new Sure Start facilities for children and families and existing community spaces.

Children's perspectives of the new space

The children's centre case study focused on a post-occupancy review, with young children, parents, practitioners and architects, of a completed space. The following account focuses on the involvement of young children (under five years old) in this process. (See Chapter 3.2 for details about working with practitioners and parents.) Reviewing the completed children's centre represented different challenges for me as a researcher from the first case study. The longitudinal nature of the school case study resulted in a dialogue with young children being established over a two-year period. There was a shared history of the design process between the children and the researcher. It was not possible to develop this shared narrative in the same way with the children in the children's centre as the building process took place before the research began.

There were several consequences of entering the design process at this later stage. One consequence was the focus of the review. This needed to be on the children's perspectives of their present 'new' environment. Another consequence was the possibility that the young children would find it disconcerting to work with a visitor if there was less time to build up a rapport with the children. This was countered by the decision to work with a practitioner on each of the research activities to provide some continuity for the children. Paula, a nursery practitioner, had made her own map of the new space, so she was familiar with the tasks (see Chapter 3.2).

Nineteen children in the nursery school were involved in this phase of the research: six of the children (three girls and three boys) were three years old; thirteen of the children (eleven boys and two girls) were four years old. This sample was comprised of almost half of the children (forty-two in total) who were in the over-threes' part of the nursery.

This direct work with the children (see Figure 2.4.4) took place over a four-week period. Preparation for this work included three days of observation in the indoor and outdoor spaces. These written observations were supported by a photographic record of the new and existing parts of the building. These

Tours of the centre (16 three- and four-year-olds)		Interviews and drawing (11 three- and four-year-olds)
	Research tools with young children	
Map making (16 three- and four-year-olds)		Observation

Figure 2.4.4 Initial research tools used to gather young children's perspectives in the children's centre case study

photographs provided a point of comparison with those taken by children, practitioners and parents in the study. Two aspects of practice in this nursery in the children's centre became clear during the observations. First, there was a free-flow system in operation; children were able to move around the indoor and outdoor spaces. Second, the nursery had a key worker system; each child belonged to a group with a particular practitioner who meet in specific parts of the room (called 'islands') at regular times each day. These were denoted by noticeboards which displayed the children's photographs and names. These photographs were carefully presented and gave these objects status within the room.

Examples of tours and map making

Working with Paula, the practitioner, and I, children were asked in small friendship groups of two or three to take us on a tour of the nursery, starting from where they came into the children's centre in the morning. I have chosen the following two accounts to illustrate a tour given by two children who were less familiar with the nursery and two who were more settled. Each of the four children spoke English as an additional language.

Jasmine and Mohammed

Jasmine (four years and one month old) and Mohammed (four years and five months old) were very familiar with the nursery and confidently took Paula and I on a tour. Mohammed began by taking a photograph of me, which seemed to reinforce that he had taken over control of this activity. Moving on from the entrance door, Mohammed and Jasmine took us to where they liked to go first thing in the morning when they first arrived. Mohammed went to the graphics table, which was surrounded by easily accessible paper and writing material. He took a photograph of this area, which Paula confirmed was where Mohammed usually chose to be when he arrived. Jasmine led us outside. She pointed out the muddy corner where children could dig. Back inside, the children took us to their islands. Paula pointed out that she could see Jasmine's name. Jasmine took a photograph of her name and then, picking up her profile book, proceeded to take thirty carefully chosen images of pages within her book, including a photograph of Jasmine when she was younger and close-up images of some of her paintings and collage. These profile books are individual child-held personal records (see Chapter 4.3). Paula confirmed that her profile book was a very important part of being in the nursery for Jasmine. Mohammed was then keen to find his profile book. His photographic record of his book included close attention to the pages which featured his siblings, parents and other family members. Jasmine and Mohammed took photographs of the computer and the block play area before going outside again, where Jasmine took her final image of the spades in the mud.

When Jasmine and Mohammed met me the following week to make a joint map of the nursery, there was a strong emphasis on images of themselves or work created by themselves. The fourteen photographs chosen for their map comprised four portraits of themselves, including two from their profile books when they were younger. There was one image of Mohammed's brother and four photographs of artwork from the profile books. The remaining five images included four images of the outside area.

Ali and Omar

Two of the younger children to take part in the tours and map making were Ali (three years and ten months old) and Omar (3 years and eight months old). These boys, in common with the majority of children in the nursery, were acquiring English as an additional language. Ali was a couple of months older, but he had only recently joined the nursery. He appeared more withdrawn in the nursery context than Omar, who was very talkative. These boys had two opportunities to take photographs of their nursery. The first time was with the nursery practitioner, Paula. She noted how Ali in particular was reluctant to move beyond the room where they began the activity. A technical problem with the digital camera resulted in these images not being able to be printed. This served as a helpful practice for a second tour with Paula and I.

On this second occasion, Ali still found it difficult to hold the camera and push the button. I decided to offer to work with Ali and to take photographs at his request in an attempt to enable Ali to stay as involved as possible. On their tour, Ali and Omar drew attention to several features about themselves. Omar remembered his profile book and photographed pages of his drawings. He fetched Ali's profile book too. Ali clutched his book close and I took a photograph. The cover shows Ali's name, date of birth and a photograph of him playing in the nursery. The boys took me to their island display and close-up photographs were taken of photographs of them and of them standing by these photographs.

During this research, Ali was not able to take his own photographs, but this was a skill he could have developed if given more familiarity with the camera. However, he was able to select which of the photographs he wanted to include on the joint map of the nursery that he made with Omar. Ali chose seven photos to add to this map. Three of these seven images were self-portraits and a fourth image was a close-up of a painting he had made (which was in his profile book).

It seemed as though in Ali's efforts to make sense of this new early childhood landscape, he was holding on to those objects which had a tangible connection to himself. The routines around the key worker system and the profile books appeared to support the building of these connections in the space.

Drawing together the material gathered by the young children about this newly completed environment, the following themes emerged. These linked to those discussed in the review of the school case study.

Physical landscape

Scale and perspective

The children paid great attention to the ground – whether inside or outside – but they paid particular attention to the mud in the garden and the insects discovered there. Soft play tiles were also photographed in close-up, revealing a surprising multi-coloured textured surface when viewed from this angle. These microscopic shots were matched by other telescopic views, which stretched up to the rooftops of the original school building and to the sky. Katie and Leo, two of the four-year-olds, both chose to turn the cameras up to take photographs of the open sky as their first chosen images. Leo's photograph, when developed, revealed the edge of a plant which had seeded itself in the guttering.

A sense of perspective was eloquently conveyed through one of the youngest children's sequence of photographs of corridors and doors taken from his height. This drew attention to the number of opaque surfaces encountered through the day.

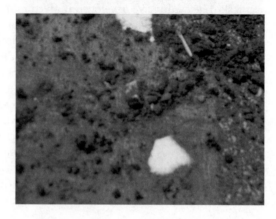

Figure 2.4.5
Board school roof and the sky

Source: Living Spaces study

Figure 2.4.6
A close-up of muddy
ground taken on a tour
led by four-year-olds

Source: Living Spaces study

Indoors and outdoors

The nursery operated free-flow play throughout most of the day. This almost continual access to the outdoors was illustrated through the frequent inclusion of a wide variety of activities taking place outdoors. These included spontaneous gatherings of older and younger children, for example gathering round a newly discovered ant, playing with water or on the bikes or singing in groups with an adult. The outdoor area was shared with the youngest children who belonged to the under-threes' part of the nursery. This resulted in adults and children from the younger groups mixing among the older children. This lack of segregation was captured in some of the children's images. Leo, for example, was delighted to see Clara, one of the practitioners, sitting outside and chatting to a baby in his pushchair. Clara and the baby turned around to smile at Leo. Both Leo and Clara appeared to be pleased to be recognised.

Forgotten spaces?

The children did not mention or photograph areas in the nursery where food was prepared. There was a pantry in the main nursery building where snacks were prepared, but children did not normally have access to this space.

The children's tours did not take us to the toilets. Each toilet had a low wooden door. The space opened onto an open area where the sinks were situated next to the coat pegs. This perhaps suggests the toilets were an area of the nursery which was taken for granted.

'Official' landscape

A strong pedagogical feature of this nursery in the children's centre was the key worker system, features of which were the regular gatherings at 'island time'. Discussion with the children suggested that this routine was an important feature of the children's day: 'It's tidy up time, it's read the story time' (Ricardo, age four).

Island time was associated with being with the individual practitioners and with stories, both reading books and listening to stories: 'It's Rachel's island. I like stories' (Chelsea, age four); 'Ewa and the books' (Jacob, age four). These were storied spaces which had been given meaning by the activities which took place there. These were also spaces which were associated with named people, unlike the nursery class in the school case study. Profile books were another element of the pedagogical practice. Here there was an overlap between the official landscape and the informal landscape as this pedagogical practice is infused with the personal.

The children in this case study did not refer to themselves as 'working' or did not use this word to describe what the practitioners were doing. However, adults were present in many of the children's photographs, engaged with small groups of children, often outside. They were a very visible presence, perhaps seen as more a part of the informal than the official in this play-based practice.

Informal landscape

Personal markers

The tours and map making had revealed strong identification with the children's profile books, which were rich child-held records of their time in the centre. Several children stopped and took many photographs of pages in their profile books. These included photographs of members of their family, as well as photographs of their younger selves with examples of their drawings, paintings and writings.

Children in this case study were more able to find traces of themselves around the nursery than children in the school case study. The island bases provided a designated area where each key worker could display individual photographs of the members of their group, clearly labelled with the children's names and mounted on different coloured card. These distinctive photographs were displayed in the particular area of the nursery where each group met. Children's profile books were also stored in these areas.

Children identified other personal markers outside. There had recently been a new border established with seeds planted by some of the children, with the children's names written on labels by the seeds. Several children included this border on their tour of the centre and added photographs of it on their maps.

Social spaces

There were similarities between the two case studies in terms of the social spaces (in the outdoor environment) identified by the children. Several children in the nursery identified particular play equipment, for example the playhouse and the 'wobbly bike', as opportunities to be with friends.

Photographs taken on the tours showed numerous examples of spontaneous gatherings of children around found objects in the outdoor play space. These included the discovery of a worm in the digging patch, which led to a crowd of interested children forming around it. There was a similar happening around an ant (which unfortunately met an untimely death in the process of being photographed too closely).

These research activities with groups of children in the nursery in the children's centre case study were part of a cycle of listening about the new spaces. Another phase of activities involved a specific focus on planned changes to the outdoor play space (see Chapter 3.3).

Discussion

'New' in the present

This chapter has discussed two examples of reviewing new spaces with young children. This has revealed details of the complex layers which combine to form learning environments for young children, whether these spaces are part of a larger school or a community facility. The concept of new spaces for young children raises questions about whether this term applies in the same way as it does for adults. The longitudinal case study in the school enabled me to revisit the new space with a group of children who had experienced the old nursery and were still members of the same school. This group of children had experienced the changes, whereas for the majority of the children I met in the children's centre case study, this prior knowledge was not part of their experience. This suggests that the purpose of reviewing a new space with young children may be more about gaining a greater understanding of how they perceive this present environment rather than expecting this task to involve comparisons with the old space. Further debate about questions of time and space are taken up in Chapter 2.5.

Who does the listening?

The role of researcher was different in the two case studies reviewing new spaces. I was the sole facilitator in the school case study, working with the young children by myself. My role changed to be one of co-researcher with the children and a practitioner in the second case study. There were several advantages to working together. The children felt at ease with the practitioner. There was a long-established practice within the nursery school for engaging young children's views, so the activities were not unexpected. It was of particular importance to be working with a familiar adult when engaging the views and experiences of the younger or shyer members of the group. A further advantage could have been gained if the children had been able to work in their home language with a practitioner who shared this ability.

The new spaces under consideration are not only environments for young children. Post-occupancy reviews need to include the perspectives of children and adults. This challenge is taken up in Part III.

2.5 Temporal spaces

Before it can ever be a repose of the senses landscape is the work of the mind. Its scenery is built up as much from strata of memory as from layers of rock.

(Schama 1995: 7)

Introduction

A study which sets out to involve young children in the process of physical change to their environment involves explorations of the concepts of time and space. This chapter focuses on three related aspects: longitudinal views of children's spaces, developing environmental literacy and evidence of compressed time. First, I look at understandings gained by revisiting children's experiences of spaces over time in more detail. How might children's priorities and interests in the physical environment develop? What areas of importance may remain constant?

Second, I explore how young children's sense of space and place can be infused with their past associations with that environment (as first discussed in Chapter 1.2). This theme links with Bachelard's notion of 'compressed time':

At times we think we know ourselves in time, when all we know is a sequence of fixations in the spaces of the being's stability – a being who does not want to melt away, and who, even in the past, when he sets out in search of things past, wants time to 'suspend' its flight. In its countless alveoli space contains compressed time. That is what space is for.

(Bachelard 1994: 8)

This exploration of the relationship between time and space is also explored by Michel de Certeau, who refers to the layering of experience in particular locations by using the metaphor of place as 'a palimpsest' (de Certeau 1988: 202). We may be familiar with this idea from our experience as adults, reflecting back on the numerous memories built up over time and in diverse circumstances which are linked to familiar places (Israel 2003). What is perhaps less familiar is the notion that young children can demonstrate a building up or layering of emotional responses to a place over time.

Third, I raise questions about young children's environmental literacy. I illustrate how this can develop through living and engaging with changes to familiar spaces. Each of these three aspects of exploring spaces over time is illustrated by examples of engaging with young children through the course of the school case study.

Taking the long view

I will begin by exploring insights to be gained from taking a long view when looking at changes to spaces with children. I have discussed the inherent complications of working with young children within the timeframe of a real building project (see Chapter 2.3). The length of time between the research phases in the Living Spaces study was dictated, to some extent, by the construction process. One result of this was that my research encounters with the children were at longer intervals than had been the case in my earlier studies. Table 2.5.1 gives an example of the length of time between my fieldwork visits to the group of children who were originally in the nursery class in the school case study.

My discussions with the children needed to grapple with the temporal nature of the study in several ways. There were discussions about new abstract environments. Children also needed reminding about the research after the long periods of time between research visits.

I decided to make a short book which would be a joint narrative of the research process so far and the next stages of the building process. It was intended to be an artefact which might help the children to reflect about the past and to more fully understand what would happen in the future. In my part of the narrative, I was keen to try to increase the children's understanding of the slow pace of change (see Box 2.5.1).

This was a difficult concept to convey to the three- and four-year-olds to whom I was talking. The following dialogue is an excerpt from an interview with Sophie. It shows her relating the length of time the building changes would take to her forthcoming birthdays:

Researcher:	'What will happen next?' Well the builders are going to start in August when you're on holiday, and ... 'Alison will be talking to you about what the playground should be like at [your school].' And then, it says, 'The new nursery will take a long time. When the new nursery is finished you are going to be older. In fact, you are going to be . . .'
Sophie:	Six!
Researcher:	Yeah.
Sophie:	Six-and-a-half.
Researcher:	Six-and-a-half, yes. So I am going to come and see you again and ask you about the new nursery.
Sophie:	When I'm six.

Table 2.5.1 Timeline to illustrate intervals between fieldwork visits to children originally in the nursery class in the school case study

Phase one (2004): October–November	6 months later	Phase two (2005): May	18 months later	Phase three (2006): November

---

Box 2.5.1 Introduction from unpublished book (2005) about the new nursery

Somethings take a very short time – like saying hello.

Somethings take a bit longer like putting on your shoes or eating your dinner.

Somethings take a lot longer like the time it takes from being three to being four.

And somethings take even longer – building a new nursery is like this.

[Your] school is going to have a new nursery and some of the children have been helping to plan what it should be like.

It takes lots of people to make a new nursery. Jennifer is the architect. Her job is to decide what the new nursery should look like and to tell the builders what to do.

Alison is a researcher. Her job is to find things out. She likes to find things out from children. Children from the nursery and the reception class helped Alison to find out lots of things about A. which she told to Jennifer.

This is the story of what happened . . . and what is going to happen next.

Hidden narratives

One of the advantages in reviewing children's perceptions of their environment over many months is seeing how these interests may change or become more visible. Sometimes adults working with young children may be aware of their predominant interests and values, but with other children these interests and values may remain hidden. The following example of Samina illustrates how revisiting children's visual narratives may reveal important details about children's lives.

Samina had just had her fourth birthday when I first worked with her during the first phase of the school case study. English was an additional language for Samina, but she was at the time almost silent in the nursery. She joined one of the other girls to take me on a tour of the nursery. Samina used non-verbal communication to indicate that she was happy to use a camera. She would respond to my questions with one-word whispers. Several of her photographs were of people. Two of them were of her friend, Sarah, one was of a boy and one was of myself. Samina took a close-up photograph of the outdoor play space with a sandpit in the background and a photograph which, at the time, I thought was of the sky. When Samina came to choose which photographs she wanted to include in her book of the nursery, I learnt a little more about her interests.

Samina chose five of her photographs. She communicated her wishes in several ways. When I showed her the photograph of Sarah her eyes brightened. She glued this photograph onto the cover of her book. Samina pointed to the photograph of the outdoor space. I asked, 'Is this the sandpit?' She shook her head. I tried again, 'Is this the ball?' There was a small basketball in the far corner, to which Samina nodded. The next photograph Samina pointed to had a close-up of myself in the foreground. The majority of the photo was taken up with the sky. A few clouds were in the centre of the image and the treetops and top storey of the school were visible along the bottom edge. Towards the right-hand edge was a small dot in the sky. I asked if this photograph was about the sky, but Samina shook her head. There was a tiny speck of an aeroplane in the distance so I asked, 'Is it the aeroplane?' Samina nodded. I wrote the caption 'the aeroplane' next to the photograph in Samina's book.

When I returned to the school two years later, Samina had completed her time in the nursery and reception class. She was now in her second year (Year One class). She was six years old. Samina came across as a vivacious child who appeared to be very at ease in school. She had one close friend. They declared to me that they were each other's best friend. These two girls took me on a tour of the completed building and made a map together. Whist on the tour, Samina took a photograph of an aeroplane flying overhead. Before assembling the map I met with Samina to review her earlier involvement in the study. I showed her (and her friend) the book Samina had made with her photographs in the nursery class. (See Chapters 1.4 and 2.2 for details about making photo books.) The following transcript is an excerpt from this review:

Samina: What's that? That's you?
Researcher: That's me. Yes this is me, and it says . . . because there's something else in the picture, I don't know if you can see it, it's very small?
Samina: Aeroplane.
Researcher: [Laughs] So two years ago you took a picture of an aeroplane and you took an aeroplane this time, as well, didn't you? I thought that was quite funny. So I decided you maybe liked aeroplanes, but I don't know.
Samina: I . . . I love . . . home and I like . . . Bangladesh . . . country.

Researcher:	Oh right, yes, and that's your country and that's why you like aeroplanes. Ah, of course, that makes a lot of sense, yes . . . Did you have to sleep on the aeroplane?
Samina:	I wasn't being asleep but my sister went fast asleep on the aeroplane.
Researcher:	Did she?
Samina:	And she didn't even eat any food.
Researcher:	[Laughs] Right.
Samina:	And I waked her up and I was so scared on the aeroplane.

Figure 2.5.1 'An aeroplane'

Source: Samina, Living Spaces study

This might have been interpreted as Samina randomly selecting an aeroplane on both tours. However, it is clear from Samina's own narrative that she was using the visual language of photography to describe an important element of her life: her sense of belonging to Bangladesh. The review confirmed that this element of her identity remained strong after two years in school. This cultural identity was a part of the narrative that Samina had constructed with me over time.

This example highlights the importance of the role of visual technology in reinforcing children's sense of identity and belonging in different environments.

Developing environmental literacy

Young children's developing competencies can be frozen in time whilst conducting a longitudinal research study. This is one of the advantages (and pleasures) of talking with the same group of young children at intervals over several years. One of the differences I have noticed has been changes in children's ability to express their views and experiences about their physical environment. Further study is needed to investigate to what extent such changes are due to their language and cognitive development and whether the revisiting of ideas about their space has contributed to this greater awareness. I refer here to what may be described as 'environmental literacy' – an ability to articulate views and experiences about physical spaces from the perspective of oneself and others. I would like to illustrate an example, which took place during the Living Spaces study of this developing competence. The following account describes two meetings (which took place two years apart) with one of the girls in the school case study.

Anna was one of the youngest children to be involved in the school case study. When I first met Anna, she was three years and seven months old. She was attending the nursery on a part-time basis. She appeared to be very quiet in the nursery context and shy when engaging with other children or adults. She had an older sister in the school. Anna took part in each phase of the study (before the new nursery was built and in the review process). I have chosen to look at her responses in more detail here as she was one of the children whose ability to articulate her views and experiences developed the most over the two-year interval in her involvement in the study.

During the first phase of fieldwork, Anna took part in several research activities (see Figure 2.5.2). During my observations in the nursery, I noticed Anna often playing by herself. I suggested she worked with one of the younger boys in the class.

Victor also came to the nursery only in the mornings. Anna and Victor began by taking me on a tour of the nursery, starting from the gate through which they entered the school site. The children took me to different parts of the school grounds rather than concentrate on any one location or activity. Several of Anna's photographs revealed an attention to the ground (with close-up shots showing pathways). Anna sat and watched the slide show of the tour on the laptop and enjoyed being in control of pressing the button to move through the photographs. She made few comments as she looked at the images, but she showed pleasure in showing the photographs of the tour to her mother.

	Tour	Parent interview
Map making	Anna (three years old)	Child interview
Practitioner interview	Slide show	

Figure 2.5.2 Research activities involving Anna in the first phase of fieldwork in the school case study

Table 2.5.2 Description of Anna and Victor's nursery photo book

Child chosen caption	Subject matter
Big children's playground	Passageway from nursery to the school playground
Path and the gate	Pathway to one of the entrance gates
I like playing with that	Dressing up corner with close-up of a handbag
No caption	Paint pots on the easel
No caption	Border of the school garden showing bushes and trees
No caption	The research bear

Anna and Victor chose six images from the tour to show on their map. Three of the six chosen images were of outdoor spaces. This included the playground where the older children played, including Anna's sister. Two aspects of the classroom were singled out: the dressing up corner (particularly a handbag with which Anna liked playing) and the painting easel. Anna and Victor also chose to include the teddy bear which accompanied me on my visits to the nursery. Children photographed the bear to practice using the digital camera. Anna and Victor then chose this image to be part of their map. It could be seen as a desire to include the present moment in the activity. There was an absence of any people in the images; this was in contrast to the maps and books produced by the other children.

My notes at the time reflected that, 'Anna did not include people whether children or adults on this map. Perhaps these places were associated with people but Anna did not express this in the interview' (extract from fieldnotes made following the tour and map making).

Interviewing Anna was a difficult process. It very quickly became evident that this was a process in which she did not feel competent engaging. Her response to each question was 'I don't know yet'. My interview with Anna's mother took place with Anna in their home, at her mother's request. I had planned to interview children's parents at school, but the home setting for this interview, with Anna present, revealed further insights into Anna and her priorities and interests.

Anna and I worked together just over two years after our first meeting. However, during this gap Anna would have seen me visit the school from time to time. Anna was now five years and eight months old. She was in the second year of the primary school. She displayed great confidence in showing me around the changes to the school, both indoors and outdoors. She showed particular skill in being able to present both a personal account and an observer's account of the environment.

Many of the images chosen by Anna for her map were about place use, for example, places to read, play football and change library books. Anna was able to detach herself from her immediate environment and comment on the space.

She was able to reflect, for example, on the gazebo: 'The gazebo is good because people can sit in it and talk to their friends.' Several of the places were

Table 2.5.3 Description of Anna's map made in Year One

Anna's chosen caption	Subject matter
The nursery can read books when they want to	Nursery reading corner
It's pretty good because the nursery and reception can sit on it	Bench around the shed
The gazebo is good because people can sit in it and talk to their friends	Close-up of the gazebo
Nursery and reception can have good things to play with	Large-scale fixed play equipment in a shared outdoor space
The stage is good. Nursery like playing on it	Close-up of window and stage built into the new nursery
H. Garden gate for people who live there	One of the entrance gates to the school
The lost property box is good when you have lost your stuff	Photo of the box
The library is quite important for people to change their books	Interior of the new library
The boys like playing football . . . that's why it is quite important	Outdoor shot of the football net

thus shown to be social spaces, but they were not shown in a way which necessarily included Anna herself. There were no intended people – adults or children – in any image. (There is a person just in one frame, but Anna's description indicated this was not a deliberate part of the photograph.) Anna referred to objects or places which could be seen to be personal markers less often than other children who were interviewed. The lost property box could be seen to be one such marker, as confirmed by her teacher who remarked on how Anna did loose her things. Another personal marker was a photograph of one of the gates through which Anna came into school. This was the same entrance she included on her earlier map. She did not choose, however, to include any images relating to her sister, her sister's class or sister's friends. This was in contrast to another girl in her class who included visits to her sister's classroom on the tour and on her map. This may be because Anna and her sister did not seek out each other's company, as her mother had discussed with me two years earlier.

Anna chose to draw attention to and comment on four of the new design features in the school. Two of these features were of internal changes. She included an image of the new library, with sunlight coming in from the new skylights, which clearly shows the new shelving, paintwork and wooden floors. Her chosen caption is about place use: 'The library is quite important for people to change their books.' However, the photograph seems to display an environmental literacy perhaps associated with older children or adults. The second internal feature Anna includes is the stage. This was a specific design feature of the new nursery. It included a protruding window to give children good visibility to the playground and to their parents. Again, Anna's comments convey her ability to consider a space from the perspective of others: 'The stage is good. Nursery like playing on it.'

The two new external features included by Anna were the shed and the fixed play equipment. Her comments display a similar ability as her comments about internal spaces to consider the appropriateness of environments for others. The outdoor play equipment is described as 'Nursery and reception can have good things to play with' and the shed with its built-in seating is described as 'it's pretty good because nursery and reception can sit on it'.

It is possible to see considerable changes in Anna's ability to articulate her views and experiences of her school environment. In particular, she appears to demonstrate an environmental literacy in her photographs and an ability to review design features from the perspective of others. Other children involved in the school study demonstrated some similar examples of an increased ability to articulate feelings about a space, but Anna demonstrated the most change over the two-year period. Perhaps, as in the development of other literacies, some children will demonstrate greater abilities than others. One of the challenges is how to nurture these skills and harness such insights for the benefit of reviewing existing spaces and creating new ones.

The final theme of this chapter on temporal spaces considers the notion of children's demonstration of compressed time in more detail.

Compressed time

What can we learn from children about how memories are linked to places and objects encountered in the present? Children involved in the studies I have carried out using the Mosaic approach have used maps to convey their memories. The clearest example of this was in the Spaces to Play study (Clark and Moss 2005). Colin (four years old) was insistent about taking me on the tour he led to an unused piece of ground for him to take a photograph. He said this was the 'show'. He then chose this photograph to be used on his map of the outdoor space and he added his own drawing of the show. Following a conversation with the practitioners in the preschool, I found out that a puppet show had taken place on that spot the previous summer (some fifteen months earlier). Even though the event had taken place many months previously it was part of Colin's narrative about the space. Another example was of one of the boys in the Listening to Young Children study who expressed his dislike of one area of the outdoor play space. He associated this with a distressing event which had taken place there. John was able to articulate this in an interview (Clark and Moss 2001: 19).

These examples challenge the notion that young children are always living in the present. The geographer Tuan (1977) writes:

> Place can acquire deep meaning for the adult through the steady accretion of sentiment over the years, every piece of heirloom furniture, or even a stain on a wall, tells a story. The child not only has a short past, but his

eyes more than the adult's are on the present and the immediate future. His vitality for doing things and exploring space is not suited to the reflective pause and the backward glance that makes a place saturated with significance . . . Young children, so imaginative in their own spheres of action, may look matter-of-factly on places that to adults are haunted with memories.

(Tuan 1977: 33)

Tuan suggests that it is not only that young children have not lived long enough to acquire much of a past, but it is their captivation with the present and the next immediate event which limits their abilities to hold memories about objects or places. Tuan indicates that young children do not demonstrate the emotional depth to hold such associations:

The child's imagination is of a special kind. It is tied to activity. A child will ride a stick as though it were a real horse, and defend an upturned chair as though it were a real castle. In reading a book, or looking at its pictures he quickly enters a fantasy world of adventure. But a broken mirror or an abandoned tricycle has no message of sadness.

(Tuan 1977: 33)

This impression appears to be at odds with more recent research involving gathering young children's perspectives (for example Cousins 1999; Brooker 2002; Carr *et al*. 2005). These studies, among others, reveal early childhood institutions to be spaces 'saturated with significance' and full of areas, people and objects which have messages of sadness and delight. This has included reminiscences about an abandoned bicycle in the Spaces to Play study (see Chapter 1.2). This layered nature of meanings in children's spaces has been explored further by other researchers within the social studies of childhood, including in the edited volume, *Children's Geographies*, compiled by Holloway and Valentine (2000). This sociological lens has provided an impetus for developing child-centred methodologies to enable children to explore and express their experiences about environments (Holloway and Valentine 2000: 8). These strategies may in turn challenge previously held beliefs about children's attachment to place and space.

Perhaps it is not as straightforward as young children having 'a short past' as Tuan suggests, but of having a concertinaed past squashed together but nonetheless capable of intense memories. This links to Bachelard's comment 'in its countless alveoli space contains compressed time' (Bachelard 1994: 8).

I have chosen to look at one of the maps produced by Jules and Natalie (see Chapter 2.2) in more detail here. This map was completed during their review of the completed building. These children were involved in each stage of the study and were among the more verbally articulate about their environment. I was interested to see whether their perspectives would provide glimpses of compressed time, and whether this would be articulated through words or images.

Table 2.5.4 Description of Jules' photographs on his joint map of the new building

Child chosen caption	Researcher's description of the subject matter
The old class of Year One	Temporary classroom that Jules and Natalie's class had been in during the building work
No caption	Close-up of display board about future careers showing Jules and Natalie dressed in their future roles
It is a map of everybody in the school	Display of everybody in the school
Miss S and N	Display showing photos of Jules' teacher and peers
This is in the library and we can choose books to read at home	Close-up of new library shelf with view out of the window
No caption	Wide-angled shot of the playground
No caption	Close-up of estate manager's flat
Ducks because if someone is not here we know they are not here	Registration cards in the shape of ducks in the nursery
So we know where all the people live	Display in nursery of a map of the world and faces connected to where people had links
No caption	Gazebo in the playground in process of being reassembled
No caption	Display of people in the nursery class

Two of Jules' captions were references to past objects and places which related to his own shared history of being in this place. The first photograph was a view into an empty room. This room was part of the new additions made to the school. It was the classroom temporarily used by Jules' class. They had been in the room for two terms. He described his photograph as 'the old class of Year One'. It seems that he acknowledged that the time spent in this classroom was part of his personal and shared history of being in this place. All physical traces of this temporary use of the classroom had been removed. It was currently being used as a family room. However, it appeared to be an important part of Jules' conceptual map of the school site; it was a reminder of the past in the present.

The second photograph with an explicit reference to the past was of the registration cards used in the nursery. These talismanic cards were identified by many of the children as important features of their existing environment in the first phase of the study (see Chapter 2.2). Jules chose to include a photograph of these duck-shaped cards on this second map made with Natalie. His caption emphasises the significant role the duck cards played in the life of the nursery: 'Ducks because if someone is not here we know they are not here'. The presence or absence of the cards signified to the children which of their peers would or would not be joining them that day. It is interesting that Jules chose to use the present tense. This brings these artefacts from the past into the present. It is perhaps one example of compressed or concertinaed time.

Other images chosen by Jules bear traces of past events, but they are not verbalised by him on the map. The gazebo is one example. He has photographed this playground structure which is in the process of being reassembled. It is one of the features of the old playground which suffered from the building work. This shared space where adults and children sat and talked was dismantled whilst the construction work was in progress and it was left half standing, surrounded by hazard tape. Jules had pointed this out to me during an earlier visit. He remarked, 'Oh that is what the builders broke.'

Jules' images made reference to the future and the past. On the map, he included a photograph of a display in his current classroom. The photograph showed Natalie and Jules dressed in their future roles. The photograph shows him holding a model of a building and looking as though his aspirational career is to be an architect!

I have discussed the images chosen by Jules which have a particular temporal dimension to them. Others emphasise the people who inhabit the present reality of being in the school: his teacher and peers and members of the nursery. These connections are conveyed through his photographs of displays of other photographs showing these people. The displays, in this sense, appear to be more than decoration as they have a tangible value in representing his social networks within the school. This theme is a strong feature of the images chosen by Natalie (see Table 2.5.5).

Several of Natalie's photographs have a biographical element which in turn emphasises her friendships within the school. She includes a photograph of her

Table 2.5.5 Description of Natalie's photographs on her joint map of the new building

Child chosen caption	*Researcher's description of subject matter*
My brother and his friends and his teacher	Close-up from display board showing brother and his class and teacher
A photo of the door of the library	Close-up showing teaching assistant waving in the doorway of the library
So we know it is about . . . Primary School	School sign on the entrance gate
My friend's name is C.	Close-up of nursery dining table showing friend's place name (in her own writing)
I like it because it is a nice picture by reception	Close-up of face of a portrait painted by a member of the reception class
My friend's little sister is in the nursery	Nursery class sitting on the carpet talking to a teacher
Where the old nursery used to be	Outdoor shot showing edge of old nursery garden with a pile of old sandtrays and chairs

brother, his peers and his teacher. This suggests that connections with her family are an important personal marker for Natalie within the school. However, it is an image of her brother in the context of his class rather than an image of an isolated figure. This suggests that her association is not only with her brother, but perhaps with his friends as well. In a similar way, Natalie includes a photograph which represents her friend in the nursery (who is two years younger than Natalie). Her friend is represented by her name card, which is written in her friend's own handwriting and is displayed as a place name on the table where lunch is served. Another image demonstrates the extent of Natalie's social connections across the school. The photograph is of her friend's younger sister sitting and talking with the nursery teacher on the mat. Natalie includes a record of her own past in the environment by displaying a photograph of the border next to the place on the site where the old nursery used to stand. The image includes some of the old equipment – sand trays and a pile of chairs – once used in the nursery but now abandoned.

Jules and Natalie's map contains both personal and shared knowledge. Christensen discusses a similar combination of children's experiences in her ethnographic study of children living in a village: 'Their emplaced knowledge is partly biographical and personal but is also collectively produced' (Christensen 2003: 20).

Natalie and Jules' personal and shared narratives reveal the school environment to be a peopled place with traces of the recent past and more distant past. There are also metaphorical lines running off the map to their future selves. Their identities appear to be embedded in their membership of this school community, with its multiple connections with peers, family members and older and younger friends.

Discussion

Retelling over time

A longitudinal study of what it means to be in a place may be seen to represent the opportunity for the children involved to revisit and retell their own narratives about themselves. This may be a rare chance to articulate their sense of self which is developed over time within a learning landscape.

Philosopher and theologian Rowan Williams (2000) discusses the importance of narratives in enabling people to construct their sense of self over time. He discusses how,

> . . . there is a way of constructing, of talking about or figuring, what's going on that is open to the questions, Why *this* reaction? Where does this sensation or response or desire belong? Or, most simply, What's it (literally) like? – and is, as a result capable of representing, however sketchily or inadequately, the time that has made a subject what it is.
>
> (Williams 2000: 142)

It is at this most basic level of 'what it is like' that the narratives constructed by the young children in the form of conversations, photo books and maps are perhaps contributing to early constructions of self through time. Children can revisit, re-evaluate and reconstruct using the documentation they produce as a springboard. Williams refers to the importance of this opportunity to revisit and re-edit through narrative:

> . . . If my narrative is simply a cumulative story of things happening, I shall treat each event as an abstract item to be catalogued, and I shall fail to see how what happens reorders what I have been as well as shaping what I shall be . . . Every 'telling' of myself is a retelling, and the act of telling changes what can be told next time, because it is precisely, an *act*, with consequences, like other acts, in the world and speech of others. The self lives and moves in, only in, acts of telling – in the time taken to set out and articulate a memory, the time that is a kind of representation (always partial, always skewed) of the time my material and mental life have taken, the time that has brought me here.
>
> (Williams 2000: 144)

The children's documentation can be seen as a series of acts of retelling. Each time they revisit the material there is the opportunity to reflect on the experiences described and on the process of documenting or 'moment of telling'. One such moment occurred when Samina reviewed her photo book constructed two years earlier. She commented, 'I wasn't even talking.' This brief comment acknowledged her recollection of her silent self in the nursery.

Opportunities for retelling formed a central part of my relationship with the children involved in the study. My point of contact with the children was not prescribed by a written curriculum but by an interest in understanding more about their local knowledge of their environment. My return visits to the children were prefixed by my return to previous interactions with the children. Each subsequent visit began with me reminding the children of what they had told me on previous visits. Their imparted knowledge formed the starting point for new conversations. Pedagogical practice which supports this type of reflection is discussed further in Chapter 4.3.

This discussion so far has emphasised the possible benefits to individual children of seeking their views and experiences of their environment over time. There are, however, wider possible advantages to a community of learners.

Longitudinal local knowledge

If children remain on the same school site for several years, they can build up accumulated knowledge about the explicit and implicit features of that environment. For some children, a school may remain the one constant feature in a changing pattern of home life between different households and locations. This knowledge may therefore hold greater significance for the individual children involved. The value of sharing acquired local knowledge may have both an organisational and individual benefit.

I have not had the opportunity to explore the possible contribution of children who have been previous users of an environment to contemporary design changes. However, this could offer a rich source of local knowledge. Perhaps classroom objects could be a catalyst for such recollection:

> Classroom objects have the potential to elicit indirect accounts of personal experience. Telling stories about objects can enable pupils and teachers to explain to an outsider the nature of school cultures, to make connections between events of yesterday and today and to locate themselves in history.
> (Burke and Grosvenor 2003: 140)

Such accumulated knowledge about an environment could also be applied to other children's spaces, including residential home and hospital wards.

Christensen discusses this accumulative nature of meaning making about environments:

> In the understanding that emerges from embodied movement through place, knowledge and perception are not separate: knowledge of place becomes part of the dialectic of perception and place that traverses the whole life course. Knowledge of place accumulates and changes over one's lifetime through inhabiting, being and becoming in a place.
> (Christensen 2003: 16)

The Living Spaces study has been a longitudinal study of children's emplaced knowledge of a changing environment. The physical area under study is small, but this does not preclude the accumulation of emplaced knowledge as the children grow, inhabit, be and become in this particular environment. Focusing on young children in the early stages of their life course may contribute to a wider understanding of how this local knowledge is developed, strengthened or challenged.

2.6 Conclusion

Part II is firmly rooted in the detailed observations of young children about their environment: existing, possible and new spaces.

Chapter 2.2 began this exploration in children's narratives about what is important to them about their nursery. Material gathered from their tours and photographs, map making and interviews reveals glimpses of the official landscape of school. However, these insights appear to be pushed into the background by the importance of informal spaces which are closely linked to the physical environment.

Chapter 2.3 tackled the difficult subject of involving young children in discussions about possible spaces. This tried to avoid falling into the wish-list trap of relying on young children to be able to articulate their environment needs and wants.

Chapter 2.4 moved back onto firmer ground by gathering children's views and experiences about built spaces. This included accounts by children who had memories of the existing spaces and those for whom the spaces are new environments. The children's documentation revealed similar strata of the official, informal and physical layers seen in the earlier phases of the research. The older children's maps, whilst showing fewer details of imaginary spaces, still paid considerable attention to personal way markers within the building.

Chapter 2.5 explored some of the relationships between space and time which have emerged. Using material from the longitudinal school case study, I discussed some of the advantages of taking the long view in listening to children about their environment. This revealed some hidden narratives about individual children's priorities and also challenged some previous assumptions about young children's inability to hold memories about spaces and places. Looking at young children's changing perspectives raises a question about environmental literacy and how this can be encouraged and employed within the design process.

The following chapters place young children's perspectives alongside those of adults who share these spaces.

Part III

Facilitating exchange

3.1 Introduction

The emphasis in Part III is on how ideas are communicated within the design process. The attention moves from the direct interactions with young children to look at how young children's interests and priorities may be the catalysts for exchanges with architects, practitioners and parents. The communication of ideas among these different participant groups requires crossing many boundaries. There are disciplinary boundaries between architecture and education. There are professional and lay boundaries between architects and education practitioners and parents. These are in addition to the generational boundaries between children and adults involved in the design process. Crossing boundaries requires time to establish common languages and understandings and to discover new modes of listening. Perhaps the hardest boundaries to cross are those which remain unarticulated, where different individuals who are involved in a process of change are unaware of others' assumptions and perspectives. Different hierarchies of power add to these complexities. What theories and practice may help facilitate exchange when designing and reviewing learning spaces?

I would like to return here to the pedagogy of listening as it has been articulated by those engaged in the preschools of Reggio Emilia and understandings about documentation as a means to facilitate the exchange of ideas about learning environments (see Chapter 1.2). Rinaldi, in discussing the pedagogy of listening, identifies three main elements:

- internal listening or self-reflection;
- multiple listening or openness to other 'voices';
- visible listening, which includes documentation and interpretation.

(Rinaldi 2005; Clark 2005b: 35)

Listening, as understood here, involves both an internal and external process. Listening to others needs to begin with an awareness of one's own ideas, assumptions and experiences. Documentation can be used as part of this process as a self-reflective tool to explore these ideas through the collection of, for example, visual images and narratives. I have discussed these ideas elsewhere in relation to young children involved in the Spaces to Play study:

Internal listening acknowledges the importance of listening as a strategy for children to make sense of their world. Listening is therefore, not just an avenue for other people receiving information but a reflective process for children to consider meanings, make discoveries and new connections and express understandings.

(Clark 2005b: 35)

The question I raise in the following chapters refers to how involvement in the design process requires adults as well as children to make sense of their world(s), whether this is their existing, future or new environment.

The complex number of participants involved in a design project brings to the fore the importance of 'multiple listening'. Rinaldi points out that this need for engaging with multiple perspectives is not limited to certain phases in the building process; it is at the centre of being a school or learning community:

This is what a school should be: first and foremost, a context of multiple listening. This context of multiple listening, involving the teachers but also the group of children and each child, all of whom can listen to others and listen to themselves, overturns the teaching-learning relationship. This overturning shifts the focus to learning; that is, to children's self-learning and the learning achieved by the group of children and adults together.

(Rinaldi 2005: 22)

Another element of listening which Rinaldi articulates is 'visible listening'. This is the means by which both the internal and multiple listening can take place. Bringing these ideas and experiences into the open supports both self-reflection and exchange.

The following chapter explores how the documentation produced by the children and by adults promoted reflection and exchange within the design process in more detail.

3.2 Working with
   practitioners and parents

Introduction

Part III of this book looks at ways of facilitating exchange within the design process. The main focus so far has been on gathering the perspectives of young children. However, the living spaces under investigation are environments shared by adults and children. It is not only young users who can be a hidden resource in the design process. The views and experiences of practitioners and parents can similarly be invisible. This study has attempted to draw these adult perspectives into discussions at different stages of the building projects.

Why might involving adult perspectives be difficult? There are possible explanations as to why this might be the case. Some of these difficulties relate to the constraints of the design process, but other, less pragmatic reasons may relate to the difficult task of asking non-design specialists to articulate their desires for a future space. However it is phrased, the question 'What do you want?' will not necessarily tap into adults' or children's feelings about existing buildings or desires about a future environment.

Through the study, there was a growing realisation that finding more creative ways of gathering practitioners' perspectives was as important as promoting methods for listening to young children. What seemed to be necessary was to enable practitioners to bring their implicit knowledge about the environment to the surface. This is a challenging task which runs counter to the majority of training which practitioners receive where the physical environment is a taken for granted element. It is as if teaching and learning exist in an invisible box which is a necessary container but does not require further study or reflection. Perhaps early childhood practitioners are at an advantage here over primary or secondary teachers due to the strong tradition of promoting the outdoor environment in particular. The Early Years Foundation Stage supports this tradition by identifying 'enabling environments' as one of the four principles in planning children's learning, development and care (DCSF, 2008a). Despite this tradition, there is still the difficulty of articulating implicit knowledge about a space in a purposeful exchange with architects and designers. There are possible questions of power to be recognised and overcome. Perhaps some practitioners feel uneasy about expressing an opinion about a topic which they feel unqualified to answer. Architecture, as in other professions, is steeped in its own language and ways of representing information. This can be daunting for those who are encountering this way of seeing the world and future worlds for the first time. Drawing plans is one example where the gulf between a practitioner's experience of an existing space and a proposed future space may require careful and repeated explanation.

As in all communication, work is required from both parties to establish an effective exchange of ideas. There seems to be the need for practitioners to make their implicit knowledge explicit and, in a sense, to think what they think. At the same time, there is the need for architects to make their own assumptions about what is required more explicit and to make their proposed ideas more accessible. This process seems of particular importance when considering multi-purpose buildings, such as children's centres. A post-occupancy evaluation of more than 100 centres identified difficulties in providing high quality buildings which met the needs of children and adults:

> Children's centres are small but highly complex buildings with relatively modest budgets. However, they need to be imaginative, inspiring and uplifting, as well as comfortable and practical. Elements that have prescribed space standards, such as children's play areas, or that have a dedicated separate budget, such as furniture and equipment, are well designed and specified and were given higher ratings by centre users.
>
> However, those elements that are not defined through standards and those without a dedicated budget, such as outdoor play areas and adult spaces, storage and environmental sustainability, were badly rated and lacking in both quality and provision.
>
> (CABE 2008: 2–3)

This study has begun to explore how the Mosaic approach may support adults, practitioners and parents, as well as young children, to explore what they think about a space. This chapter focuses on reviewing the completed building in the children's centre case study.

Starting with adults: practitioners' perspectives

This second case study began by working with adults. First, the aim was to familiarise the practitioners with the research tools before the nursery practitioners used the activities with the children. Second, the aim was to give practitioners the opportunity to stop and reflect on their own working environment. The hope was that the combination of the visual and reflective approaches would provide a necessary space to think and make their implicit knowledge explicit. This way of working provoked a high level of engagement and reflection across diverse groups of practitioners from different professional backgrounds (see Chapter 1.3). The core group of adults involved included nineteen members of the nursery team and ten Sure Start practitioners.

Tours of the centre		Group reviews in staff teams
Interviews	Research activities with nursery practitioners and Sure Start team	Collaborative workshop with nursery practitioners and Sure Start team
	Map making	

Figure 3.2.1 Research activities with nursery practitioners and Sure Start team

Tours and map making

Walking, reflecting and photographing can provoke different conversations than a static interview. I adopted walking interviews as part of the Mosaic approach with young children. The principle, however, was adapted from international development (see Chapter 1.4), where walking tours have been used to gather adults' experiences of their locality, and subsequently, children's perspectives. I decided to reapply this technique with practitioners in the new children's centre. Working with the nursery school staff and later with the Sure Start multi-disciplinary team, I asked practitioners to take time to walk around the children's centre and to record their tour. (I was not able to accompany practitioners on these tours due to the numbers involved.) The idea was to visit familiar spaces and less well-known areas. I asked the participants to take photographs during their tours to illustrate what was important to them in the centre. Some of the images were positive and others showed negative aspects which they wished to raise.

It was important to explain the purpose of the tours and photographs to practitioners despite not being able to meet as a group beforehand. The letter to practitioners was intended to reduce anxieties about the activities whilst at the same time being clear about the public nature of the documents that were being produced. The aim was to display the maps as part of establishing a dialogue about the completed building and therefore would need to not just be seen as private.

I was not able to make observations during the tours as practitioners carried these out by themselves. This removed one source of research data. However, it did provide perhaps a greater level of importance to the interviews in which practitioners' explained their choice of images. These interviews were, in most

Box 3.2.1 Extract from a letter to practitioners explaining the research activity

Taking photographs
- During the next few days take photographs of the places within the building and outside where you spend time.
- Decide 'what are the important places for you here?'; 'where do you enjoy being?'; 'where do you feel uncomfortable or don't like?'
- When you have finished the film or taken as many photos as you like please return the camera to the office.

Making a map
- Alison Clark who is the researcher organising the study will meet with you for a half hour session. The idea of this meeting is to talk about your photographs and to make a map using your photos.
- You don't have to be creative to make a map!
- The maps will be displayed where other adults and children can see them.
- There will be a review with the nursery and the architect to look at all the maps made by children and adults in July.

cases, undertaken individually to discuss their developed photographs and to make a map using a selection of their images. The nursery school practitioners had access to digital cameras, but they were not necessarily familiar with their use. The research became an opportunity for practitioners to use the technology to express their points of view. This new skill could later be shared with the children. The Sure Start practitioners did not have access to digital cameras, so I decided it was more practical to use single-use cameras with this group. Once developed, these photographs were saved as digital images, thus increasing the possibilities for reflecting on these perspectives.

Examples of the maps

The maps produced reflected a range of personal and shared meanings, as had been detected with the children's maps in the first case study. The formats of the maps were highly individual, particularly among the nursery school practitioners. Two practitioners chose to use their own cameras; one of these practitioners printed the images in black and white. The map making became a creative activity in which aesthetic judgements about the presentation of the material became part of the knowledge construction. Some practitioners decided to make separate maps for positive and negative images. Others made their maps into collages of images and comments.

Examples of nursery practitioner maps

Three female practitioners decided to make the map making a collaborative exercise. They were each new members of the children's centre staff, having started work in the nursery school three weeks before taking part in the research. They were therefore still in the process of becoming familiar with their new environment and with each other. One of the three had only recently moved to the United Kingdom, so she was adapting to a different culture at the same time.

Having discussed the activity together, this group of women decided to each take photographs and then produce two maps together. The first was to illustrate the places which they 'liked most' and where they enjoyed working. The second was to illustrate places they disliked, highlighting specific areas they thought could be improved.

The positive images, which they arranged in an oval, includes many spaces where direct activities take place with the children, such as the home corner (for role play), the sand tray and the garden. Other places on their map related to their use of the space as adults. They drew attention to the staff room, the security system on the main door, which made them feel safe, and the staff information board, which, as new members of the team, helped them to know what was happening each day.

The four negative images highlighted very specific areas in the nursery school which they felt could be improved: the outdoor toy store, the area for spare clothes, the music cupboard and the children's cloakroom. This group added a written description of their own solutions to each of these problems on the map. The maps, through the combination of visual and verbal languages, became a way of raising their voices within a large team.

Example of Sure Start practitioner map

One of the maps was made by a midwife who was one of the health representatives on the Sure Start team. She had a desk in the open-plan office which was part of the new build element of the project. She demonstrated a high level of sensitivity to the space and was able to clearly express her perspectives on the positive and negative aspects of the building. This awareness included professional and personal insights. The nature of her work meant that she used a number of rooms in the course of her week, including the shared office, the interview room and a community room for a post-natal group. The midwife had been a wheelchair user in the past and currently came to work on a bicycle. Both these factors seemed to be important to her interpretation of the completed centre.

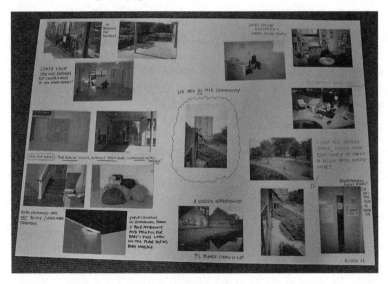

Figure 3.2.2 Example of a Sure Start practitioner's map

Source: Alison Meinel, Living Spaces study

Gathering parents' perspectives

I decided to explore whether the tools used in the Mosaic approach might facilitate discussions with parents about the children's centre. A group of six parents participated in this part of the study. Each had experience of the children's centre in some way. Several came to parent groups as well as having children in the nursery. One of the parents was a member of the parent council and also a cleaner on the premises. I asked the parents to go on a tour of the building, taking photographs of what was important to them, including, if appropriate, positive and negative images. Following the tour, I met with the parents individually to interview them about their choices and to make a map.

Each map represented an individual account of their experiences in the centre. Some of the parents concentrated on the few rooms with which they were familiar, whereas others illustrated the relationship between the centre and the wider environment. The parents' maps displayed the same individuality as the practitioners in how they approached the activity. One of the parents made the journey to the children's centre an integral part of her map of the centre. Her visual narrative placed the new and old parts of the children's centre in the context of its local community. This parent made her youngest daughter, who was about to start at the nursery, the particular audience for her map, thus adding a very personal narrative. This is an example of what can happen in participatory research. The researcher places the frame in the hands of the participants, who may chose to discuss a very narrow or broad view of the topic under discussion or choose to depict a different view altogether.

Another example of this re-framing occurred in the Spaces to Play study when one of the boys chose to include indoor photographs in his book about the outdoors (Clark and Moss 2005: 36)

Frameworks for reviewing spaces

It is a complex task to present different perspectives about a completed building. Among others, the Design Quality Indicator (DQI), including a version produced for schools, has been developed by the Construction Industry Council in conjunction with the Commission for Architecture and the Built Environment (CABE) to provide a tool for assessing the design quality of buildings. There are three critical areas of the DQI: function, build quality and impact. This framework has provided a way of drawing together both visual and verbal comments made by the practitioners and parents about the new children's centre. There is, however, some overlap between the three identified themes; some comments can be seen to convey insights into more than one of these areas.

Function

The following comments refer to room use, accessibility and storage as different aspects of discussing the match between the intended purpose of the building and how this is supported by the design.

Room use

Practitioners were articulate about how the way the spaces were working in practice. Consistent references were made to the under-threes' rooms, which were the new provision for the youngest children in the centre. The following comments were made in interviews with practitioners based on discussing their maps. These practitioners spent a high percentage of their day in these spaces.

Figure 3.2.3
Practitioner maps on display in the new building

Source: Living Spaces study

You can see cars and legs and at children's height. I spend time there. I feel connected to the outdoor space.

(Nursery assistant)

You can look out. There is lots going on. You can see the road and . . . the different sounds from the environment.

(Nursery officer)

It is big enough for big furniture. The glass doors mean you can look through to the main road. The patio doors mean the babies can see out.

(Senior nursery officer)

These illustrate how the new design was perceived as helping both practitioners and children feel connected to the wider environment. The furniture enabled the environment to be a living space for both adults and young children. The rooms were large enough for comfortable armchairs.

Practitioners' maps also conveyed messages about multiple functions of spaces. There were photographs taken, for example, of an office door covered in notices. The room operated as a multi-purpose space, including an office, a breastfeeding room and an interview room. The number of notices on the door represented these multiple, competing functions.

Figure 3.2.4 Internal view of the rooms for children under three years old
Source: Anne Thorne Architects Partnership

Changing functions emerged as a design issue. Some of the rooms were designed for generic community use and subsequently hosted specific activities which were not ideal for the space. This was highlighted by the example of baby massage classes, which were taking place in a room with overhead strip lighting. This was, of course, not the function which the architect had envisaged for this room, but it was the result of the changing nature of community provision.

Accessibility

Practitioners and parents expressed opinions about the accessibility of the facilities. A platform lift had been installed, due to cost constraints. It was creating problems for those with pushchairs. The lift needed to be operated by holding down a button inside the lift whilst it was in use. This was difficult for a parent to do whilst in the lift with a pushchair and a young child. Adults also discussed accessibility issues surrounding the entrances, which needed to cater for a large volume of buggies, bicycles and wheelchair users.

Storage

The availability of sufficient storage space is an important aspect of the function of a children's centre. There is a recognised need for the safe storage of indoor and outdoor equipment in early childhood provision and for children's and adults' storage space (see Dudek 2001: 42). This need is multiplied in centres which house a diversity of groups for parents and children. One of the Sure Start practitioners drew attention to this difficulty on her map by including a photograph of enormous bean bags used in a parent and baby class. This demonstrated the scale of the equipment which needed to be hauled around and stored.

Build quality

This is the most technical of the themes identified in the DQI. It refers to issues such as the type of material used, sustainability and health and safety issues. However, practitioners and parents did have a considerable number of observations to make about these topics.

Material used

As discussed, there were positive comments made about the new provision for children under three years old. This included references to the high standard of design and materials used in this section of the building. Conversely, some practitioners were critical when the finish was not of the highest standard. As one practitioner remarked, 'It's the difference between the Savoy and a Comfort Inn!' This practitioner drew attention to this on her map by including a close-up photograph of a switch. The instruction 'press to exit' was already wearing off after a few months of use. Practitioners displayed their acute awareness of temperature. Several people took photographs of room thermo-meters displaying temperatures of over 30 degrees centigrade.

Sustainability

Sustainability was an issue which had been taken seriously in this building project, both in terms of materials used and information to users. There were wind turbines, for example, on the roof of the new offices. This dimension to the building work was drawn to attention by several practitioners, including a participant (who was a parent and a member of staff) who included a photograph of the turbines on her map.

Health and safety

Health and safety issues discussed included internal and external features. One of the social work students took a photograph of a stair gate and another safety gate to indicate two important features for her in the children's centre. The phone entry system was mentioned by several practitioners as a positive safety feature. There was also a security guard on site. One of the practitioners included an image of the guard at his desk with the caption 'feeling safe – even at night'.

Impact

This third theme in the DQI refers to impact: the influence the building has had in terms of perceptions of its feel and special qualities. This theme is harder to quantify. The impact may involve an individual's personal response to a change in the environment or wider considerations of change on an organisation and its links with its surrounding community. One of the feelings expressed was one of connectedness. The midwife placed a photograph of the view from one of the upstairs windows, showing a nearby block of flats on her map. Her caption read, 'We are IN the community.' A nursery practitioner included the following captions on her map: 'vistas and connections: wonder-ful long views through to the rest of [the centre]'; 'feeling connected to the rest of the world'; and 'open to view – nothing to hide – feeling in touch with what is going on, having a sense of what is happening . . . and disconnections, barriers, solid, final'. This list shows how responses to different parts of a building can provoke contrasting reactions. A complex organisation, particu-larly one which incorporates new and old elements, may create a range of responses even within the same individual. It is important, therefore, to allow sufficient time for participants to step back and reflect on their firsthand experience of an environment. As one Sure Start practitioner commented, 'I hadn't realised there were some things I liked and some things I didn't.'

There were certain qualities which practitioners valued in their environment which emerged from the visual narratives. These included personal spaces, liveable spaces and ambiguous spaces for adults and children. Other rooms received contrasting reactions.

Personal spaces

Sometimes the qualities looked for in the environment were improvised by the practitioners rather than designed. Photographs taken by practitioners illustrated some of these different responses. A social work student photographed the disabled access toilet and described this as her 'quiet zone'. Her bag was photographed as representing her 'office'. She had shared access to the staff room and the parent room, but she identified her bag as one of the most important places in the children's centre. A nursery practitioner photographed her new office, which she had gained as a result of the building work. A Sure Start practitioner photographed her desk: 'my creative space – very important'.

Liveable spaces

A liveable space might be described as one which enables both adults and children to feel human. As described earlier, this was the response prompted by practitioners to the new facilities for the youngest children:

I enjoy going in there. It is relaxing.

(Nursery assistant)

It looks relaxing and comfortable.

(Nursery officer)

Warm and cosy, comfortable, comforting and safe.

(Head teacher)

Ambiguous spaces

The kitchen or staff room was one of the rooms that provoked different reactions. It was liked by certain groups of practitioners (who saw it as social space or a 'chatty space'), but it was avoided by others (who preferred to eat at their desks). Even the different names for the same room hinted at some of the complex understandings which existed among the different staff teams. The room officially described as 'the parent room' acted as an unofficial staff room, particularly for some newer members of staff. The board room received a mixed reaction. Again the choice of name conveys a certain function and feel. This room contained a large oval table and meeting room chairs. Some practitioners liked the formal style. This layout was familiar to many of the Sure Start team. However, for the nursery practitioners, the oval table represented an alien work culture that was very different from the easy-chair feel of many staff rooms. This illustrates one of the complexities of bringing together multi-disciplinary teams in children's centres. The choice of furniture conveys implicit meanings about how work is viewed.

These examples are indications that the evaluation of rooms relates to the social practices which take place there and to the physical characteristics of the space. Practitioners' photographs and comments revealed the different official landscapes which were present within the same physical space, as well the informal landscape of the personal and private. The map making provided an opportunity for some of these layers to be articulated.

The map making and interviews were central parts of working with practitioners and parents. Local knowledge had been gathered and constructed through this process. It was important, however, to attempt to debate some of the issues raised across the different staff teams.

Whole-group discussions

A workshop was chosen as a forum for discussing the review of the completed children's centre. This event, which took place as part of a training and development day, was jointly led by the lead architect and I. Twenty-five practitioners across the different teams within the children's centre took part. The aim was to promote discussion in the context of practical activities with a focus on the physical environment. This included tours of the building, model making about changes to the outdoor environment and reflection on the essential ingredients of a children's centre.

Tours of the building

The aim of the activity was to broaden participants' understandings of how different members of the children's centre felt about and valued the building. Working in twos or threes, participants took turns leading others on tours of the building, pointing out what they felt to be important places, both positive and negative. Another member of the group took notes on the tours and then group members swapped roles, as time allowed. The Sure Start and nursery teams worked in mixed groups on this activity, so a social worker might lead a tour with two members of the nursery. This enabled practitioners to begin to see the same building through different eyes and, in some cases, discover unfamiliar parts of the centre.

Some of the brief comments on the tours echoed feelings shared in more detail in the maps and interviews carried out earlier in the research. Positive comments were made in particular about the new under-threes' part of the nursery, as a pleasant place to be for staff and children and the new outdoor garden. Negative comments included insufficient storage, the courtyard, the children's toilets and the lift.

Courtyard activity

The courtyard was a shared space which led to the nursery and the Sure Start facilities and other community rooms. The architect had identified this as one of the final areas needing further work. This was reinforced by comments made by practitioners during the tours. This next activity brought participants together to discuss initial thoughts about the courtyard before dividing into groups to plan possible changes.

Although at the start of the discussion the feelings expressed were negative, the discussion revealed how many different uses the courtyard had and the range of different groups who walked across the courtyard looked onto the space or could hear what was happening there. It was used by parents to socialise after bringing their children to the nursery and by youth users of the centre. The space was used for private talks and mobile phone conversations.

After this initial discussion, participants worked in small groups to explore possible changes to the space. The activities were designed to draw on different expressive languages. Two groups made a poster with drawings and captions about changes to the courtyard. These became three-dimensional rather than two-dimensional creations. Two groups worked with a cardboard model of the courtyard, using plasticine and play dough to create sculpture forms. The final group worked outside in the courtyard, using chairs and chalk to try out different ideas for arranging the space.

Key features emerged. All five groups mentioned planting a tree or flowers and shrubs and introducing seating to include benches. Three of the groups designed a buggy park, one with an awning. Adding steps from the crèche to the courtyard was mentioned by three of the groups. Another common feature was an information board.

Additional design features suggested included using mirrors and murals on the walls, adding a clock, placing animal models on the roof and adding floor markings in the form of footprints to show the way to different parts of the centre. Considerable thought was given to how to make the courtyard more welcoming. One group demonstrated how the reception door could show the word 'welcome' in different languages and how a tree in the courtyard could be a 'welcome' tree bearing messages in different languages.

What are the essential ingredients for a children's centre?

Discussing meanings and values is an important part of the design process. One of the aims of engaging with practitioners has been to support them in articulating their implicit knowledge about their environment. This last activity was developed to provide another opportunity for practitioners to reflect on their views and experiences in order to inform future buildings. The practitioners were divided into three groups to think about the essential ingredients for a children's centre for three groups of users: children, practitioners and families. This was a short brainstorming activity. Each group was

Box 3.2.2 Essential ingredients of a children's centre, compiled during workshop discussions

Participants' list of essential ingredients for children in a children's centre

1. to have fun – be bright and colourful
2. space – to be able to move freely
3. child-sized – low-level windows, sinks and toilets, coat pegs
4. outside space – interesting and varied
5. security – be safe and feel secure
6. representative of local community – able to be adaptable
7. easy access – wheels friendly light doors that can be opened easily
8. quiet spaces – can be made homelike
9. organisation – able to identify own spaces as well as well-organised space with adequate storage
10. local – near where you live

Participants' list of essential ingredients for practitioners in a children's centre

1. welcoming
2. practical – getting in – how children use it
3. to facilitate day-to-day routine
4. staff room
5. integration of physical space (links with 13)
6. parking
7. storage, lockers, resources
8. meeting room
9. resource room – for staff working
10. private spaces for working with parents
11. secure throughout day (staff arriving for early shifts or leaving late)
12. toilets – more toilets
13. central reception area

Participants' list of essential ingredients for families in a children's centre

1. parents room
2. signage to be aware of accessible areas
3. access to information
4. physical impact to have a feel of a children's centre
5. welcoming for whole family
6. suitable furniture for all age groups
7. booklet showing staff members

asked to compile a list of ten or more factors. The lists are not intended as definitive statements but as a starting point for discussion by other practitioner groups who may be embarking on similar building projects.

Discussion

From indicators to dialogue

This chapter has explored ways of facilitating exchange within the design process between different adult groups. This has demanded tools which enable practitioners and parents to stop and reflect on the meanings they hold about the spaces they know well and share with children. This reflective process has involved handing over the tools developed to gather the views and experiences of young children to adults.

The Design Quality Indicators have provided one analytical framework for gathering this information together. The categories of 'form', 'build quality' and 'impact' are not necessarily easily accessible terms for reviewing an environment. The use of visual participatory methods has brought these issues to life, providing opportunities for adults to view the environment anew with others. Maybe what we are seeing here can be understood in terms of a joining of 'activity systems', where the visual materials produced act as 'mediating artefacts', aiding communication between the participants in different groups (Cole and Engeström 1997; Daniels 2001). This theory, developed from the work of Vygotsky, has been applied to facilitating communication within a range of workplace settings, including health environments (Engeström 1999) and teaching and learning institutions (van Oers 2005; Edwards 2008).

Facilitating exchange is not a process which is neatly bound or leads to tidy answers. The series of engagements described in this chapter have formed an ongoing dialogue which has involved differences of opinion and argument, as well as some consensus. This is in keeping with Dahlberg and Moss' description of 'discursive spaces' (2005). The map making, tours and workshops are not end products; they are markers in a conversation about change. One of the challenges of developing listening in this way remains how to keep these channels of communication open (see Chapters 4.2 and 4.3).

3.3 Working with architects

In any experiment the possibility of producing innovation is triggered by the ability to see problems and solutions from new points of view, using people with different skills.

(Malavasi and Pantaleoni 2008: 49)

Introduction

There appear to be few opportunities for architects, whether they are in training or in practice, to interact with the world of young children. When the demands of a design project result in limited time to meet with clients and users, it is understandable that engagement with young children is unusual. Establishing a common language between professionals and users can take time. The youngest or most vulnerable members of a community may present the greatest challenges in terms of establishing communication and gaining perspectives.

This 'picturing a world', discussed by Sacks in Chapter 1.2, however, can offer new ways of seeing existing environments. It may lead to possibilities for future spaces. An important step towards achieving such new solutions may be to create more opportunities for architects to picture the worlds of young children both directly, through face-to-face encounters, but perhaps more significantly through material produced by young children. One of the aims of the Living Spaces study has been to create spaces for exchange between architects, practitioners and young children in several ways. These exchanges have been direct encounters involving talking, listening and making together and have happened through documentation produced by children and practitioners. This chapter describes both types of encounters in each case study and discusses issues raised for facilitating exchange within the design process.

First encounters

It was important for this study to choose architects with established reputations in early childhood design and participatory approaches to design. Both

practices chosen valued clients' perspectives and were open to new interpretations of user involvement.

My first meeting with John Jenner from Greenhill Jenner Architects, the
architects responsible for the first case study, served as a reminder of the
cyclical nature of early childhood policy. John described a number of early
childhood centres he had designed in the late 1970s and early 1980s. These
included the Patmore Centre, Battersea in South London for which the practice
won a RIBA Community Architect Award. The Patmore Centre, despite its
award-winning facilities was closed as a consequence of changes to government funding, but it has since been re-opened as a children's centre. Good
consultation is part of a wider political landscape, which may be a stronger
influence than local involvement in the long-term survival of an initiative.
This theme is one which became a particular feature of the second case study
in this Living Spaces study.

Two images remain with me from this first meeting. The first image was of
a playhouse imaginatively constructed on several levels, providing the children
with hideaway spaces, in an early childhood centre. The image, however, did
not show young children exploring the space or watching their peers from the
playhouse as it was being used as a storage unit due to health and safety issues.
There had been a change of practitioners since the centre was first opened.
A subsequent head was concerned about the height of the structure and so its
original purpose was lost. This highlights several of the themes which
reappeared throughout the Living Spaces study. Good design can be attributed
to many factors, including the partnership between architects and those who
live and work in the spaces. However, the adults and children who use the
building will change, so there needs to be an ongoing dialogue between users
and their environment.

The second image from this first meeting illustrated what can happen when
an imaginative partnership between architects and practitioners is established
and sustained. The photograph is of the 'beach' at Pen Green in Corby. This
early childhood centre in a disadvantaged ex-mining community is led by
Margy Whalley (for example Whalley 2002). Greenhill Jenner won a RIBA
Regional Award for the design of the new centre, which included a courtyard
filled with a sixteen-metre square beach:

> Overall, the development designed by Greenhill Jenner Architects, is
> extremely successful. The 'beach' provides an exciting and inspirational
> focus for the centre and a clear statement about its values: children and
> the importance of play and learning.
>
> (CABE 2008: 8)

The idea for the beach was partly inspired by a visit by Margy Whalley to early
childhood centres in New Zealand. This is an example of what can happen
when inspired leadership from early childhood practitioners comes together
with imaginative design.

John raised three main issues about involving young children in design. First, would children be disappointed if their ideas did not happen? This raises the question of what kind of consultation was going to happen. Consultations which rely on a wish-list approach (discussed earlier) can lead to children or adults feeling let down by a consultation process (Marchant and Kirby 2004). This conversation reinforced the importance of exploring broader participatory methods which emphasised personal and shared meanings and perspectives on place use rather than limiting discussions to what adults and children wanted. Second, John asked about the views of adult stakeholders. John's experience of working with a variety of stakeholder groups pinpointed the importance of finding ways to engage with adults as well as young children. This became an increasingly important issue as the Living Spaces study progressed (see Chapter 3.2). Third, we discussed the possibility of young children's voices being lost in complex projects where there were many diverse professional and community voices involved, as well as teams involved in the design and the construction of new provision. John described a Sure Start project being undertaken in a regeneration area. Stakeholders in this project included a local school, local church and numerous other community groups.

Images were used to facilitate these discussions about past projects. John produced storyboards which illustrated chosen photographs and plans. These architects' narratives presented a summary of design perspectives on completed projects in a similar way to the maps which were to be produced through the study by children, parents and practitioners. This highlighted the importance of strengthening visual languages as means for architects, practitioners and children to share understandings and experiences of a place.

The decision to work with the second architects' practice was, first, led by finding a local authority who had recently completed children's centres and was willing to take part in research. Second, having identified such a local authority, an architects' practice with a strong record in early childhood design and in participatory approaches was chosen.

Meeting points

Facilitating communication between architects and young users can be problematic for several reasons. There is the generational gap between adults and children which is widened if the children in question are young children rather than adolescents. Memories of our own childhood become less distinct even if becoming a parent may be one way of rekindling these memories. There is also a professional gap between architects and the users of the environments they create, which again can be magnified if the users are young. The question remains: What kind of meeting points may support communication across these divides to improve design?

Direct engagement: observing, listening and talking

The first meeting points for exchange in the Living Spaces study were through supporting activities which brought architects and young children together. The activities included both research activities based on listening and talking and interactive workshops. Each was designed, however, to play to young children's strengths rather than play to those of the architects or researcher.

During the first six months of the school case study Jennifer, the lead architect, took part as an observer in several of the research activities with children in the nursery and the reception class. One morning, Jennifer and I were joined by another member of the architects' practice who was starting to work on this design project. Over six-feet tall, he was at a certain disadvantage in a nursery classroom. He observed the interviews, which were taking place in the reading corner of the classroom, from the uncomfortable perch of a small child-sized chair. This illustrates how the onus was on the adults adapting to the children's familiar environment rather than the young children adapting to an adult-orientated space, such as the architects' office.

The interviews with children provided one direct meeting point between architects and children facilitated by me as researcher. Children had taken part in child-led tours, book making and map making, so they were becoming familiar with me as a researcher who did not know very much about their school and wanted to find out more. The interviews provided the chance for children to review their maps to think through what were the most important places for them in the school and to consider the new nursery (see Chapter 2.2). During one interview at which Jennifer was present, I asked one of the five-year-olds, who had recently moved to the reception class from the nursery class, 'Where is your favourite place inside the school?'

Researcher:	Where is your favourite place inside school?
Claire:	In the writing area.
Researcher:	Okay. And why is it a favourite place?
Claire:	Because you get to write and I take it home and then my mum says it's good, and that you can write in a book and she does it at home.
Researcher:	Oh right, so you get to write in a book.
Architect:	The writing area is where the tables and chairs are and you sit down and you write?
Researcher:	Can you see anything from there? Can you see anything else from the writing bit? What can you see from there?
Architect:	A park and . . .
Researcher:	You can yes, and you can also see out the window. I like that, when I work in an office I like it when I can see out the window.
Architect:	Yeah, do you like to look out the window? What do you like to look at?
Claire:	I look at my Mum and my Nan and my Dad when they come and take me home, and when they take Julie to school.

Researcher: I think we need to write all this down, okay . . . I can see my Mum
                and my Nan, was that? Dad? . . .
Claire: And my mum. And my sister Julie, she's four. I say hello to them.
Researcher: And you can see them through the window?
Claire: Yeah.

This exchange with Claire illustrates how the interviews became, on occasion, a three-way discussion between Jennifer (the architect), me and a child (or sometimes a group for children). I was interested in Claire's initial response to the question and how she drew attention to the writing area. This was a space in the classroom which looked out on a landscaped border and a pathway around the school which led to the nursery. There were low windows along the length of this side of the classroom.

Claire, in her first reply, linked this favourite place with the curriculum activity in which she took part there. She appeared to be drawing attention to the official landscape of school (see Chapter 2.2). She was unusual in making a direct reference to a reading or writing activity in her responses. However, as the conversation developed, it became clear that this space was associated with both the official and the informal. The writing activities were associated by Claire with a strong link with home – Claire could take the writing home and be praised by her mother. Perhaps if Jennifer had not been present, I would have moved on in the interview to the next question, but Jennifer asked a supplementary question about the location of the writing area. This moved the discussion on from the writing task and led to a valuable insight from Claire. This insight demonstrated that this area was a favourite place not only because of what children could do there, but also because of what children could see from there: 'I look at my Mum and my Nan and my Dad when they come and take me home, and when they take Julie to school.' These low windows enabled Claire to feel connected to her family, including her younger sister who attended the nursery. The nursery children started later than the reception children, so Claire would have been able to watch her family walking round to the nursery. Similarly, at the end of the day, Claire and other children were able to tell the end of the school day was approaching as parents walked to the classroom door.

This encounter with Claire was a clear indication of the complex layers of meaning children carry about the physical environment, which can be supported or hindered by design. If this classroom had been designed on the lines of a Victorian board school, Claire's experiences would have been very different. She might have identified her desk where she did writing practice as a favourite place, but the windows would have been too high to see siblings or other family members from the classroom.

Direct engagement: making together

Observing, listening and talking together are one approach to creating a meeting point between architects and young children. Another method can be

Figure 3.3.1
Box-building activity
Source: Living Spaces study

to devise opportunities for both groups to engage in creative activities, such as making play structures together. The exchange relies on exploring materials and shapes rather than a grasp of spoken language. This was the route chosen in the children's centre case study for several reasons. Fran, the architect, had experience leading design workshops with children, including young children, during an earlier phase of the children's centre design. This active approach seemed particularly well suited to a setting in which a high percentage of the children began in the nursery with English as an additional language, including some children who were in the first stage of learning English. A research method which relied on language skills in English would have placed many children in this group at a disadvantage.

The box workshop created a meeting point between architect, practitioners, children and me as the researcher. The modes of communication were construction and movement. The young children could choose their own way of (not) engaging with the activity. Some enjoyed sticking tape onto the large cardboard boxes to make larger structures. Others added string and, with the help of adults, made a window flap which opened and closed. Once assembled, more children joined in and used the boxes to crawl through or hide inside.

Some children preferred to keep their distance, adopting an observer role. Two children pulled up a small sofa which was nearby and sat and watched what was taking place. The roles of the adults in this process were changed by the practical, creative nature of the workshop. The open-ended encounter enabled the architect, practitioners and I to play alongside the children, observing and following the children's leads.

Indirect engagement

There may be several reasons which might prevent architects from directly engaging – through observing, talking and listening or through creative activities – in activities with young children. Time and budget may be important factors here. There is an unpredictability of working with young children. This can result in surprising responses which may not sit easily with tight adult timeframes. Such encounters require an engagement between the architect and young children. Some architects may feel uncomfortable and unprepared, even with the support of an early childhood practitioner or researcher. Indirect engagement may provide an important alternative. Children's documentation can provide a bridge between architects and young children. The client, who is the funder, needs to support the process, which requires a procurement programme that has children as its priority (see Chapter 1.2). This way of working also challenges architects to approach consultation not as a top-down design process, but as an ongoing dialogue.

There were two workshops (held at the architects' practice in the first case study) which centred on children's material; one was at an early design stage and the second was after the building work had been completed, as part of a post-occupancy review of the project. These were devised as small internal events for the lead architect and her colleagues. The purpose of the first workshop was twofold: first, for me as the researcher to explain the research process and emerging themes resulting from ongoing discussions between Jennifer and I; second, for me to listen to architects' reactions to the children's work.

I began the workshop with a short talk explaining the origins of the research and the methodology together with a description of the first phase of the study. The architects were then given the opportunity to look at the documentation produced by the children. Research material was drawn together and brought to the meeting. Maps produced by the three- and four-year-olds who were involved in the first phase of the Living Spaces study were on display. The maps were discussed by the group to see what insights they might contain about young children's priorities, interests and perspectives on their existing environment. These discussions were supplemented by other documentation produced by the children. Examples of photo books made by children in the nursery were available for the architects to read. There was a slideshow of images from a number of child-led tours and extracts from interviews with children. There were storyboards of still images which had been taken by

Figure 3.3.2
Architects reviewing children's documentation during phase one of the Living Spaces study

Source: Living Spaces study

Observations	Photo books made by children in the nursery	Child-led tours by children in the nursery and reception class
Interviews with children in the nursery and reception class	Research material drawn together for the workshop with architects	Photo boards of images taken from the tours selected by the researcher
Interviews with practitioners	Photographs of model making	Individual and group maps made by the children

Figure 3.3.3 Research material drawn together for the workshop with architects

children on their tour. I compiled these storyboards as part of my initial analysis to raise possible design issues which had become apparent during the fieldwork alongside Jennifer.

The workshop aimed to raise the status of the children's perspectives within the design process. The display boards in the architects' office represented this point. The children's maps of the nursery were placed alongside early architect's plans of the site and storyboards of photographs, sketches, drawings and images compiled by the architect. This juxtaposition illustrated the bringing together of different ways of seeing which was being undertaken here.

The differences in perspectives were instantly apparent from examining the children's and architect's work together. The architect's photographs focused on the buildings, whereas the children's images drew attention to the spaces in between, including the pathways, stretches of tarmac and the sky. Another distinguishing feature related to how the children's maps showed children and adults and objects within the space. Children were visible on the map through their names, drawings and presence in photographs. These were maps of personal spaces and experiences (see in Chapter 2.2).

The documentation provoked conversations about the specific design issues of scale and perspective, privacy and the quality of floor surfaces and ceilings. Engaging with the children's material raised wider philosophical questions about the nature of school: Is it about children coming to terms with the adult world? Is it about children as becomings or about children as beings? These discussions did not end in agreed solutions or single viewpoints. As one of the architects involved in the initial workshop commented, 'This opens up more questions than it answers.'

This style of workshop was repeated in a similar format at the end of the design process in both case studies when the new building work had been completed. These indirect encounters included documentation of adults' and children's perspectives. Slideshows of photographs taken by children and adults on their tours of the settings provided a platform for discussion about designing for these complex inter-generational spaces (see Chapter 3.2).

Architects' reflections on the research process

Weinstein and David explain in the edited volume *Spaces for Children* (1987) how they did not want to make prescriptive accounts of what environments for young children should be like. They want to enable designers to make decisions informed by better understandings of children. This different way of seeing has been identified as one of the results for the architects of engaging in the Living Spaces study:

> What has come out of this is the way that children see compared to the way that we see.
>
> (John Jenner, architect)

> The structured consultation process has informed the process of design. It has allowed the architects to 'see differently' – to better understand spatial design from the perspective of the child through interaction with the researcher and children alike. It has allowed the architects to work with the children to understand not only what they 'want', but, perhaps more importantly, the thought processes behind these ideas. This becomes the 'window' into the child's way of seeing. This process has allowed the architects to move beyond the preconceptions of children's design (i.e. bright colours, spatial and functional organisation) to a new level of thinking about designing for children.
>
> (Jennifer Singer, architect)

Sometimes this different way of seeing has given a new emphasis to an established design principle:

> It was partly just the actual reality of the things we all know, like young children are smaller and so their eye height is different to our height. We all know that . . . and we've been designing buildings for children with low level windows for a long time. But actually seeing some of those photographs just reminds you about scale. It's not just that they're lower but also adults are very big . . . seeing what the children were doing, it reminded [me] of how they look so carefully and how little things can have a lot of meaning.
>
> (Fran Bradshaw, architect)

A different way of seeing does not invalidate the professional lens with which architects explore an environment, but it adds another dimension. I feel I have undergone a similar process as the architects through engaging with the children in this way. My repertoire for exploring a new environment has been stretched. I am more aware, for example, of small details at floor level, the numbers of solid or transparent doors I encounter and what attention (if any) has been given to the ceilings.

The children's attention to detail was felt, by the architects, to add weight to some of their own design decisions, supporting the quality of their proposals:

> Furthermore, the consultation process has encouraged the client to value the process of design and the input of the building users (particularly the children) – and (from a practical point of view) invest time, energy, and money into this. Hopefully this collaboration will allow the process of children's consultation in design to develop and continue into future projects.
>
> (Jennifer Singer, architect)

The emphasis on living spaces emphasised the need for child-centred design which was also human-centred:

> Taking part in the study was about being reminded that children are just young versions of ourselves. They do need calm spaces and they need reassuring spaces and they need happy, running about, jumping up, whatever, spaces . . . I think the way that you break down the different spaces into private spaces, personal spaces, social spaces according to the qualities of spaces is a helpful way to think about designing.
>
> (Fran Bradshaw, architect)

Engaging in research has offered an opportunity for the different participants within design projects to step back and reflect on the process. This has appeared to be of particular value at the post-occupancy stage:

> I think this process could be extrapolated to cover design at other scales – i.e. special needs, disabled, even older children – it's almost 'a way of thinking' about design and respecting the building 'users' . . . It is so important to have a formal review following the building work, the chance to relook at the process . . . as [this study] shows the process is probably as important as the design/building itself and it's a very organised way of discussing what worked and what did not. The post-occupancy review seems to have provided some sense of completion – it's such a great way to step back and articulate our thoughts in a rational way.
>
> (Jennifer Singer, architect)

What might be the possibilities for architects to adapt facilitating exchange using the Mosaic approach in future projects? Jennifer Singer, the lead architect in the school case study, has since tried the map-making tool as a way of engaging older children in the initial stages of a new design project. Here the architect has been engaged as a design consultant with a Jewish secondary school embarking on a new build project. Jennifer has been working with children and young people from ten to fourteen years old, including the oldest class in the existing primary school and two classes in the secondary school. A key starting point has been asking, 'What does it mean to be in this place?' The exact wording used was 'What is important to you about being Jewish at [this] School?' This enabled the participants to consider the connections between their faith and place. The maps of the younger children (ten to eleven years old) revealed insights into the importance of specific markers of their Jewish faith around the school. There was a similarity here with the specific personal markers identified by the children in the Living Spaces study. The older children's maps, however, raised complex issues and thoughts about their experience of Jewish identity within their school environment which at times went beyond the physical aspects of their school to consider the spaces in between and the potential of experience within that space:

> The visual and written information contained in the maps provided a springboard (rather than a design template) for discussions about living and learning in the existing and future space and how the design project might structure the aspirations for the project. The children's drawings and photos have introduced a way of talking about feelings about school and faith which may not have emerged in this way through a focus group or questionnaire approach.
>
> This experience showed that the Mosaic approach is a dynamic tool that can adapt to different stakeholder groups but the facilitator must keep an open mind about the outcome, and how it might influence the design approach, rather than the design itself.
>
> (Jennifer Singer, architect)

Discussion

Bridging communication

If we consider the indirect exchanges in the workshop for architects described in this chapter, the children's documentation can be seen to have played a key role. Communication across boundaries requires the establishment of common languages. Architects are part of a community with closely defined sets of routines and rules. It is a diverse community in which expression through visual languages is recognised and given status and in which attention is given to detail, colour, scale and perspective. The documentation produced through the research process, such as the children's maps, is based on the visual languages of photography and drawing. These visual art forms also enable children to emphasise their attention to detail, colour, scale and perspective. These similarities are brought to the fore through the use of media. This level of communication would have been impossible if exchanges were conducted through the written or spoken word.

Communication can be hindered by power differences. Architects belong to a community which has status within the design process. The level of perceived status may vary depending on the nature of the construction process and according to internal politics, which may operate within any cost-driven enterprise. The architects' position, however, will be of greater status than those of the users, whether children or adults. This power difference can add a further stumbling block to communication. It would, for example, have made it difficult to arrange a meeting at the architects' offices with the children and practitioners present. However, the documentation in the form of the maps and photo books mediated their perspectives or voices. The maps acted as a way of reconsidering preconceptions about the learning environment at each stage of the design process.

This process could be seen as enabling architects to see the official, informal and physical learning landscapes of the young children. The role of researcher was an important part of the mediation which took place between the architects and this documentation. Without this bridge, more of the children's interpretations would have remained inaccessible. One example of this facilitation occurred during the first workshop with architects. This was provoked by a photograph taken by one of the four-year-olds on his tour of the nursery. The architect commented, 'What is this about? Is it about their home? Would they like home to be like this?' On this occasion I was able to bring another perspective to this discussion by referring to comments made by Jules' mother. These responses are taken from my interview with her, where she reviewed the material produced by Jules:

Researcher: What does he enjoy doing at home inside or outside?
Mother: Cars, kitchen corner with his little sister, cycling and running, football. Cartwheels on the sofa, pole jumping with a broom.
Researcher: What did you learn about from the photographs and other activities he has taken part in?
Mother: He can take photographs – it confirms his interest in cycling, the balls, the home corner and water games.

The home corner images could therefore be understood as a confirmation of the freedom for imaginative play to which Jules drew attention on his tour.

A researcher may be able to act at times as a bridge between architects and children, but there is a risk that some of the children's original meanings will be lost in translation. It is necessary to keep returning to the children's words, drawings and photographs and, where possible, to look again with the children at the documentation they have produced. Facilitating indirect engagement emphasises the role of interpretation in the process as the authors of the narratives are not present to clarify their intended meanings. Pedagogue Laura Malavasi and architect Luciano Pantaleoni highlight the need to check meanings in participatory design projects and review and revisit material:

Synthesising and attributing meaning to these requests was a complex task, which led us to make a first series of assumptions and then go back to the schools so that we could test our findings against the children again. We were dealing here with interpretative processes.

(Malavasi and Pantaleoni 2008: 45)

The role of visual narratives in facilitating exchange is returned to in Part IV of this book.

Wider exchange

In this chapter I have discussed the roles of both indirect and direct encounters between architects and young users involved in real building projects. This raises a further question about the possible value of setting up exchanges between architects, practitioners, children and researchers beyond the constraints of individual projects. One possibility for such an exchange emerged during the Living Spaces study. A study tour was organised to the preschools in Reggio Emilia to focus on architecture and pedagogy. The participants included architects, artists, early childhood practitioners and academics. Two questions emerged for me as a result of this visit. First, raising questions about architecture and pedagogy at an international level increases the need to establish a common language or vocabulary. Second, children's and adults' documentation about living and working in an environment may open up possibilities for new conversations which cross professional, national and generational barriers. However, the more public the arena, the greater the importance of considering the ethical implications of making different perspectives visible.

The wider implications of participatory approaches to design, learning and research are the focus of Chapters 4.2, 4.3 and 4.4.

3.4 Conclusion

Part III began by proposing the value of different forms of listening within the design process, taking Rinaldi's (2005) description of listening as a starting point: 'internal listening' or self-reflection, 'multiple listening' across different boundaries and 'visible listening' in which implicit knowledge is made tangible. This encompasses key issues in involving learning communities in changes to the physical environment: how to enable children and adults to articulate their views and experiences and how to exchange these understandings with others.

Chapter 3.2 explored different possibilities for creating 'discursive spaces' (Dahlberg and Moss 2005) for practitioners and parents to make their views and experiences about a newly completed environment explicit. This began with the opportunity for internal listening, where two of the tools used with young children (i.e. tours and map making) have been explored with adults. The resulting maps have become the focus for multiple listening across teams of practitioners from a range of professional backgrounds. This multiple listening acknowledges that the design process should not only be two-dimensional (based around drawings and plans) but a three-dimensional process (alive to different viewpoints and expertise).

Chapter 3.3 took facilitating exchange with architects as its focus. Encounters with the different perspectives of users, both children and adults, have taken place through direct meetings and through documentation. Architects have listened to young children talk about their views of existing and possible spaces and they also met to review children's material. The process has challenged some preconceived ideas about what environments for young children should contain. Children have not been turned into architects, but architects have been able to bring new perspectives to designing for children. Questions about changing roles within the design process are explored further in Part IV.

Part IV

Ways forward

Narratives of learning spaces

4.1 Introduction

Part IV looks at some of the possibilities and challenges raised by this study in terms of the design process, learning communities and research with both young children and adults. Each of Chapters 4.2, 4.3 and 4.4 revisits the central question 'What does it mean to be in this place?'. Emphases on perspectives and experience are explored in relation to their relevance to architects, designers, education practitioners and researchers.

Constructing narratives has been a recurring theme through the study. First, I will revisit the place of narratives in the design process. How have these narratives constructed by young children and adults facilitated an inter-generational approach to involving end users of different ages in the design process from design brief to post-occupancy reviews? Possibilities and obstacles are discussed in establishing this 'narrative communication' (Landry 2000) in order to examine if the means of dialogue explored in this book could become tools for facilitating exchange in other design projects.

Second, in Chapter 4.3, I examine the role of narratives as explored in the study in relation to learning communities, including early childhood institutions. This chapter explores the implications of creating opportunities for both styles of communication within learning communities involved in change. This is linked to issues about democracy and listening. Can schools and early childhood institutions become living spaces for children and adults which are more attuned to each person's capabilities and needs? How might visual participatory methods contribute to building 'people-centred schools' (Fielding 2004: 213)?

Third, Chapter 4.4 reflects on the implications of working with visual, participatory narratives for researchers, particularly those seeking to involve young children in research. What part should researchers play in narrative construction? Who are the narrators in these accounts? Are there other facilitators who could produce more appropriate tools?

4.2 Narratives in the design process

Design can be defined as a translation of experience, the translation of inspiration. In order to create extraordinary spaces with integrity and atmospheric presence we need to identify what we find valuable, what we are moved and inspired by.

(Lewis 2007: 228)

Introduction

There is a danger that participation can become tokenistic. This risk applies in the field of architectural participation, as in many other areas (for example Percy-Smith 2006). Blundell Jones, Petrescu and Till sound this warning:

At the level of lowest common denominator architectural participation can be defined as the involvement of users at some stage in the design process. Too often this involvement is token, bringing a degree of worthiness to the architectural process without really transforming it.

(Blundell Jones *et al*. 2005: xiii)

This is an increasing risk in a climate of policy interest in stakeholder views and participation. Consultations can be carried out in order to satisfy funding requirements without leading to any reflection and change on the building projects involved. In this chapter, I argue how participation needs to be approached differently, seeking answers to the question 'What does it mean to be in this place?'. This places participation in the context of a reciprocal process, understanding the reality of living in a space. This way of working challenges a more technical approach to building that focuses on physical aspects in isolation from social, psychological or philosophical considerations. As Lewis comments, extraordinary spaces can require seeking out 'what we find valuable, what we are moved and inspired by' (Lewis 2007: 228). This requires participants to explore and articulate what they find of value in terms of the physical, official and informal landscapes in which they live and work. There is an element of self-discovery here, reconsidering one's own perspectives and those of others. This requires the ability to listen on many levels and to use different languages. If architects have more opportunities to reconsider their own perspectives and those of the users of different ages who experience their buildings, then assumptions may be challenged and possible new solutions (or past solutions) may be found. New insights may lead to innovative design or a renewed interest in solutions from previous decades which have become overlooked. A view of participation which is based on reconsidering values and meanings can change consultations from isolated, abstract events to a process of engagement.

This suggests the need to experience different perspectives rather than just record points of view. Therefore, participation becomes a reciprocal process of architects engaged in finding out about children's lives and children involved in the design process.

Experiencing things differently

Physical landscape

One important way to rethink space is to experience the physical landscape differently. Snug and Outdoors, an artist-led organisation who design play spaces, organised a symposium at the Royal Institute of British Architects. The diverse audience included civil servants, artists, teachers, landscape architects and academics. The audience members were encouraged to work in pairs to explore the environment from a different perspective. One person in each pair rested a small mirror against their upper lip, facing the mirror up to the ceiling. Concentrating on the mirror, this inverted image of the ceiling was their only perspective on the space whilst their partner led them around the building. It was a perplexing, disorientating and surprising way to explore the space.

Architects engaged in a project to design a new special school in Scotland for visually impaired children wore sight-restricting glasses to feel their way around a school building. This physical engagement enabled the architects to gain more understanding of how to design way finders within the school.

As discussed in earlier parts of this book, there have been examples in the Living Spaces study where the visual narratives constructed by children and by adults have enabled the architects involved to experience the physical environment from other perspectives. This has particularly been the case in terms of scale and perspective. Young children's photographs of the ceiling and the sky, together with close-up images of carpets and mud, served as one example of this. Another example came from the map made by the student social worker in the children's centre case study (see Chapter 3.2). She included a photograph of the toilet as her private space. Experiencing physical spaces differently can be achieved indirectly through documentation produced by users and through direct encounters, which may be harder to achieve.

Physical, official and informal landscapes

What other opportunities are there for adults, including architects, to re-think children's spaces? Some of the most innovative approaches have arisen from partnerships with artists. One such project was Grown-up School:

> The workshops used a combined arts approach, incorporating drama, visual arts, creative writing, information technology and discussion to develop the children's ideas on what adults needed to learn and what they could teach them.
>
> (Storer 1999: 1)

> Grown-up School is for different sized people to see what different sized people do.
>
> (Storer 1999: 2)

This project, initiated by performance artist Bobby Baker, was a collaboration between artists, an arts organisation and a primary school. A class of nine- and ten-year-olds used a range of expressive languages to think about a school for adults. It can be seen as a project about imaginary narratives about school. This starting point succeeded in revealing unexpected understandings about how those involved viewed adults, adulthood and school. The children designed a 'Dream room' in the school as there were some interesting possi-bilities presented for the physical landscape:

> Grown-up School looks like a castle, because it should be extravagant and colourful. Not everyone can make their house as beautiful as they would like. We have designed this so that they will like school.
>
> (Lauren Brennon and Imogen Ball, students, quoted in Storer 1999: unpaginated)

This comment reveals a strong connection between the physical appearance of school and well-being. A similar level of maturity and insight is offered in the following remark:

> I would like grown-ups to know that there is always somewhere to go. A place where they can meet people and create things.
>
> (Lauren Watts, student, quoted in Storer 1999: unpaginated)

The children in the Grown-up School project demonstrated how their views about the physical appearance of school linked to the informal landscape of friendship, caring or bullying. The official landscape was considered by designing a curriculum and considering uniforms for adults. The artists facilitated this enquiry, enabling the children to think differently about school and adults. In so doing, they increased understandings about how children view their own experiences in school.

Design and views of childhood

Grown-up School is an example of children considering 'What would it mean to be an adult in this place?'. I wish to return to the question 'What does it mean to be a child in this place?'. This opens up wider issues about how a society views children and childhood. The environments which are created for children are linked to the beliefs which are held and assumptions which are made about children and their needs and capabilities.

The study by James and Curtis (Curtis 2007) of children and young people's views and experiences of hospital spaces draws attention to assumptions about children and childhood which the hospital design conveyed. The participants included children from four to sixteen years old in three hospitals:

> The ideas of childhood that are embedded within hospital décor are, over-whelmingly, those associated with the infant child, a resonant babyish-ness that child patients, aged between 7 and 16, tolerate, rather than appreciate.
>
> (Curtis 2007: 19)

This 'babyishness' included references to artwork made by younger children and the use of cartoon figures on the walls. Images of clowns received negative comments and were seen as frightening, even by some of the older children.

This poses the question about what a child-friendly environment could look like when providing for a wide age range of children and young people in difficult circumstances. Curtis discusses the need for both private spaces and social spaces for children in hospitals (Curtis 2007: 20). Interestingly, some of the youngest children in the study expressed the importance of some form of privacy being provided by the curtains around the bed: 'you can draw those curtains around if you need a wee' (Curtis 2007: 20).

Two contrasting examples of a link between design and how young children are viewed derive from Iceland. I discussed earlier (see Chapter 2.2) how Einarsdottir's (2005: 534) study revealed the children's use of the child-only room in an Icelandic preschool. This unsupervised space reflects a view about young children which values their independence and the importance of peer relationships. A different set of views about children and childhood appeared to be reflected in a new preschool I visited in Iceland. Based on a particular philosophy about children, the architecture conveyed the need to supervise children and to train them to behave in an orderly way. Corridors had lines and arrows painted on the floor to indicate where children could walk and in what direction.

Architect Mark Dudek (2000) discusses how early childhood environments reflect a range of understandings about childhood and child development. He makes a distinction, for example, between a design which sets out to be a 'home from home' and others, such as the Luginsland kindergarten in Stuttgart, Germany, which embody a view of the child as explorer and creator (Dudek 2000: 156). This unconventional structure takes the form of a tilted boat, complete with portholes and masts, tethered to the ground by 'mooring ropes' which look like they are preventing the kindergarten floating away. Dudek comments, 'Stuttgart gains a distinctive symbol of civic pride, underlying the importance placed on children in the city; secondly, the children have a building that immediately challenges their conventional view of architecture' (Dudek 2000: 156). This remark is a reminder that buildings designed for young children can convey the status that is given to children within the wider community. Are early childhood environments seen as places peopled by valued members of society, both in terms of the adults and children present?

Italian housing project Coriandoline represents another striking example of how the value placed on young children and families can be conveyed through architecture. Coriandoline is a housing co-operative on the outskirts of the small town of Correggio in northern Italy. Here the designs of the houses and landscaping are the result of a long-standing engagement between the architects, twelve nursery and infant schools and two child psychologists. The development is described in Italian as 'le case amiche dei bambini e delle bambine' which has been translated as 'friendly houses for girls and boys'. Both the design process and the final buildings conveyed that young children were key participants rather than tokenistic players. The first phase of the research resulted in the launching of a Manifesto of Children's Living Needs:

This is how I would like my house to be:

Transparent . . . so I can look outside if it is sunny or raining.

Hard outside so it will never break. If a bad man comes along he will hurt himself on it.

Soft inside . . . the house is lovelier, it would be soft and warm.

Decorated . . . I would put precious stones so the house is nicer.

Intimate . . . I would like a secret place to go into and come out of whenever I liked.

Peaceful . . . not trafficky.

Playful . . . a house with stairs and slides

Big . . . so that when Emanuel and Mattia come they can stay over . . . so they can ride around it with their bikes.

Childsize . . . I would like a bell button with my name on it.

Magic . . . I want a special wall with . . . so that when I put my hand on it it took me on journeys.

(Malavasi and Pantaleoni 2008: 8–9)

At one stage, the town square was invaded by numerous cardboard houses: 'The kids' town occupies the grown-ups' city (and the kids symbolically take over the city with their imagination' (Malavasi and Pantaleoni 2008: 5). Each house has been developed with an individual name and character, such as 'the house with the roof held up by trees' and the 'transparent house'. The houses in Coriandoline convey a community in which children and living with children is placed centre stage:

> We used the 'child's point of view' as a measurement of quality. These are 'real houses' in which families have constructed life projects and have invested their economic resources . . .

> Giving importance, legitimacy and interest to the contributions and ideas of children is the most revolutionary aspect of the research. Listening to their needs and taking in their comments: welcoming, playful . . . richness, transparency . . . These are the words that have disappeared from the vocabulary of those who actually build houses.
>
> (Malavasi and Pantaleoni 2008: 28; 33)

Before moving on, I would like to add a final reflection. Revisiting views about children and childhood may not necessarily lead towards increasingly elaborate buildings. The forest kindergarten movement is one example where the expression of views and values about childhood has led to an increasing number of kindergartens which are based outdoors (Knight 2009).

I have been discussing here how ways of viewing children and childhood can influence design. But a participatory approach involves both reflecting on how children and childhood are viewed and engaging with perspectives gained from children. This next section focuses on how narratives produced by children, including the visual narratives developed in the Living Spaces study, may provide new ways of children's own views becoming part of a dialogue about the design and review of buildings.

Design and children's views: past narratives

An important part of listening to children's perspectives about learning spaces is to engage with what children have already said. This accumulative local knowledge provided by children over several decades can be brought alongside current engagement with children in individual projects. 'The School I'd Like' project (Burke and Grosvenor 2003) is a valuable resource in this respect as it draws on the views and experiences of children and young people at two points in recent history: 1967 and 2001. A competition was the catalyst for both sets of data, as the authors explain:

> It was the *Observer* newspaper that sponsored the competition in 1967, which received 943 entries. This competition had as its focus the future of the secondary school. In 2001, the *Observer's* sister newspaper, agreed to host the competition and received multiple entries from over 1,500 schools and hundreds of individuals.
>
> (Burke and Grosvenor 2003: xii)

The competition in 2001 received writings, drawings and models from over 15,000 children from four to eighteen years old. Dea Birkett, a journalist who was involved in the competition, compiled the following children's manifesto based on a summary of the entries:

> The school we'd like is:
>
> A beautiful school with glass dome roofs to let in the light, uncluttered classrooms and brightly coloured walls.
>
> A comfortable school with sofas and beanbags, cushions on the floors, tables that don't scrape our knees, blinds that keep out the sun, and quiet rooms where we can chill out.
>
> A safe school with swipe cards for the school gate, anti-bully alarms, first aid classes, and someone to talk to about our problems.
>
> A listening school with children on the governing body, class representatives and the chance to vote for the teachers.
>
> A flexible school without rigid timetables or exams, without compulsory homework, without a one-size-fits-all curriculum, so we can follow our own interests and spend more time on what we enjoy.
>
> A relevant school where we learn through experience, experiments and exploration, with trips to historic sites and teachers who have practical experience of what they teach.
>
> A respectful school where we are not treated as empty vessels to be filled with information, where teachers treat us as individuals, where children and adults can talk freely to each other, and our opinion matters.
>
> A school without walls so we can go outside to learn, with animals to look after and wild gardens to explore.
>
> A school for everybody with boys and girls from all backgrounds and abilities, with no grading, so we don't compete against each other, but just do our best.
>
> (Birkett 2001)

This manifesto illustrates how gathering children's narratives about a future, imagined school stretched beyond bricks and mortar to emotional and social needs as well as to questions of pedagogy. This body of material deserves to be taken seriously in ongoing projects to transform education, providing a compass for thinking about learning and design.

The final section of this chapter investigates what contribution narrative communication can play in promoting this thinking.

Discussion

Ongoing narrative communication

The documentation produced by the young children and adults in the Living Spaces study can be seen as a collection of narratives about present, anticipated and new spaces. Narratives have been adopted as a strategy for gathering different perspectives in regeneration projects. Architect and academic Prue Chiles sets out a case for narrative as a form of engagement in community participation in this context: 'a device to help us develop a set of background ideas, an identity for a place – a "there" for somewhere that was not there before' (Chiles 2005b: 187–206).

There is a strong future direction in Chiles' use of narrative as these stories have been constructed in the context of regeneration – to be part of the process of recreating a sense of place. She emphasises the importance of identity building in constructing narratives by referring to the work of Dolores Hayden: 'Narratives locate us as part of something bigger than our existences, make us feel less insignificant, sometimes give us partial answers to questions like who am I? Why am I like I am?' (quoted by Chiles 2005b: 187). This sense of identity building has particular relevance when the people concerned are young children, who are actively involved each day in working out who they are.

Chiles proposes the importance of narrative communication in contrast to iconic communication, as explained by Landry:

> Narrative communication is concerned with creating arguments; it takes time and promotes reflection. Its 'bandwidth is as wide' as its scope is exploratory and linked to critical thinking; it is 'low density' in the sense of building understanding piece by piece.
>
> (Landry 2000: 64)

Iconic communication for Landry (2000: 65) is about making a high impact, a trigger for action. Such exchange would not be looking to explain deeper meanings or underlying principles. He describes the example of a children's charity fundraising campaign as an example of iconic communication. A design project may require both forms of knowledge sharing during the lifetime of a project. A statement or image may be used to galvanise support, but there may be a more lasting value in promoting reflection through the construction and exchange of narratives.

Architect students in Sheffield have explored different approaches to creating or provoking narratives. Carolyn Butterworth describes how conceptual art practice has provided an alternative set of tools for gathering narratives about a place (Butterworth 2007: 148). Site surveys have been the focus of the students' work. Traditionally, according to Butterworth, an architect would use a camera, architectural drawings and physical, historical and social data to conduct a site survey. The students have replaced these tools with storytelling, performance, game playing and conversation. One example is of an architectural student performing a Mexican dance in front of Accrington Market Hall. This event opened up a range of conversations about past activities which had taken place in the space. This type of encounter led to the sharing of 'fine-grained' detail which would not have been possible from secondary data or through the architect's lens alone:

> Architects are not the experts in understanding a place; to approach any level of expertise, they themselves need to become users. In contrast to the information gathered by conventional survey techniques, the stories told of people uncover hidden possibilities, speaking of the imagination and the metaphorical and not just the measurable.
>
> (Butterworth 2007: 151)

There is a distinction between declaring 'architects are not the experts' and 'architects are not the experts in understanding a place'. The architect maintains the expertise in terms of conceiving the designs, but it is in the understandings of what it means to be in this place from which architects can gain insights to inform their work. Narratives produced during the Living Spaces study have opened up new possibilities through demonstrating the imaginative and the metaphorical and valuing the difficult to measure. Young children's views and experiences about existing, possible or new environments are hard to quantify. For example, understandings about personal, social and private spaces (see Part II) are not easily tied down or quantified, but they do provide a way into seeing how spaces are understood by their young users. Blundell Jones *et al.* remind us of the contested nature of architectural participation: 'Participation is not always regarded as the guarantee of sustainability within a project, but as an approach that assumes risks and uncertainty' (Blundell Jones *et al.* 2003: xiv).

This chapter has raised questions about the nature of participation in the design process. I have emphasised the possibility of participation which is reciprocal; children can be involved in different stages of the design and architects can become engaged with the views and experiences of children. This way of thinking about participatory design:

- discusses meanings and values;
- promotes reflection;
- bridges disciplinary boundaries;
- fosters the hundred languages of children and adults;
- involves children and adults, users and professionals;
- includes ongoing encounters rather than one-off consultation.

The Mosaic approach can provide one framework for working in this way. In Chapter 4.3 I consider the connections between participatory design and pedagogy and the contribution of pedagogical documentation to questions about being in this place.

4.3 Narratives in learning communities

Introduction

This study has been carried out within the context of learning communities. These are not neutral spaces. They are environments which come with a particular range of expectations from both children and adults. Carrying out research during the design process using visual participatory methods in these contexts has raised questions and possibilities. This chapter considers what contribution this way of working may make to listening to both young children and adults within school and early childhood environments. In Chapter 4.2, I examined what impact the question 'What does it mean to be in this place?' may have within the context of architectural participation. This ended with thinking about participation as involving risks and uncertainty. Participation within a learning context can be challenging too. It may confirm well-established views about children and childhood, but it also raises questions and surprises.

Young children's narratives

A sense of belonging

A study which has set out to involve young children in the design process suggests research with an emphasis on future spaces. However, some of the most enduring insights have focused on how young children view and experience their current social environment. These understandings may support practitioners in reflecting on their pedagogy and their physical setting. The question 'What does it mean to be in this place?' is not only a valid question to ask in the context of a building project. Listening to children in this way can be embedded in practice (Clark *et al.* 2005).

Perhaps the most significant understanding gained has been about how children have expressed a 'sense of belonging' to a place (Woodhead and Brooker 2008). Children across both case studies and at different ages have drawn attention to details, to personal markers, which are about themselves or their families, in the environment. It is as if the nursery class or children's centre is criss-crossed with invisible string which links the children to different objects, places and people within the space. Woodhead and Brooker (2008) discuss the importance of this 'sense of belonging' to children and adults in early childhood environments:

> Belonging is the relational dimension of personal identity, the funda-
> mental psycho-social 'glue' that locates every individual (babies, children
> and adults) at a particular position in space, time and human society and
> – most important – connects people to each other.
>
> (Woodhead and Brooker 2008: 3)

Sometimes these connections may remain hidden from adults who work with children. Gathering children's perspectives on being in a place can make some of these associations more visible, increasing the possibility for respect to be shown to what is of value to the children in an environment.

Profile or portfolio books appear to be of particular significance in terms of a way of making children's narratives visible. There is a distinction to be made in a UK context between the teacher-held Early Years Foundation Stage Profiles, which are required to be completed on every child during their fifth year (DCSF 2008a), and a child-held record, which can be visual and verbal records compiled with the help of young children and their families to document their journey through nursery. One nursery school I visited recently distinguished between the Early Years Foundation Stage Profile, which was compiled by the early childhood practitioners and kept on a high shelf, and 'special books'. These child-held records were stored at floor level for children to access. They were children's narratives and family narratives with episodes added to the book by the children, older siblings, grandparents and parents. Driscoll and Rudge (2005) describe how these narratives can provide children with 'cues for remembering, cues for thinking and cues for discussion' (Driscoll and Rudge 2005: 92). It is these child-held records which have been drawn attention to by children who have taken part in studies using the Mosaic approach (whenever this form of documentation has been practiced). Children in the children's centre in the Living Spaces study photographed page upon page from their portfolios, discussing examples of their work and images of their extended families (see Chapter 2.4). However, this form of documentation was not practised in the nursery class. Many children in this environment seemed to draw attention to their name cards and photographs by their pegs.

Early childhood practice in New Zealand brings together the two functions of a teacher-held formal assessment and a child-held record in the form of portfolios based on 'learning stories' (Carr 2000; Carr *et al*. 2005). Margaret Carr and colleagues discuss how these visual and verbal narratives of children's learning become significant objects which are treasured by young children and their families: 'Portfolios can become an artefact of belonging, signifying the relationship between the learner and the setting' (Carr *et al*. 2007: 2).

One example is given of a child, Suelisa, who is finding it hard to settle into kindergarten. Her portfolio (or 'file', as it is described in her centre) and the photographs and stories it contains of her family provide a tangible link between her home and her new environment: 'The file provides the initial scaffolding that can sometimes be left behind as other "enablers" are added. (New relationships are developed with other children, and a new activity is initiated and encouraged.)' (Carr *et al.* 2007: 23).

Sometimes the children's portfolios stretch to several large volumes. These can provide schools with a rich narrative of children's learning before starting school. This raises the question of whether children feel less of a sense of belonging to a place in which there are few traces of themselves to be found.

Portfolio books are one of several examples of how children's personal markers can be strengthened in a place. Personal hand puppets are another example (see Wunschel 2003); practitioners have made individual puppets which look like each child and are embroidered with their name. As Ilse, a practitioner, comments:

> Our children are now between two and a half and three and a half years old and they dearly love the little look-alikes that bear their names. For some children these have replaced the stuffed animals they slept with at nap time . . . We have realised that the children love their personal puppets dearly. They are taken to bed, to meals, to playing times and also on weekend trips. The puppets accompany the children in our group until they reach school age, and are then taken home.
>
> (Wunschel 2003: 21–22)

Joining in official narratives

Inspections are one example of an official narrative where the voices of the youngest children may be invisible. This may become increasingly less of the case in the United Kingdom, where inspections carried out by the Office for Standards in Education, Children's Services and Skills (Ofsted) require examples of how children's views are heard and acted upon. This raises the question of how practitioners can document where this has taken place.

Documentation produced by children in the form of photo books, maps and interviews, such as illustrated in the Living Spaces study, may provide tangible evidence of work being carried out in this area. A head teacher recently recounted to me how she had been able to support her claim that children's views were heard. The nursery school had been involved in a small study using the Mosaic approach to gather children's views about their existing environment in preparation for a new building (Knight and Clark 2006). The children's maps, which were co-constructed with practitioners, showed how listening to children was an integral part of the change process.

Building as a catalyst for change

At the start of the Living Spaces study, it was difficult to predict whether the research in the school case study would remain a discreet piece of work within the Early Years Foundation Stage or whether there would be any wider impact of the study. My earlier study using the Mosaic approach (Clark and Moss 2005) revealed examples of how young children's views and experiences could facilitate dialogue with children and adults about how an outdoor play space could be redesigned. However, the Spaces to Play study was carried out in a preschool rather than with the youngest children within a primary school. It felt more subversive to be there to listen to the three- and four-year-olds in a school setting than it had felt carrying out the identical role in the preschool. The presence of a researcher interested in the views of the youngest children could be interpreted as making these groups more visible within the school system.

The first surprise was to see the reaction of the school community to the youngest children's maps (see Chapter 2.3). These were displayed in the hall as part of the whole-school consultation organised by the architect. Other activities included a slideshow of possible design features. It was led by the oldest children in the school (ten- and eleven-year-olds). There were also displays of the architect's early drawings and models. The authors of the maps appeared to enjoy seeing their work being given status in this way. Older children seemed to engage with interest in the younger children's contribution.

The children's maps and photographs were part of a presentation I (separately) made to the staff team and to a team within the local authority with responsibility for school buildings. This led to funding by the local authority to carry out an additional consultation within the school, with older children (from five to eleven years old). This funding was in itself significant. It was a strategic-level acknowledgement of the value of listening to children's perspectives. The focus of this consultation was the redesign of the play-grounds. The school council was chosen as the group with whom the researcher would work. This work was supplemented by activities conducted by class-room teachers with whole classes. This consultation gave the opportunity to experiment by using the youngest children's maps as the starting point for the older children to consider 'What does it mean to be in this place?'. Having carefully considered what they could learn about the youngest children's priorities and interests outside, the school council then carried out their own audit of the playground and visited other play spaces before contributing ideas for changes to the space. Spending time engaging with material produced by three- and four-year-olds in the school community reversed the hierarchy of knowledge which is embedded in most schools. The maps and photographs produced by the nursery and reception class provided the means to cross pedagogical boundaries and enabled children of different ages to co-construct meanings.

At the end of the first year of the Living Spaces study, the head teacher made this observation about the research:

> Working with Alison has really opened our eyes as far as involving even our youngest children in consultation about important, whole-school issues. Some members of staff were sceptical at the beginning of the exercise about how informed and sensible our Nursery and Reception pupils' ideas were going to be and how useful this research was going to be to us as a school. After getting half way through the project, Alison's approach has radically changed the way that we include all of the children in making whole-school decisions; we now try to see them as 'the experts' in their experiences, adapting some of the ideas that Alison used with the Reception and Nursery to inform our plans for the future. I hope that this way of working will become an integral part of our normal everyday practice and it becomes a legacy to future generations of children, parents and staff at [this] School.
>
> (Head teacher, school case study)

During an evaluation of the study (carried out at the end of the three years) the head teacher commented:

> The idea of seeing children as experts is obvious but it crystallised our thinking as a learning community.
>
> If another Head said 'should I do it?', I'd thoroughly recommend that they do. It develops your thinking of how schools can work. Today members of the staff say, as a matter of course, 'what do the children think?'. This shows how embedded the approach has become.
>
> (Head teacher, school case study)

The phrase 'children as experts' appears to represent a change in how children were viewed within this school. This phrase comes from a comment by a Danish colleague, Ole Langsted, in an article about deciding on quality in early childhood provision:

> But what about the influence of the primary users – the children themselves? Is anyone interested in the kind of daily life the *children* want? Does anyone regard children as experts when it comes to their own lives?
>
> (Langsted 1994: 29; original emphasis)

This comment is echoed in the 'student voice' literature when Rudduck and Flutter refer to children as 'expert witnesses' (for example Rudduck and Flutter 2004: 14–28). This leads us on to consider the links between listening to young children and wider democratic practice.

Democratic practice

Can listening to young children's perspectives lead towards more democratic practice in schools? It seems there may be an impetus for more democratic practice in schools approaching from multiple directions: student participation initiatives with older students (for example Fielding 2004) and early childhood education (for example Dahlberg and Moss 2005; MacNaughton 2003). This is not to say that every early childhood institution is a site of democratic practice; this is still a relatively new development in the field. However, even small changes have the potential to quickly be transferred upwards into schools as rapidly as young children grow older and move on through the education system.

This is difficult territory under discussion here. Both 'democracy' and 'participation' are slippery words which can allude precise definition and prove difficult to tie down in practice. Fielding's (2004) work illustrates what democratic practice could look like in an education system for younger or older children. He sets out four different types of school organisation: schools as impersonal organisations, schools as affective communities, schools as high performing learning organisations and schools as person-centred learning communities. The contrast between the third and fourth types are of particular interest in reflecting on democratic practice. In Fielding's model, schools which are high performance learning organisations may harness student voice to make schools more effective: 'Student voice operating within the "high performance" mode is largely an instrumental undertaking orientated towards increased measurable organisational performance' (Fielding 2004: 211).

This differs from schools as person-centred learning communities – living spaces – in which the aim is to promote dialogue between children and adults which encompasses widely defined educational goals. A person-centred school acknowledges aspirations for schools to be places which respect the humanness of teachers and students: 'It is about ensuring student voices and teacher voices are also the voices of persons in relation to one another in the quest for a deeper and more fulfilling humanity' (Fielding 2004: 213).

'Student voice', in this last example, is not about promoting children's views and experiences in isolation from adults but promoting them 'in relation to one another'. This links to ideas about participation as a reciprocal process, (see Chapter 4.2). This raises the question of what structures or spaces can be created to promote such exchanges. Several writers have proposed different possibilities for creating such 'discursive spaces' (for example Cruddas and Haddock 2003; Marchant and Kirby 2004; Moss and Petrie 2002; Percy-Smith 2006). Moss and Petrie, to take one example, articulate these possibilities for new exchanges as a desired move from 'children's services' to 'children's spaces' (Moss and Petrie 2002: 101–112).

The process of 'documentation' may offer a 'physical and metaphorical space' (Fielding 2004: 213) where dialogue can take place. Adopting methods which enable children and adults to make their perspectives visible is a starting point, but change happens when this leads to respectful exchange of ideas which informs practice. Dahlberg, Moss and Pence (1999: 144) suggest how documentation can be an important ingredient in promoting democratic practice in early childhood education. Dahlberg and Moss, in subsequent work, push these ideas further, raising the possibility of early childhood institutions as spaces for 'minor politics' (Rose 1999: 279–280 quoted in Dahlberg and Moss 2005: 121–122). This notion refers to locally-based democratic practice which is rooted in the everyday. Rose's phrase 'little territories of the everyday' (Rose 1999: 279–280) seems to apply to early childhood institutions. Dahlberg and Moss use the Mosaic approach to illustrate one possible way of creating such local narratives:

> The Mosaic approach opens up a space for listening to young children, and a creative methodology for their inclusion in minor politics. Children's perspectives – their perspectives on the institutions created for them by adults – can place a stutter in adult narratives about preschools and pedagogical work, and offer more local narratives spoken by children. They can be a provocation to an outcome-focused instrumental rationality, by reminding us that preschools are places where children increasingly live their childhoods, and which may be valued by children for social, emotional, aesthetic and many other reasons not necessarily defined by adults as desirable outcomes.
>
> (Dahlberg and Moss 2005: 164)

Perhaps the research in this book has examples of how to create 'a stutter in adult narratives' about children, preschools and schools. Herein lies one of the major challenges to promoting such democratic practice. A stutter can be disempowering for the individual concerned. Viewing children in a different way and considering their perspectives can leave adults feeling threatened, especially when their own perspectives and roles are challenged in new ways. Perhaps this is why it felt subversive to be listening to young children in the primary school. It was creating a stutter in the official school narrative.

This suggests that the structures and methods which are needed are 'person-centred' (to use Fielding's phrase) and value and respect children and adult members of each learning community. Perpetua Kirby and colleagues refer to this goal as 'building a culture of participation' (Kirby *et al.* 2003). They refer to the following comment by a senior member of staff: 'The principles of pupil voice are something that extend throughout the whole school community. It is not just listening to children, it's respecting the views of everybody in the organisation. Because schools are just people' (Senior manager quoted in Kirby *et al.* 2003: 32).

Listening to adults

A seminar was held, at the end of the Living Spaces study, which focused on post-occupancy reviews. One of the participants who worked in an advisory capacity with early years settings talked about her experiences of projects which have focused on listening to young children. She encountered practitioners who wanted to listen to the views of young children but at the same time felt their own views and experiences were not acknowledged. It was as if the increased interest in listening to young children brought into sharp relief their own feelings of disempowerment.

There is growing support for practitioners in terms of practical ways of listening to young children in the United Kingdom. The Young Children's Voices Network has been established at a national and local level to promote listening within the early years (Clark and Williams 2008). Perhaps there needs to be further development work and training to explore values, structures and methods which support listening to both adults' and children's perspectives. This links to approaches to leadership and teamwork. A hierarchical leadership model may preclude other members of early years teams contributing their views and skills to ongoing practice and future initiatives (for example Rodd 2006). However, a model of distributed leadership (Benson 2006; Siraj-Blatchford and Manni 2007) may enable more individuals within an institution to feel they are valued and contributing positively. This links with creating a culture of listening which includes children, adults, parents and practitioners.

A head of a children's centre who has been a member of the Young Children's Voices Network described how she had worked to promote a listening culture which included both children and adults. She explained, 'It is not just a case of "Every Child Matters" but Every Person Matters' (Clark and Williams 2008).

Crossing professional boundaries

Multi-agency working has become an increasing feature of early childhood practice in the United Kingdom. This has led to early childhood environments often being the meeting point for individuals from an array of professional backgrounds, including social work, health and education (Weinberger *et al.* 2005). The physical environment provides the arena within which these encounters take place. However, there may be very different professional and personal viewfinders being used to work with the same young children and families.

The review of the children's centre described in the second case study (see Part III) brought together different professional groups to reflect on the physical environment. The visual task of taking photographs and making maps provided an accessible common ground on which to discuss everyday practice within the shared space. This in turn revealed differences in work culture. The meeting room, for example, was familiar to some practitioners from office-based jobs, but it represented an approach to discussion that was too formal for some of the early childhood practitioners. Gradually implicit views about children and childhood were made explicit. Sometimes these followed professional lines; sometimes they represented different personal approaches to a similar role. This raises the possibility of the Mosaic approach being adapted to facilitate exchanges between different professional groups working with young children.

In this chapter, I have explored how gathering young children's narratives about being in a space can be embedded in practice through pedagogical documentation. This can underpin learning and support children's sense of belonging and relationships. Here we can see the link between participation and belonging, which Carr has described as two sides of the same coin (Carr quoted in Hipkins *et al.* 2005). Questions around participation lead to wider questions around politics and democratic practice. Here we can see how discussions around older children's student voices can now be joined by younger children's narratives as visual and verbal methods are combined. Listening to younger children within learning communities has led to some reconsidering of how to also listen to adults' views and experiences. As Hart explains, this presents us with a challenge: 'We need to go beyond simple strategies for listening to children's voices if we are to build more democratic communities. We need to consider how children and adults come together, and could come together in meaningful dialogue' (Hart 2009: 24).

4.4 Narratives and narrators
The role of researchers

Introduction

This book has focused on research carried out with learning communities undergoing change. Collecting narratives within the context of design projects has led me to reflect on the role of the researcher within this process. What part should researchers play in narrative construction? Who have been the narrators? Could others develop the role in different ways? This chapter discusses questions which have arisen about the roles of researchers and participants involved in visual, participatory research projects.

I have made references throughout this book to a way of viewing children – including young children – as experts in their own lives. The inclusion of this principle acknowledges that there is a place for subjective accounts in research. I have explained how this standpoint is not intended to undermine adults' particular professional expertise, but it is intended to recognise and give value to children's own perspectives. This may, however, be perceived as a threat to adult roles in the design process (see Chapter 4.2) and in learning communities (see Chapter 4.3). I examine here whether this approach presents a similar threat to researchers. For researchers, what are the risks or benefits of working in a participatory way with children?

Adult researcher: losing my voice?

My professional career in education began as a teacher. One of my lasting memories of my first term as a probationary teacher was of becoming voiceless. I had a class of thirty-five young children. By December, I had lost my voice. It was a frustrating and disempowering predicament. Does the adoption of participatory research methods runs the risk of rendering the researcher voiceless?

I will refer to the camera as an illustration. The sharing of power within this study may be symbolised by the handing over of the digital camera to the young children. Young participants, such as Samina (see Chapter 2.5), who was almost silent in the nursery, made their perspectives visible through the mediated use of this tool. However, in doing so, had I lessoned my own means of communication within the research process? I was no longer the 'lady with the camera', as children sometimes refer to me, in a research setting; I became the observer of children's use of the camera. This change in relationship within the study was taken a step further when I became the focus of children's photographs.

Samina, on one occasion, took a photograph of me and her friend sitting in a playhouse outside. I am caught in the photograph pulling a face, feeling uncomfortable with being in the picture. Samina, as the photographer, is in control of who is included in the research and who is given meaning. This was not a one-off incident. Several children chose images of me to go onto maps about their nursery, which in turn became artefacts for parents, practitioners, architects and other children to discuss. In so doing, my place in the study as a participant was cemented by the children. The researcher became the researched (see Chapter 1.4).

It is important for researchers who are working within a participatory framework to be clear about their role as a researcher within the process. There is still the need to bring expertise to the study, just as I have discussed the need for architects and practitioners to bring their own skills to discussions with children.

I give examples here of how I have maintained my voice as researcher through this study.

Fieldwork and voice

There are several strategies available for researchers to develop their own voice through the research process. I discuss here research journals, photography, advisory groups or supervisions and the role of public speaking. I would argue that a research journal may become of particular significance to a researcher in a study which involves engaging with many voices. This can be a space for an internal dialogue to take place. The experiences of listening to children and adults in different professional roles can be examined and held alongside ideas discussed with colleagues or read in articles. The journal should be a creative opportunity where researchers can experiment and improvise. It is not intended as a public document, although extracts may help to illuminate themes which emerge from the data. This experimentation may involve researchers in taking on new verbal or visual languages. It seems important that researchers become as aware of the hundred languages of expression as children. As a visual artist, I have become increasingly aware of bringing drawings, writings and photography together in my research journals. This has been of particular value when I have visited different schools and nurseries, in several countries, throughout the study. There is a similarity here with how some architects reflect on the buildings which they visit, incorporating written accounts with drawings and photographs. Dudek (2000) includes examples of his own drawings of kindergarten architecture alongside architects' plans and

Figure 4.4.1
Researcher's collage
of the completed
building

Source: Living Spaces
study

photographs. John Bishop (2001), another architect, brings his own drawings of Reggio preschools into his account of his visit there.

Early on in the study, I visited a primary school as part of a different research group. This helped me to reflect on the role and voice I had established for myself within the early stages of the Living Spaces study. I went on the visit with a multi-disciplinary team of colleagues, including architects, historians and educationalists. One of these colleagues began by documenting the classroom we had entered by photographing the room from each point of the compass, moving systematically from corner to corner. He explained how he always recorded a new classroom in this way, thus building up a bank of images upon which to reflect. This approach highlighted for me the importance of researchers being confident in keeping their own narratives of a space and of the research process, at the same time as learning from those constructed by research participants of whatever age. Participatory methods involve an epistemological humility which values the narratives of others. However, the researcher needs to balance this with a confidence in their own narrative which will eventually be co-constructed into a narrative of other narratives.

The research journal is primarily a private space to develop a researcher's voice. There are other, more public arenas. An advisory group may be one arena which can open up opportunities for debate and, in so doing, develop a researcher's narrative. An account in my research journal reminded me of when

I began to articulate how important the advisory group had become to me in developing my ideas:

> It is as if the 'real work' happens in the gaps between what you think you doing. So there is a parallel with children's images of the nursery [listening to young children study]. Gary's image of the 'round the back of the shed and the hedge by the fence'. This seemed to him where the action was – and in the corridors, 'fruit time' and not in the more formal language activities.
>
> Similarly with the Living Spaces project – exciting work in the case studies – and the advisory group is a necessary part of the structures *but* it seems that the advisory group actually is a very strong part of the project . . .
>
> All invention and progress come from finding a link between two ideas that have never met, bringing foreign bodies together [Zeldin, 1995].
>
> (Research journal notes, April 2006)

Through my study, I began to realise that the function of the advisory group had changed from a formal arrangement required by the funder to an important opportunity for exchanging meanings and constructing narratives. The creativity of the group was magnified by its multi-disciplinary nature. Policy-makers debated with architects, historians, artists, head teachers and academics from early childhood and childhood studies. I found this group, which met annually through the three-year study, to be a catalyst for new ways of thinking about the research. There was an opportunity within the course of the meeting for different members to present some of their own current work. These presenting members included, on the first occasion, Michele Zini, an Italian architect whose own work on young children's environments provided an alternative lens for looking at the children's narratives (for example Ceppi and Zini 1998). This arena proved a creative discursive space for other members of the group (see Chapter 3.3).

As Zeldin described above, new narratives may be formed when two ideas which have never met are brought together. An advisory group can be one opportunity to bring these different ideas together, although this invention is not guaranteed. There needs, perhaps, to be an understanding that these multi-disciplinary groups are valued as part of the meaning-making process of research rather than as a monitoring body. Forming an advisory group is a requirement of many research grant-making organisations. This support is not available in this formal way for research students, however, research supervisions can, at their most creative, be an opportunity to bring together ideas which have perhaps not met in this way before. The likelihood of this occurring may be increased when a student has more than one research supervisor and supervisors from different disciplines or areas of expertise.

Public speaking has been an important avenue for developing my researcher's narrative through this study. This has included discussing this research throughout the three years of the study and beyond during the writing process. These opportunities have included speaking to groups from different disciplinary backgrounds, including education, architecture and family therapy, and in different countries. These encounters, particularly at the smaller gatherings, have provided a rich source of questions. These questions have in turn challenged me to look in new ways at the narratives I had gathered. These talks have not been presentations of the final story, but they have been part of an ongoing revisiting of the texts. The public nature of these encounters has raised issues about ethics. It is important, in bringing participants' narratives to a wider audience, to consider what is appropriate to discuss in these arenas. Some information will only be appropriate to discuss with children, parents and practitioners at a local level, within the nursery or school (for example, where an issue of concern is raised by a child). Other themes can be linked to similar accounts by other children in other studies and brought to a wider audience, where there is permission to tell others about the research.

One example of how the questions I encountered helped to strengthen my researcher's narrative occurred at a research seminar with practitioners and researchers working in a hospital. A person asked how the multi-method nature of the approach would be viewed by a medical research ethics committee. Her concern was that giving children several means of communicating their views and experiences might be seen as placing unnecessary strain on the children involved. This question helped me to reflect on the tension between viewing a multi-method approach as a positive feature to increase inclusion within a children's rights framework and a welfare framework which may see a diversity of methods as harmful.

I have discussed the need to develop a researcher's voice when working within a participatory research framework, through a range of visual, verbal and oral means. The following discussion examines how building on this basis the role of researcher may need to be reconstructed in the light of changing boundaries between the researcher and the researched (see Clark forthcoming).

Changing roles of the researcher

Researcher as novice

A researcher who shares power with children is relinquishing the need to know all the answers. I have referred to the idea of researcher as authentic novice who acknowledges a lack of understanding about a particular setting or routine (see Chapter 1.4). The tour demonstrates this relationship with children or with adult participants. The researcher asks to be walked around an environment and tries to see it through the eyes of those who are in charge of the tour. One question which arises is whether this role of authentic novice is only open to an external researcher who undertakes research in an environment or whether this attitude can be adopted by practitioners. This question arose at the end of the Spaces to Play study:

We have discussed . . . the advantages for researchers of the role of 'novice'. However, one disadvantage for researchers is that they do not have a long-term relationship with the children that would enable them to use their insights into children's priorities and interests into children's ongoing learning. Perhaps the key question is not about who is doing the listening but about what is the individual's expectations of the children and what skills and resources they have at their disposal to support children's self-expression?

(Clark and Moss 2005: 98)

When the focus of a project is the physical environment, I think it is more possible for practitioners to adopt a novice role to seek to see the environment through new eyes. This is maybe more possible when the practitioners have themselves had the opportunity to step back and look afresh at their own living and working space and to reflect on the viewpoint of others (both the children and adults with whom they share this environment).

Researcher as teacher and learner

The redrawing of boundaries between adults' and children's roles can lead to a greater freedom for both children and adults. One result for adult researchers may be the opportunity to acknowledge a wider range of personal skills within the research process. This may be linked to a greater honesty about what researchers know and their gaps in knowledge. It is far easier for a researcher in the position of an authentic novice or interested adult to be honest about their strengths and weaknesses than a researcher in the role of adult expert. The way is laid open for researchers to acknowledge that they are learning, as well as, perhaps, teaching, within the boundaries of a research study.

This intermingling of adult roles occurred within each of the research studies using the Mosaic approach. The following incident is taken from the Living Spaces study. The decision was taken by the research team to introduce digital technology into this study. The three- to five-year-olds were using digital cameras as one of the tools for exploring their perspectives. This was combined with introducing a photo printer so the children could select and print out their own photographs. At first, I was in the role of teacher, explaining to the children how the camera worked, how to use the liquid crystal display (LCD) screen rather than the viewfinder and how to review photographs once they had been taken. Most of the children did not have any direct experience of using a digital camera to call upon, but they had watched the researcher (and, in some instances, their parents) use such cameras. This was an apprenticeship model of teaching; the children watched and understood the purpose of the activity and then experimented and, in most cases, became competent in using the tool.

The photo printer was the second piece of equipment which needed to be mastered. This presented me with a challenge when, despite a rehearsal and reading the handbook, I failed to print from the camera's memory card the first time round. Rather than hiding, I admitted to the children there was a problem and re-read the instructions. Demonstrating my role as learner felt like an honest and important part of the process. This technical learning was in addition to the ongoing learning of young children's priorities and interests, which was a day-to-day feature of the fieldwork. The blurring of distinction between teacher and researcher has been articulated in the theory and practice of the preschools of Reggio Emilia:

> That is why I have written so often about the teacher as a researcher . . . [I]t's not that we don't recognise your [academic] research, but we want our research, as teachers, to be recognised. And to recognise research as a way of thinking, of approaching life, of negotiating, of documenting.
>
> (Rinaldi 2005: 192)

This broad definition of the role of research as a 'way of thinking' appears to open up new possibilities for researchers and for teachers. This is a definition which does not constrain either profession within tight boundaries; it acknowledges common threads. This includes a thirst for understanding and a desire to negotiate rather than dictate meanings.

Researcher as artist or artist as researcher?

Research using participatory methods may sometimes blur the boundaries between researcher and artist in the research process as some of the skills required can be seen to be similar. An artist can also be seen as engaged in a 'way of thinking, of approaching life, of negotiating, of documenting', to use Rinaldi's above phrase. An artist engages with a range of media in order to explore meanings. This links the use of visual and verbal methods to explore meanings within participatory approaches. Documenting is an important part of this endeavour, making thinking processes concrete (Clark 2005b). Children's map making is one example from the Mosaic approach in which children can explore their feelings and attachments to a place by documenting what it means to be in this place. This focus on reflexivity is an important benefit of using participatory methods with children (Christensen and James 2008) and with adults (Reason and Bradbury 2006).

The development of the Mosaic approach was influenced by my ways of thinking as a practising visual artist. This led to an openness about possible methods and a willingness to explore both visual and verbal means of communication. This emphasis on visual modes of communication was in keeping with my preferred ways of exploring ideas and perhaps helped to engage with young children who have emergent verbal skills.

This openness about methods was matched by an openness about outcomes. There was the possibility that some of the methods would fail or prove of limited value – which they did. Role play, for example using miniature figures with two-year-olds, gave some insights (Clark and Moss 2001: 31). However, it seems, on reflection, to be too ambitious as a research tool with this age group. However, an openness to new possibilities led to the development of the map making and tours with children under five. Artists are risk takers. This implies an ability to explore uncertainty. This characteristic (if applied within an ethical research framework) can open up new possibilities for research methods.

Researchers may find themselves drawing on skills associated with artistic practice. Artists, in a similar way, may find themselves adopting a role as researchers. This boundary crossing can be seen to have taken place in the production *For the Best*, a play produced by the Unicorn Theatre in collaboration with Mark Storor and Anna Ledgard:

> 'For the Best' began in September 2008 with Mark Storer working as an artist in residence on the Dialysis Unit (at Evelina Hospital School, London). He worked with the children, hearing their stories and enabling them to create poems and to think of images.
>
> (Unicorn Theatre 2009: unpaginated)

The artists explain how they assembled the piece of theatre from the children's shared narratives:

> The original work with the children was created in personal and intimate circumstances, and we are attempting to find a way to create a piece of work that can be shared by more people whilst retaining its intimacy. We are taking the stories, keeping the essence of them and making something new and fresh which has the children's voices absolutely at the heart. That's why the way in which we make the work is so important; going back to the source material all the time, with artists bringing their experience to it.
>
> (Unicorn Theatre 2009: unpaginated)

There are several parallels here with the role of a researcher using participatory methods. These include the need to construct a public narrative from often personal encounters with children and to desire to keep children's voices at the centre of the work and, finally, to do so by repeatedly returning to the source material.

Researcher as translator and facilitator?

Working in multi-disciplinary environments can highlight the need for translators who can support groups in understanding each other's different perspectives and professional languages. Part III of this book looked at some practical examples of how a researcher may find themselves immersed in the complex process of translation. A translator can be seen as someone who makes meanings known from one language to another. One aspect of this has been listening to the children's own accounts of their images and then describing these narratives in such a way as to make the meanings accessible to other audiences. This complex process involves interpretation. There is the need to continue to revisit the material with the authors and with others. A similar process has taken place when working with the material created by adults. The need for a translator was emphasised in the second case study, where several different professions were sharing the same new environment (see Chapter 3.2).

Facilitation has been another feature of the researcher's role, particularly when sharing the narratives created by the children. As described, some of these encounters between architects and children have been face-to-face encounters, but the majority have been mediated through the children's materials. Here the role of researcher has moved beyond translation to facilitation, bringing different sources of knowledge together. This has played an important part in the design process described in this book. This facilitator role did not appear to be a specific part of the brief for any of the other professionals – whether architects or education practitioners – involved. Further examples are needed to examine whether there should be the opportunity to include this researcher as facilitator role as an established part of design projects.

. . . and sometimes the narrator

There are limits to participatory methods. Sometimes the most effective way to understand what it means for individuals to live in a particular environment is to observe (see Warming 2005). This is of particular importance when researching with babies. Detailed observations of how they interact with their environment and how others interact with them are crucial narratives. There may be older children and adults who are ill or who have complex communication needs where the observations of others, including researchers, may be of particular significance. This book began with a reference to Oliver Sacks' account of the lives of his patients. Some of these individuals were able to add their own narratives through interviews with Sacks. However, others were disabled by their illness in such a way that it is Sacks' own narrative and reflection which portrays their lives in the institutions or 'pictures their world' (Sacks 1973: xviii).

A further example concerning the lives of disabled children in institutions in the 1970s comes from the research of Maureen Oswin (1971). Her meticulous ethnographic accounts were gathered as she observed disabled children in four residential institutions:

> It was decided to observe the life of the children during the week-ends, because this would be a time when they would be free of school routines,

and entirely in the charge of nurses or houseparents; and, assuming that the nurses and houseparents (unlike the teachers) would have some duties concerned with the domestic running of the establishment, then it might be seen how the children fitted into domestic routines when not having school. Particular attention was paid to standards of mothering and home-making, which included daily routines, the communication between staff and children, occupations and play, socialization, the physical environment of the institutions and the behaviour of the children. The following diaries record the week-end lives of some handicapped children and give a brief glimpse of what it is like to be a small child in an institution.

(Oswin 1971: 41–42)

These diaries provide a revealing narrative of the official, informal and physical landscapes which she experienced. Her book, *The Empty Hours*, was met with opposition in some quarters due to the bleakness of the life which she in some of the case studies described. The account contributed to changes to the provision of disabled children in hospitals.

Multiple roles in a community of practice

Shifting roles within childhood research could be seen as advocating children and adults swapping roles. This is too simplistic an interpretation and masks the complexity of the reality of carrying out research with children. It is perhaps more constructive to think about the multiplicity of roles which adults and children can play within the research process. This blurring of boundaries can be a freedom for both parties without placing unnecessary responsibilities on children or abandoning adults' professional expertise. There is a parallel between the role of researcher within participatory research and the following quotation about the teacher's role. Rinaldi refers to this description made by Loris Malaguzzi, the founder of the Reggio municipal schools:

> . . . we need a teacher who is sometimes the director, sometimes the set designer, sometimes the curtain and the backdrop, and sometimes the prompter. A teacher who is both sweet and stern, who is the electrician, who dispenses the paints, and who is even the audience—the audience who watches, sometimes claps, sometimes remains silent, full of emotion, who sometimes judges with scepticism, and at other times applauds with enthusiasm.
>
> (Malaguzzi quoted in Rinaldi 2001: 89)

Within the Mosaic approach, the role of researcher changes from being the set designer providing the research tools to an audience for the children's words and images to a silent observer; it rarely changes to the role of a prompter.

There appears to be a need to find a theoretical framework which can cope with the complexities of the continually changing roles between children and adults and within adults' roles in research with children. One possibility is to see researchers in some studies as part of a 'community of practice' (Wenger 1998). Wenger describes a community of practice as being formed by people who participate in a process of collective learning within a shared domain. The research process, as articulated here, is a process of collective learning within the confines of a particular research setting. Collective learning acknowledges that adults and children are at times learners as well as teachers. Wenger describes the process of moving from an outsider role to that of insider within a community of practice in detail. This could be seen to have parallels with the Mosaic approach, where the researcher begins as an outside observer and is gradually introduced to the local practices of the early childhood community (or communities) through the tutoring of the children. This might include such sub-groups as the community of three-year-olds or the community of bike users, for example. The tools used in the Mosaic approach used to explore what it means to be in this place can be seen as a means of reification:

> I will use the concept of reification very generally to refer to the process of giving form to our experience by producing objects that congeal this experience into 'thingness'. In so doing we create points of focus around which the negotiation of meaning becomes organised.
>
> (Wenger 1998: 58)

Reflexivity has been a key ingredient for the children and adults involved in this study. Perhaps reflexivity is one of the important skills which researchers using participatory methods in childhood research can offer the communities of practice in which they work. This is the means by which to express one's own perspectives whilst being made aware of the perspectives of others.

Researchers are members of many communities of practice. Research groups may function in this way if shared interests are pursued. Considering researchers to be members of the communities of practice, their research promotes the idea of researcher as insider, embedded in a community rather than parachuted in. This is possible for longitudinal ethnographic studies (for example Pahl 1998; Brooker 2002; Christensen 2004). This poses challenges, however, for short-term consultations, which may use participatory methods but are constrained by time restraints.

Releasing the researcher from the role of expert has opened new possibilities for reconfiguring the role of children and adults within the research process. This final chapter has focused on the greater freedom but perhaps vulnerability which adult researchers may experience if children – including young children – are enabled to play an active part in research. It is not as straightforward a question as swapping roles. It is a question of finding methodological and theoretical frameworks which can cope with the diversity and flexibility required. The Mosaic approach presents one opportunity to enable both children and adult researchers to take on a multiplicity of roles within the research process with the capacity to play to different children's and adults' strengths. This in turn may lead to more reciprocal relationships being established between the researched communities and the researcher.

4.5 Conclusion

Part IV took the central question 'What does it mean to be in this place?' and explored its relevance within the design process. Lewis (2007), at the start of Chapter 4.2, reiterates the importance of considering what is of value in design: 'In order to create extraordinary spaces with integrity and atmospheric presence we need to identify what we find valuable, what we are moved and inspired by' (Lewis 2007: 228). This search for what adults and children find valuable in their learning communities takes participation beyond tokenism, looking for sustained ways of maintaining dialogue and proposing principles which may be helpful in establishing such listening.

Chapter 4.2 looked at different ways for architects to reconsider what it means to be a child in this place. Some of these methods have involved architects using other languages, including sensory and creative languages, to experience spaces differently. Artists have played a key role in several of the projects described to help in this task of experiencing differently and revisiting ideas about childhood spaces. Experiencing physical spaces differently can also be achieved through engagement with documentation which is produced by children and which is from both contemporary and older sources.

Participation runs the risk of being tokenistic within learning communities and within the design process. Chapter 4.3 discussed some of the structural issues which have supported or hindered the establishing of dialogue across age groups, generations and professions. The role of narratives has been explored at organisational and individual levels. Young children's narratives, in particular, in the form of portfolio or profile books, illustrate how making perspectives visible can strengthen a child's sense of belonging to an environment and to a community of learners.

Researchers can also be involved in the process of constructing narratives. Working in a participatory way with young children and adults and across professional boundaries has created new narrators. This in turn challenges the role of the researcher to reconsider what languages and forums are appropriate or develop a voice within the research process. Multi-disciplinary advisory groups are discussed as possible discursive spaces for exchange. This raises the question of how such points of debate, challenge and co-construction can be established across the education and design field beyond the confines of individual research studies.

Epilogue

I began Chapter 1.2 with a fictional account of a boy who carries under his arm in a window frame his way of seeing the world. My original interest was in gaining new insights into how young children 'picture their worlds'. I was interested in increasing my own awareness of young children's views and experiences of their learning environments and showing this view to others, including architects.

This 'picturing a world' has been for a practical rather than abstract purpose. This has been listening for real in the design and review of learning environments. The aim has not only been to provide a set of static views into the landscapes of a nursery class and children's centre, but to enable young children and adults to explore their own ways of seeing, to form their own narratives and to listen to the narratives of others. This has led to a continual movement between children's and adults' images, conversations and reflections. My hope is that the result will contribute to new understandings about the landscapes of being experienced by young children within the designed environment and also reflective design practices which make tacit knowledge explicit.

What has emerged at the end of this study has been a greater awareness of the value of a model of dialogue which enables adults and children – including young children – within learning communities to reconsider 'What does it mean to be in this place?'. This remains a central question, whether an organisation is embarking on a building project or reviewing everyday practice.

As Mannion advocates:

> There is a need to deal with the intergenerational aspects of the processes we are investigating if we are to more fully understand them. This may mean collecting data from or with young people and from adults but data can also come in the form of objects, pictures, practices and other processes that are implied in how children, adults and spaces come together (or move apart). Without a focus on the relations between adults and children and the spaces they inhabit we are in danger of providing a narrow view of how children's 'voice' and 'participation' are 'produced'.
>
> (Mannion 2007: 417)

The physical environment provides one tangible arena within which to reconsider the views and experiences of others. These considerations are at the heart of participatory design and participatory living. This brings us back to the wider questions which have been discussed here about the nature of democratic practice and of politics. Young children, and those who share the spaces in which they learn, can be part of this dialogue.

Glossary

Board school   Victorian schools built by local authorities after the 1870 Education Act.

Children's centres   Provision bringing together range of early years services for children and families including early education and childcare.

Early Years Foundation Stage (EYFS)   Statutory framework for England, introduced in 2007 to set standards for development, learning and care of children from birth to five, replacing earlier frameworks such as *Curriculum Guidance for the Foundation Stage*, *Birth to Three Matters* and *National Standards for Under 8s Daycare and Childminding*.

Key person   A named practitioner with whom a child has more contact than other adults.

Office for Standards in Education (Ofsted)   Government agency which inspects children's services including schools, early years settings and local education authorities.

Practitioner   Adults who work with children in a setting.

Reception class   First year pupils usually begin infant school at the age of four.

Sure Start   Government-led initiative to provide a range of services for children under five and their families, including childcare, focusing on disadvantaged areas.

Year One   Year group of five- to six-year-olds.

Year Two   Year group of six- to seven-year-olds.

Bibliography

Altman, I. (1975) *Environment and Social Behaviour: privacy, territoriality, personal space and crowding*, Monterey, California: Brooks Cole.

Bachelard, G. (1994) *The Poetics of Space*, Boston: Beacon Press.

Banks, M. (2001) *Visual Methods in Social Research*, London: Sage.

Benjamin, W. (1931/1979) *A Small History of Photography in One Way Street and Other Writings*, London: Verso.

Benson, L. (2006) 'Leading and managing others' in Bruce, T. (ed.) *Early Childhood: a guide for students*, London: Sage.

Berger, J. (1972) *Ways of Seeing*, London: Penguin.

Birkett, D. (2001) 'The school we'd like', *Guardian*, June 5. Online at <http://www.guardian.co.uk/education/2001/jun/05/schools.uk7>, accessed October 2009.

Bishop, J. (2001) 'Creating places for living and learning' in Nutbrown, C. and Abbott, L. (eds) *Experiencing Reggio: implications for pre-school provision*, Maidenhead: Open University Press, 72–79.

Blades, M., Blaut, J., Darvizeh, Z., Elguea, S., Sowen, S., Soni, D., Spencer, C., Stea, D., Surajpaul, R. and Uttal, D. (1998) 'A cross-cultural study of young chidlren's mapping abilities', *Transactions of the Institute of British Geographers*, 23, 2: 269–277.

Blundell Jones, P., Petrescu, D. and Till, J. (eds) (2005) *Architecture and Participation*, London: Spon Press.

Brooker, L. (2002) *Starting School: young children learning cultures*, Buckingham: Open University Press.

Brosterman, N. (1987) *Inventing Kindergarten*, New York: Harry N. Abrams Inc.

Bruner, J. (1990) *Acts of Meaning*, London: Harvard University Press.

—— (1996) *The Culture of Education*, London: Harvard University Press.

—— (2006) *In Search of Pedagogy Volume II: The Selected Works of Jerome Bruner, 1979–2006*, London: Routledge.

Burgess, R. (1985) 'In the company of teachers: key informants and the study of a comprehensive school' in Burgess, R. (ed.) *Strategies of Educational Research: qualitative methods*, Lewes: Falmer.

Burke, C. (2004). 'Theories of childhood' in Fass, P. (ed.) *Encyclopedia of Children and Childhood: in history and society*, New York: Macmillan Reference USA.

—— (2005a) 'The edible landscape of school' in Dudek, M. (ed.) *Children's Spaces*, Amsterdam/London: Architectural Press.

—— (ed) (2005b) 'Containing the school child: architecture and pedagogies', *Paedagogica Historica*, 41, 4 and 5:489–494.

—— (2007) 'The view of the child: releasing visual voice in the design of learning environments', *Discourse: studies in the cultural politics of education*, September 28, 3: 359–372.

—— (2008) 'Play in focus: children's visual voice in participative research' in Thomson, P. (ed.) *Doing Visual Research with Children and Young People*, London: Routledge.

Burke, C. and Grosvenor, I. (2003) *The School I'd Like. Children and Young People's Reflections on an Education for the 21st Century*, London: RoutledgeFalmer.

Butterworth, C. (2007) 'Of all we survey: drawing out stories of place' in Littlefield, D. and Lewis, S. (eds) *Architectural Voices: listening to old buildings*, Chichester: John Wiley & Sons, 148–151.

CABE Education/Architecture Centre Network (2003) *Engaging Places: architecture and the built environment as a learning resource*, London: CABE Education.

CABE (2008) *Sure Start Children's Centres: a post-occupancy evaluation*, London: CABE.

Calvino, I. (1997) *Invisible Cities*, London: Secker and Warburg.

Carr, M. (2000) 'Seeking children's perspectives about their learning' in Smith, A., Taylor, N. J. and Gollop, M. (eds) (2000) *Children's Voices: research, policy and practice*, Auckland: Pearson Education, 37–55.

Carr, M., Jones, C. and Lee, W. (2005) 'Beyond listening: can assessment play its part?' in Clark, A., Moss, P. and Kjørholt, A. *Beyond Listening: children's perspectives on early childhood services*, Bristol: Policy Press,129–150.

—— (2007) 'Kei tua o te pae. Assessment for learning: early childhood exemplars', resource prepared for the Ministry of Education. Book 11. Wellington, New Zealand: Ministry of Education, Early Childhood Education.

Carnegie Young People's Initiative (2001) *Taking the Initiative: promoting young people's involvement in public decision-making in the UK: UK Overview report*, London: Carnegie Young People's Initiative.

Casey, E. (1996) 'How to get from space to space in a fairly short stretch of time: phenomenological prolegomena' in Field, S. and Basso, K. (eds) *Senses of Place*, Sante Fe, New Mexico: School of American Research.

Ceppi, G. and Zini, M. (1998) *Children's Spaces and Relations: metaproject for the environment of young children*, Reggio Emilia: Domus Academy Research Center/ Reggio Children.

Chawla, L. (ed.) (2002) *Growing up in an Urbanising World*, Paris and London: UNESCO publishing/Earthscan Publications.

Children in Europe (2005) 'The stakeholders: a snap shot of different perspectives on space' in *Children in Europe*, April, 8: 21.

Children in Scotland (2008) *Adventures in nature*, Edinburgh: Children in Scotland.

Children's Play Council (2002) *More than Swings and Roundabouts: planning for outdoor play*, London: Children's Play Council.

Chiles, P. (2005a) 'The classroom as an evolving landscape' in Dudek, M. (ed.) *Children's spaces*, London: Architectural Press, 101–113.

Chiles, P. (2005b) 'What if? . . . a narrative process for reimagining the city' in Blundell Jones, P., Petrescu, D. and Till, J. (eds) *Architecture and Participation*, London: Spon Press, 187–206.

Christensen P. (2003) 'Place, space and knowledge: children in the village and the city' in Christensen, P. and O'Brien, M (eds) (2003) *Children in the City: home, neighbourhood and community,* London: RoutledgeFalmer.

—— (2004) 'Children's participation in ethnographic research: issues of power and representation', *Children And Society,* 18, 2: 165–176.

Christensen, P. and James, A. (2008) 'Childhood diversity and commonality: some methodological insights' in Christensen, P. and James, A. (eds) *Research with Children: perspectives and practices.* Second edition. London: RoutledgeFalmer, 156–172.

Christensen, P. and O'Brien, M. (eds) (2003) *Children in the City: home, neighbourhood and community,* London: RoutledgeFalmer.

Clark, A. (2004) 'The Mosaic approach and research with young children' in Lewis, V., Kellett, M., Robinson, C., Fraser, S. and Ding, S. (eds) *The Reality of Research with Children and Young People,* London: Sage, 142–161.

—— (2005a) 'Talking and listening to young children' in Dudek, M. (ed.) *Children's Spaces,* London: Architectural Press, 1–13.

—— (2005b) 'Ways of seeing: using the Mosaic approach to listen to young children's perspectives' in Clark, A., Moss, P. and Kjørholt, A. *Beyond Listening: children's perspectives on early childhood services,* Bristol: Policy Press, 29–49.

—— (2005c) 'The silent voice of the camera? Young children and photography as a tool for listening', *Early Childhood Folio,* 9, 28–33.

—— (2007) 'Views from inside the shed: young children's perspectives of the outdoor environment', *Education 3-13,* 35, 4: 349–363.

—— (2008) *Early Childhood Spaces: involving young children and practitioners in the design process,* The Hague: Bernard van Leer Foundation.

—— (2009) 'Undertaking research with children' in Maynard, T. and Thomas, N. (eds) *An introduction to Early Childhood Studies.* Second edition. London: Sage, 218–229.

—— (Forthcoming) 'Young children as protagonists and the role of participatory, visual methods in engaging multiple perspectives', *American Journal of Community Psychology.*

Clark, A., McQuail, S. and Moss, P. (2003) *Exploring the Field of Listening to and Consulting with Young Children,* Research Report 445, London: Department for Education and Skills.

Clark, A. and Moss, P. (2001) *Listening to Young Children: the Mosaic approach,* London: National Children's Bureau for the Joseph Rowntree Foundation.

—— (2005) *Spaces to Play: more listening to young children using the Mosaic approach,* London: National Children's Bureau.

Clark, A., Moss, P. and Kjørholt, A. (eds) (2005) *Beyond Listening: children's perspectives on early childhood services,* Bristol: Policy Press.

Clark, A. and Percy-Smith, B. (2006) 'Beyond consultation: participatory practices in everyday spaces', *Children, Youth and Environments,* 16, 2: 1–9.

Clark, A. and Statham, J. (2005) 'Listening to young children: experts in their own lives', *Adoption and Fostering,* 29, 1: 45–56.

Clark, A. and Williams, L. (2008) 'Beyond listening: translating research into practice', unpublished paper presented at the 18th EECERA Conference in Stavanger, Norway, September.

Clark, H. (2002) *Building Education: the role of the physical environment in enhancing teaching and research,* London: Institute of Education.

Cole, M. (1996) *Cultural Psychology: a once and future discipline,* London: Harvard University Press.

Cole, M., and Engeström, Y. (1997) 'A cultural-historical approach to distributed cognition', in Salomon, G. (ed.) *Distributed cognitions: psychological and educational considerations*, New York: Cambridge University Press, 1–46.

Construction Industry Council (2002) *Design Quality Indicators*, Online, at <http://www.dqi.org.uk/website/default.aspa>, accessed October 2009.

Corsaro, W. (1985) *Friendship and Peer Culture in the Early Years*, Norwood, New Jersey: Ablex.

Corsaro, W. and Molinari, L. (2008) 'Entering and observing in children's worlds: a reflection on longitudinal ethnography of early education in Italy' in Christensen, P. and James, A. (eds) *Research with Children: perspectives and practices*, Second edition. London: Falmer Press, 239–259.

Cousins, J. (1999) *Listening to Four-year-olds: how they can help us plan their education and care*, London: National Early Years Network.

Cruddas, L. and Haddock, L. (2003) *Girl's Voices: supporting girls' learning and emotional development*, Stoke on Trent: Trentham Books.

Curtis, P. (2007) 'Space to care: children's perceptions of spatial aspects of hospitals: Full Research Report', ESRC End of Award Report, RES-000-23-0765, Swindon: ESRC.

Dahlberg, G. and Moss, P. (2005) *Ethics and Politics in Early Childhood Education*, London: Routledge.

Dahlberg, G., Moss, P. and Pence, A. (1999) *Beyond Quality in Early Childhood Education and Care*, London: Routledge.

Daniels, H. (2001) *Vygotsky and Pedagogy*, London: Routledge.

Daycare Trust (1998) *Listening to Children. Young Children's Views on Childcare: a guide for Parents*, London: Daycare Trust.

de Certeau, M. (1988) *The Practice of Everyday Life*, Berkeley: University of California Press.

Delfos, M. (2001) *Are You Listening to Me?; communicating with children from four to twelve years old*, Amsterdam: SWP Publishers.

Department for Children, Schools and Families (2008a) *Statutory Framework for The Early Years Foundation Stage*, London: Department for Children, Schools and Families.

Department for Children, Schools and Families (2008b) *Early Years Foundation Stage Resource Cards*, London: Department for Children, Schools and Families.

Dewey, J. (1897) 'My pedagogic creed', *The School Journal*, LIV (3) (16 January): 77–80.

Driscoll, V. and Rudge, C. (2005) 'Channels for listening to young children and parents' in Clark, A., Moss, P. and Kjørholt, A. (eds) *Beyond Listening: children's perspectives on early childhood services*, Bristol: Policy Press, 91–110.

Dockett, S. and Perry, B. (1996) 'Young children's construction of knowledge', *Australian Journal of Early Childhood*, 21, 4: 6–11.

—— (2005) 'Researching with children: insights from the Starting School Research Project', *Early Child Development and Care* 175, 6, August: 507–521.

—— (2007) *Transitions to School: perceptions, expectations, experiences*, Sydney: UNSW Press.

Dockett, S. and Simpson, S. (2003) 'This is school . . . where people come to learn for school: what children need to know when they start school', *Early Childhood Folio*, 7, 14–17.

Donaldson, M. (1979) *Children's Minds*, New York: Norton.

Dudek, M. (2000) *Kindergarten Architecture: space for the imagination*. Second edition. London: Spon Press.

—— (2001) *Building for Young Children: a practical guide to planning, designing and building the perfect space*, London: National Early Years Network.

Drummond, M. J. (1998) 'Observing children' in Smidt, S. (ed.) *The Early Years: a reader*, London: Routledge, 99–106.

East Riding of Yorkshire (England) Education Committee (1967) *The Condition of the Primary Schools in the East Riding of Yorkshire*, Beverley: East Riding of Yorkshire (England) Education Committee.

Edwards, A. (2008) 'Activity theory and small-scale interventions in schools', *Journal of Educational Change*, 9: 375–378.

Edwards, C., Gandini, L. and Forman, G. (eds) (1998) *The Hundred Languages of Children*. Second edition. Norwood, New Jersey: Ablex.

Einarsdottir, J. (2005) 'Playschool in pictures: children's photographs as a research method', *Early Childhood Development and Care*, 175, 6, August: 523–542.

Elfer, P. and Selleck, D. (1999) 'Children under three in nurseries. Uncertainty as a creative factor in child observations', *European Early Childhood Research Journal*, 7,1: 69–82.

Emond, R. (2005) 'Ethnographic research methods with children and young people' in Hogan, S. and Hogan, D. (eds) *Researching Children's Experiences: approaches and methods*, London: Sage, 123–139.

Engeström, Y. (1999). 'Innovative learning in work teams: analyzing cycles of knowledge creation in practice' in Y. Engestrom *et al*. (eds) *Perspectives on Activity Theory*, Cambridge: Cambridge University Press.

Fasoli, L. (2003) 'Reading photographs of young children: looking at practices. Contemporary issues' *Early Childhood*, 4, 1: 32–47.

Fielding, M. (2004) '"New Wave" student voice and renewal of civic society', *London Review of Education*, 2, 3: 197–217.

Fine, G. and Sandstrom, K. (1988) *Knowing Children: participant observation with minors. Qualitative Research Methods series 15*, Newbury Park, California: Sage.

Foucault, M. (1972) *The Archaeology of Knowledge*, New York: Pantheon Books.

Geertz, C. (1973) *The Interpretations of Culture*, New York: Basic Books.

—— (1983) *Local Knowledge: further essays in interpretative anthropology*, New York: Basic Books.

Gordon, T., Holland, J. and Lahelma, E. (2000) *Making Spaces: citizenship and difference in schools*, London: Macmillan Press.

Gray, A. (2003) *Research Practice for Cultural Studies*, London: Sage.

Greene, S. and Hill, M. (2005) 'Methods and methodological issues' in Greene, S. and Hogan, D. (eds) *Researching Children's Experience: approaches and methods*, London: Sage, 1–21.

Greene, S. and Hogan, D. (eds) (2005) *Researching Children's Experiences: approaches and methods*, London: Sage.

Grosvenor, I. and Lawn, M. (2001) 'In search of the school: space over time', *Bildung und Erzhung*, 1, Spring: 55–70.

Hammersley, M. and Atkinson, P. (1995) *Ethnography: principles in practice*, Second edition, London: Routledge.

Harding, J. and Meldon-Smith, L. (2000) *How to Make Observations and Assessments*, London: Hodder & Stoughton.

Harmon, K. (ed.) (2004) *You are Here: personal geographies and other maps of the imagination*, New York: Princeton Architectural Press.

Hart, R. A. (1979) *Children's Experience of Place*, New York: Irvington Publishers.

—— (1997) *Children's Participation*, UNICEF and London: Earthscan.

—— (2009) 'Charting change in the participatory settings of childhood' in Thomas, N. (ed.) *Children, Politics and Communication: participation at the margins*, Bristol: Policy Press, 7–29

Hatch, J. (1990) 'Young children as informants in classroom studies', *Early Childhood Research Quarterly*, 5, 4: 251–264.

Heaney, S. (2002) *Finders Keepers: selected prose 1971–2001*, London: Faber and Faber.

Higgins, S., Wall, K. and Smith, H. (2005) '"The visual helps me understand the complicated things": pupil views of teaching and learning with interactive whiteboards', *British Journal of Educational Technology*, 36, 5: 851–867.

Hipkins, R., Boyd, S. and Joyce, C. (2005) 'Documenting learning of the key competencies: what are the issues?' A discussion paper. Wellington, New Zealand: Council for Educational Research.

Holloway, S. and Valentine, G. (eds) (2000) *Children's Geographies: playing, living, learning*, London: Routledge.

International Child and Youth Care Network (2005) Berg, L. and Duane, M. CYC-ONLINE, September, 80: no pagination.

Israel, T. (2003) *Some Place Like Home: using design psychology to create ideal places*, Chichester: Wiley.

James, A. and Prout, A. (1997) *Constructing and Reconstructing Childhood*, Second edition, London: Falmer.

Kaplan, I. (2008) 'Being "seen", being "heard": engaging with students on the margins of education through participatory photography' in Thomson, P. (ed.) *Doing Visual Research with Children and Young People*, London: Routledge, 175–191.

Kinney, L. (2005) 'Small voices, powerful messages' in Clark, A., Moss, P. and Kjørholt, A. (eds) *Beyond Listening: children's perspectives on early childhood services*, Bristol: Policy Press, 111–128.

Kirby, P., Lanyon, C., Cronin, K. and Sinclair, R. (2003) *Building a Culture of Participation*, London: Department for Education and Skills.

Kjørholt, A. T. (2001) '"The participating child": a vital pillar in this century?', *Nordisk Pedagogik*, 21: 65–81.

Kjørholt, A. (2005) 'The competent child and "the right to be oneself": reflections on children as fellow citizens in an early childhood centre' in Clark, A., Moss, P. and Kjøholt, A. *Beyond Listening: children's perspecties on early childhood services*, Bristol: Policy Press, 151–174.

Knight, A. and Clark, A. (2006) 'Consulting the children at Comet Nursery School, Hackney', Unpublished report, London: Thomas Coram Research Unit.

Knight, S. (2009) *Forest Schools and Outdoor Learning in the Early Years*, London: Sage.

Lancaster, P. and Broadbent, V. (2003) *Listening to Young Children*, Maidenhead: Open University Press.

Landry, C. (2000) *The Creative City: a toolkit for urban innovators*, London: Earthscan.

Langsted, O. (1994) 'Looking at quality from the child's perspective' in Moss, P. and Pence, A. (eds) *Valuing Quality in Early Childhood Services: new approaches to defining quality*, London: Paul Chapman Publishing.

Lave, J. and Wenger, E. (1991) *Situated Learning: legitimate peripheral participation*, Cambridge: Cambridge University Press.

Lawn, M. and Grosvenor, I. (eds) (2005) *Material Cultures of Schooling: design, technology, objects, routines*, London: Symposium Books.

Lewis, S. (2007) 'Epilogue' in Littlefield, D. and Lewis, S. (eds) *Architectural Voices: listening to old buildings*, Chichester: John Wiley & Sons.

Lewis, V., Kellett, M., Robinson, C., Fraser, S. and Ding, S. (eds) (2004) *The Reality of Research with Children and Young People*, London: Sage.

Littlefield, D. and Lewis, S. (eds) (2007) *Architectural Voices: listening to old buildings*, Chichester: John Wiley & Sons.

Lynch, K. (1960) *The Image of the City*, Cambridge, Massachusetts: Massachusetts Institute of Technology.

MacNaughton, G. (2003) *Shaping Early Childhood: learners, curriculum and contexts*, New York: McGraw-Hill.

Malavasi, L. and Pantaleoni, L. (2008) *Coriandoline: le case amiche dei bambini e delle bambine. Friendly houses for boys and girls*, Correggio, Reggio Emilia: Andria.

Mannion, G. (2007) 'Going spatial, going relational: why "listening to children" and children's participation needs reframing', *Discourse: studies in the cultural politics of education,* 28, 3, September: 405–420.

Marchant, R. and Kirby, P. (2004) 'The participation of young children: communication, consultation and involvement' in Willow, C., Marchant, R., Kirby, P. and Neale, B. (eds) *Young Children's Citizenship: ideas into practice*, York: Joseph Rowntree Foundation, 92–163.

Markus, T. (1993) *Building and Power: freedom and control in the origin of modern building types*, London: Routledge.

Matthews, H. (1995) 'Culture, environmental experience and environmental awareness: making sense of young Kenyan children's view of place', *Geographical Journal*, 161, 3: 285–295.

Mayall, B., Bendelow, G., Barker, S., Storey, P. and Veltman, M. (1996) *Children's Health in Primary Schools*, London: Falmer.

McAuliffe, A., Linsey, A. and Fowler, J. (2006) *Childcare Act: the essential guide*, London: National Children's Bureau.

McMillan, M. (1919) *The Nursery School*, London: J. M. Dent & Sons.

Miles, M. and Huberman, M. (1994) *Qualitative Data Analysis: an expanded sourcebook*, London: Sage.

Montessori, M. (2004) *The Discovery of the Child. Revised and enlarged edition of the Montessori Method*, Delhi: Aakar Books.

Moss, P. and Petrie, P. (2002) *From Children's Services to Children's Spaces: public policy, children and childhood*, London: Routledge.

van Oers, B. (2005) 'Promises and problems of collaborative innovation in early childhood education', unpublished key note address, Warwick: University of Warwick.

Oram, H. (1984) *In The Attic*, London: Andersen Press.

Orellana, M. (1999) 'Space and place in an urban landscape: learning from children's views of their social worlds', *Visual Sociology*, 14, 1 and 2: 73–89.

Oswin, M. (1971) *The Empty Hours: a study of the week-end life of handicapped children in institutions*, London: Penguin Press.

Pahl, K. (1999) *Transformations: children's meaning-making in a nursery*, Stoke on Trent: Trentham Books.

Parker, C. (2001) 'When is she coming back?' in Abbott, L. and Nutbrown, C. (eds)

Experiencing Reggio Emilia: implications for pre-school provision, Buckingham: Open University Press.

Pearse, I. and Crocker, L. (1985) *The Peckham Experiment: a study of the living structure of society*, Edinburgh: Scottish Academic Press.

Percy-Smith, B. (2006) 'From consultation to social learning in community participation with young people', *Children, Youth and Environments*, 16, 2:153–179.

Pink, S. (2001) *Doing Visual Ethnography: images, media and representations in research*, London: Sage.

—— (2006) *The Future of Visual Anthropology: engaging the senses*, London: Routledge.

Plester, B., Blades, M. and Spencer, C. (1998) 'Children's understanding of environmental representations: aerial photographs and model towns' in Spencer, C. and Blades, M. (eds) *Children and Their Environments: learning, using and designing spaces*, Cambridge: Cambridge University Press, 42–56.

Powell, K. (2001) *Will Alsop. Book 1*, London: Lawrence King.

Project Zero/Reggio Children (2001) *Making Learning Visible: children as individual and group learners*, Reggio Emilia: Reggio Children.

Probyn, E. (1993) *Sexing the Self: gendered positions in cultural studies*, London: Routledge.

Proshansky, H. M. and Fabian A. K. (1987) 'The development of place identity in the child' in Weinstein, C. and David, T. (eds) *Spaces for Children: the built environment and child development*, New York/London: Plenum, 21–40.

Prosser, J. (ed.) (1998) *Image-based Research: a source book for qualitative researchers*, London: Falmer Press.

Prosser, J. and Schwartz, D. (1998) 'Photographs within the sociological research process' in Prosser, J. (ed.) *Image-based Research: a source book for qualitative researchers*, London: Falmer Press, 115–130.

Reason, P. and Bradbury, H. (eds) (2006) *Handbook of Action Research*, London: Sage.

Reggio Children (2004) *Children, Art and Artists: the artistic language of Alberto Burri*, Reggio Emilia: Reggio Children.

Rinaldi, C. (2001) 'A pedagogy of listening', *Children in Europe*, 1: 2–5.

—— (2005) 'Documentation and assessment: what is the relationship?' in Clark, A., Moss, P. and Kjørholt, A. (eds) *Beyond Listening: children's perspectives on early childhood services*, Bristol: Policy Press,17–28.

—— (2006) *In Dialogue with Reggio Emilia*, London: Routledge.

Robson C. (2002) *Real World Research: a resource for social scientists and practitioner-researchers*, Second edition, Oxford: Blackwell.

Rodd, J. (2006) *Leadership in Early Childhood*, Third edition, New South Wales, Australia: Allen and Unwin.

Rogoff, B. (2003) *The Cultural Nature of Human Development*, New York: Oxford University Press.

Rose, N. (1999) *Powers of Freedom: reframing political thought*, Cambridge: Cambridge University Press.

Rudduck, J. and Flutter, J. (2004) *How to Improve your School*, London: Continuum.

Rudge, C. and Driskoll, V. (2005) 'Channels for listening to young children and to parents' in Clark, A., Moss, P. and Kjørholt, A. (eds) *Beyond Listening: children's perspectives on early childhood services*, Bristol: Policy Press, 91–110.

Ryder Richardson, G. (2006) *Creating a Space to Grow: the process of developing your outdoor learning environment*, London: David Fulton.

Sacks, O. (1973; 1990) *Awakenings*, New York: Harper Perennial.

Schama, S. (1995) *Landscape and Memory*, London: HarperCollins.

Siraj-Blatchford, I. and Manni, L. (2007) *Effective Leadership in the Early Years Sector: the ELEYS study*, London: Institute of Education, University of London.

Smith, A. Duncan J. and Marshall, K. (2005) 'Children's perspectives on their learning: exploring methods', *Early Child Development and Care* 175, 6, August: 473–488.

Sontag, S. (1979) *On Photography*, London: Penguin Books.

Sorrell, J. and Sorrell, F. (2005) *Joinedupdesignforschools*, London: Merrell Publishers.

Storer, M. (1999) *Grown-up School Created with Year 5 Pupils at Brecknock Primary School*, London: Lift 99.

Thomas, N. (ed.) (2009) *Children, Politics and Communication: participation at the margins*, Bristol: Policy Press.

Thomson, P. (ed.) (2008) *Doing Visual Research with Children and Young People*, London: Routledge.

Thomson, S. (2003) 'A well-equipped hamster cage: the rationalisation of primary school playtime', *Education 3-13*, 31, 2: 54–59.

Titman, W. (1994) *Special People, Special Places: the hidden curriculum of school grounds*, Godalming: World Wildlife Fund/Learning Through Landscapes.

Tolfree, D. and Woodhead, M. (1999) 'Tapping a key resource', *Early Childhood Matters*, February, 91: 19–23

Trancik, A. M. and Evans, G. W. (1995) 'Spaces fit for children: competency in daycare center environments', *Children's Environments*, 17, 3: 311–319.

Tuan, Y. (1977) *Space and Place: the perspective of experience*, Minneapolis, Minnesota: University of Minnesota Press.

Unicorn Theatre (2009) '*For the Best*. Unicorn Theatre in collaboration with Mark Storer and Anna Ledgard.' Programme notes, London: Unicorn Theatre.

United Nations Committee on the Rights of the Child, United Nations Children Fund and the Bernard van Leer Foundation (2006) *A Guide to General Comment 7: implementing children's rights in early childhood*, The Hague: Bernard van Leer Foundation.

Vecchi, V. (1998) 'What kind of space for living well in school?' in Ceppi, G. and Zini, M. (eds.) *Children's Spaces and Relations: metaproject for the environment of young children*, Reggio Emilia: Domus Academy Research Center/Reggio Children.

Vecchi, V. (2001) 'The curiosity to understand' in *Making Learning Visible: children as individual and group learners*, Reggio Emilia: Project Zero/Reggio Children, 158–213.

Viola, B. and Violette, R. (1995) *Reasons for Knocking at an Empty House. Writings 1973–1994*, London: Thames and Hudson.

Vygotsky, L. S. (1978) *Mind in Society: the development of higher psychological processes*, Cambridge, Massachusetts: Harvard University Press.

Wagner, J. (2004) 'Fishing naked: Nordic early childhood philosophy, policy and practice', *Young Children*, 59, 5: 56–62.

Walker, R. (1993) 'Finding a silent voice for the researcher: using photographs in evaluation and research' in Schratz, M. (ed.) *Qualitative Voices in Educational Research*, London: Falmer Press, 72–92.

Ward, C. (1978) *The Child in the City*, London: Architectural Press.

Warming, H. (2005) 'Participant observation: a way to learn about children's perspectives' in Clark, A., Moss, P. and Kjorholt, A. (eds) *Beyond Listening: children's perspectives on early childhood services*, Bristol: Policy Press, 51–70.

Weinberger, J., Pickstone, C., and Hannon, P. (eds) (2005) *Learning from Sure Start: working with young children and their families,* Maidenhead: Open University Press.

Weinstein, C. and David, T. (eds) (1987) *Spaces for Children: the built environment and child development*, New York/London: Plenum.

Wells, G. (1986) *The Meaning Makers: children learning language and using language to learn*, London: Hodder & Stoughton.

Wenger, E. (1998) *Communities of Practice: learning, meaning and identity*, Cambridge: Cambridge University Press.

Wertsch, J. (1991) *Voices of the Mind: a sociocultural approach to mediated action*, Cambridge, Massachusetts: Harvard University Press.

Whalley, M. (2002) 'Working as a team' in Pugh, G. and Duffy, B. (eds) *Contemporary Issues in the Early Years: working collaboratively for children,* Third edition, London: Sage, 125–145.

Williams, R. (2000) *Lost Icons: reflections on cultural bereavement*, London: T & T Clark.

Woodhead, L. and Brooker, M. (eds) (2008) *Developing Positive Identities: diversity and young children. Early Childhood in Focus: 3*, Milton Keynes: Open University.

Woolner, P., Hall, E., Higgins, S., McCaughey, C. and Wall, K. (2007) 'A sound foundation? What we know about the impact of environments on learning and the implications for Building Schools for the Future', *Oxford Review of Education*, 33, 1: 47–70.

Wunschel, G. (2003) *From Car Park to Children's Park*. Working Paper 30, The Hague: Bernard van Leer Foundation.

Zeldin, T. (1995) *An Intimate History of Humanity*, London: Vintage.

Index

Note: Page numbers in *italics* refer to tables. Page numbers in **bold** refer to figures.